FAVELA CHILDREN

A Brazilian Diary

by Ute Craemer

Translated from the German
by Frank Thomas Smith

ANTHROPOSOPHICAL PUBLICATIONS
FREMONT, MICHIGAN USA

Favela Children

Translated by
Frank Thomas Smith

Edited by
Marylin J. Kraker

Cover designed by
James D. Stewart

This book is not a work of fiction. Names, characters, places, and incidents are diarized events of the author's actual experiences.

Printed in the United States of America

First Printing: Aug 2022
The e.Lib, Inc.
Anthroposophical Publications
https://AnthroposophicalPublications.org/

ISBN-13: 978-1-948302-42-5 paperback
978-1-948302-43-2 eBook

CONTENTS

INTRODUCTION

During the summer of 1979, I visited the large Waldorf School in São Paulo, Brazil. Previously a friend had told me that one of the teachers there intended to open a school in a favela (slum). I asked if I could speak with that teacher, Ute Craemer. Although she still taught in the São Paulo Waldorf School, her heart was in the "escolinha" (little school) situated about seven miles away in a favela inappropriately named *Monte Azul* (blue hill). The favela was not on a hill, but in a muddy depression; it wasn't blue either, but gray-brown. But names are mysterious things and somehow it fits in this case, at least it does now. And the school wasn't a school in the proper sense either. The escolinha was a barrack-like house on a small piece of land above the favela. It was divided into rooms where various activities took place: dance, painting, theater, cooking, sewing. There was also a carpentry, a kindergarten and a playroom. The children, between three and sixteen years of age, attended the escolinha before or after their "official" school hours. They were the poorest of the poor and naturally could not pay for the lessons and care they received.

How do you finance all this? I asked Ute.

Yes, that's a problem, she said. She told me how at first she taught the children in her own home, a few blocks from the favela, and that someone in Germany heard of her work and donated ten-thousand German marks, with which she built the escolinha and bought materials.

Since that time the work has greatly expanded and has even spread to other favelas. It is all financed by donations from individuals, business firms, charities and a subsidy from the city of São Paulo. Nevertheless, "Yes, that's a problem" is more true now than ever, for expansion creates new costs and world-wide recessions affect non-profit making institutions just as much, if not more, than profit making ones.

*

That visit and subsequent ones partially answered a question which had long occupied me: How can the educational and social impulses which Rudolf Steiner introduced to the world be expanded to include the poor?

Many years ago I was involved in the founding of a Waldorf School in Argentina. The first years were financially very difficult, which is practically a normal situation. But the school developed and is now a well-established institution for middle and upper-middle class children. The number of poorer children who can be accepted is limited by economic realities and the understandable reluctance of the poor to send their children to schools dominated by another social class.

For two reasons this seemed to be a tragically unavoidable contradiction, for the Waldorf educational method as practiced the world over was not meant only for the well-to-do, but also for the under-privileged. One could even say especially for the latter, for these schools emphasize the human aspect of education, the intensive artistic character of the teaching process, the spiritual non-denominational atmosphere, the dedication of the teachers and more, all of which the weak need more than the strong. The second reason is ironical rather than contradictory: The first Waldorf School, founded in Germany in 1919, was for the children of the workers in a cigarette factory. Its subsequent development has been very different, however. As soon as the founder's financial support was no longer available, it was transformed into a school for those who could afford to pay. My experience in many countries has shown that this situation is universal, even in those countries where the schools are partially subsidized by the state.

The escolinha in São Paulo was the first educational institution to apply the Waldorf method based on anthroposophical spiritual science to concentrate on serving the poor, the forgotten, the degraded – and under extremely difficult conditions.

*

This book is a translation of Ute Craemer's *Favela Kinder,* which first appeared in German in 1981 and went through several editions, and parts of her second, later book, entitled *Favela Monte Azul*. It is neither theoretical nor ideological, but is a true story from her diary, written as the events were occurring. But it is more than these things. It is a kind of modern mystery drama about the opposing forces of good and evil. During the Saint Michael's Day celebration in the Waldorf Schools (described in the book), the children lay their crystals on the scales of the good and, with the help of the archangel, that side always wins. In today's world, however, outside the Waldorf School, the scales seem to be tipping the other way. This book, then, is the story of a small group of people who are fighting against the dragon of ignorance, egotism and social indifference in an effort to give more weight to the scale of the good.

Frank Thomas Smith

FORWARD

In this book the reader will find diary entries made from the time I first set foot in a Brazilian favela, or slum, as a social worker in 1965. It also covers the later years when I started a favela project together with students from a Brazilian Waldorf School, which continues to this day. It shows how such a project can become a life's work, and how experiences from childhood, adolescence and adulthood can acquire meaning.

As a child during the Second World War, while begging for food in the Austrian countryside, I realized how valuable a slice of bread can be, how good it smells and tastes, but also how humiliating it can be when the farmer's wife turns her back and you have to try somewhere else.

During my adolescent and young adult years, I often thought about the injustices in the world and how one might remedy them. I thought especially about the "underdeveloped" countries, in which I had lived many years. So in 1965, when the "German Development Service" was founded, I volunteered immediately. You could work for two years in Asia, Africa or Latin America in slums, in the countryside, hospitals or trade training centers, for which you were paid some pocket money. This was the way I intended to make my contribution to the elimination of the world's injustices. However, the problem continued to worry me and from my present place of domicile and work, São Paulo, Brazil, I am still trying to make my contribution — but with an essential difference. Favelados (occupants of Brazil's urban slums) and the poor in general have long since become more than mere hardship cases. They are human beings through whom I can become a human being myself. While I am trying to help them in their development, they make their contribution to my understanding of myself and the world.

When you open the newspaper and read statistics your flesh creeps at the revelation of so much cruelty. Here, for example, are some facts about Brazil: There are thirty-six million needy children. Seven million of them live on and from the street Approximately a half million children are housed in state orphanages. Thirty-five per cent of the population has had no schooling. Of the seven million underage criminals, sixty per cent are from broken homes. Thirty per cent of the population lives a nomadic existence, continually looking for work.

Such statistics can go on forever. But what good are they if they only serve to paralyze our will and create psychological defense mechanisms? Nevertheless, this feeling of complete helplessness and impotence can awaken a strength that lends us wings and stimulates us to action. The inventory of facts and their translation into reality then makes sense.

In order to make sense of this avalanche of horror, injustice and inhumanity, two different theories can be applied. The first contends that in order to eliminate injustice from the world the institutions, forms of government and laws must first be changed. The other says that you must first change people in order to develop a humane world.

Once you have worked and lived for many years in a favela and have attained an insight into the social structures and the secret wishes of the people who live here, you understand that the truth lies somewhere in the middle. Why? A slum, a favela, is the result of an unjust social-economic system in the country and in the whole world. It is capitalism's final destination. This historical fact is given a very personal, mostly painful stamp in a favela inhabitant's life.

From the situations I have tried to describe in this book one can easily come to the conclusion that the system must be changed. During the years I have worked in favelas as part of the Monte Azul Community Association I have noticed, however, that phenomena such as exploitation, displays of power, manipulation and discrimination against those who are different are also practiced in them. In every favela there is a shopkeeper who overcharges for food and other essentials and exploits those who must buy on credit. There are those who are somehow cleverer, more favored by destiny, perhaps even more diligent than others, who despise those who aren't able to rise above the lowest level of existence. Those who are different, such as homosexuals, are discriminated against by the so-called "normals". These are just a few examples.

The insight grew stronger in me that only a transformation of the individual in the direction of a loving empathy towards other human beings can result in a lasting, meaningful reduction of misery in the world. It is self-evident that worthy schools, hospitals, trade-schools and dwellings are necessary; that is, social institutions that respond to the inner human need for personal development. It is also self-evident that people should participate in voluntary initiatives for better health, dwellings, cheaper and healthier nutrition, agrarian reform, child protection laws, etc., in order to create the framework for a more human existence. However, in my opinion the history of the past decades has shown that these outward changes and improvements will only have a lasting effect if they go hand in hand with a profound understanding of the miracle of man — knowing the human being not only in his visible physical form, but also in his original spiritual essence. To recognize in every individual a creative, spiritual Self who has come to the earth in order to evolve toward freedom and love and to carry this result into future lives on earth, is an enhanced point of departure for today's social work, social art, social science.

Once this conviction has impregnated our human encounters, the struggle for each individual soul can develop into a multiplying movement which is a formidable opposition to the forces that are based on hunger for power, self-destructive influences and contempt for humanity. The scenes of future conflicts aren't battlefields visible to the eye, but the souls of men - even though, as an extension, outward warlike conflicts will arise. The antidote for power-hunger, hate, sectarianism and fundamentalism is a loving approach to the other, an understanding of his differences, sympathy for his capacity to learn and develop, thanks to his individual spiritual essence.

Love even evil — so speak
wise souls well,
For even the scoundrel
was once woven of light.

Christian Morgenstern

DIARY 1965-1967

Antwerp, August 20, 1965

Rudely awakened at five in the morning by the noise of the ship being unloaded, jumped out of bed, put on jeans and a sweater and went out on deck. I watched the unloading of meat from Argentina and then took a stroll through the harbor area where I discovered a wonderful Flemish Gothic church.

Le Havre, August 25

We've started to save money and now use the menus as post-cards. It feels as though we're on vacation and it takes a great mental effort to realize that in three weeks we'll be working in the favelas. But now we're being drowsily rocked on deck by long, softly rolling waves.

At sea between Le Havre and Vigo (Spain), August 26

A storm today! Waves all around, unbridled, spraying water on deck and a wavelet in our cabin. Quite fitting for Biscaya. Wrapped in leather coats, our bodies at a 45-degree angle, we went for a "stroll" on the deck of the Laennec.

Lisbon, August 27

We sweat in a Portuguese café, tired from the heat, which is gradually taking on Brazilian characteristics, and try out our newly acquired Portuguese phrases for the first time. Portugal is a true developing country – wonderful flowering gardens and villas, liberally laid out streets, beautiful Gothic churches from Portugal's heyday. And, alongside them, beggars scavenging, abandoned children. It seems not quite European. But it probably depends on your perspective. Coming from Brazil, the fact that one gets a feeling of history and tradition because of the churches and monuments makes it part of Europe.

Today we leave Europe!

Rio de Janeiro, September 7

After the ten-day Atlantic crossing we are feverish to have land under our feet again. Rio, the *cidade maravilhosa* (wonderful city), is in sight under a blue veil of haze. Miles of white beach devoid of life. Seemingly hostile forests cover the mountains in the background. It's difficult to imagine the nearby metropolis. Entry into the harbor is really beautiful: the Sugarloaf, the many inlets and islands, behind them the skyscrapers of Copacabana and, like a frame, the thick rain forest with its unknown trees surging exuberantly up the mountains from the sea. The first impression is of an American city lost in the tropics. The "white" face of Brazil is the first to be seen. The black one presents itself immediately afterwards however, in the form of the many black workers who unload our ship.

Estamos chegando ... o Rio. (We are arriving in Rio.) The phrase from our language book has become reality.

Santos, September 11

We left the Laennec for good and have been hanging around Santos for two days, ill-humored and numb, with our crates and suitcases. Yesterday the customs officials ransacked my lovingly packed bags and temporarily confiscated my tape recorder. Finally Nivea cream and Otto's opera records served as bribes. Tomorrow we continue by bus, a twelve-hour drive to the interior, to Londrina.

Londrina, mid-September 1965

Our reception here was touching: the house was decorated with little flags, a rocket was launched as we descended from the jeep; three children, fit representatives of racial mixture, one blond, the other brown and a third black, gave us flowers. Frei Nereu, a Franciscan monk who has taken on the favela's sanitation problems, gave an impassioned speech full of genuine Latin pathos. All this under the eyes of television and the Londrina newspaper, in which we are to be admired on the front page of today's edition.

*

The day before yesterday the bishop of Londrina was here in all his finery, including lilac stockings, and last night the criminal police inspector came to visit and offer us his services — you can never know! He learned from the newspaper that we were living in Londrina's worst quarter. Right behind our favela is one of Brazil's most infamous red-light districts. Whereas in the favela the women only show their breasts when nursing infants, the women in that district do so while the men pass through on their way to work, even when in the company of the priest. As the police inspector made a very unpleasant impression — he is of German descent and looks like a Nazi storm trooper — we believed only half of what he told us about the many gangsters, muggings and robberies here. As far as we can tell so far, the favelas are not meeting places for criminal elements. The *favelados* are simply poor due to lack of employment and schooling; and they are possessed by an irrepressible wanderlust that pushes them on to another city with all they own as soon as they have earned enough money.

*

I must tell the story of the rats. Our house previously belonged to a Japanese *fazendeiro* (farmland owner) who disappeared when his debts became too big. The house stood empty for many years and the cellar became the undisturbed meeting place for Londrina's animal world. During the second night, awakened by a scratching sound, I carefully switched on the light and saw a fat rat scramble away from a carrot a foot from my head. I ran to our men who, armed with a broom and club, drove the wildly scurrying creature away. I was far from calm however, as the beast had bored a hole through the floor from the cellar and was surely only the advance guard of an army. The animal life in our house is active indeed: flying, clothes-eating cockroaches, hordes of mosquitoes, mice, a hairy poisonous spider, fleas and beetles.

The favela is depressingly poor, but even such poverty is relative; the favelas in Rio or the slums in India are worse. Even the poorest seem to have someone poorer than themselves. Horrible holes serve as dwellings for countless children and their parents. A family of five lives in a discarded bus together with chickens, a dog, a sewing machine and an open cooking fire. The father gets up every morning a 4 a.m. to collect scrap paper from the street and sell it. They came, as did most of the favela residents, from Brazil's impoverished northeast. The favela residents aren't anti-social, but simply poor people who, because of their low income, cannot afford decent housing and therefore nail together huts made of boards on the edge of the city. The wives' additional income doesn't suffice for a better life. Many women and children work at picking coffee beans. They earn about a dollar for a thirty-pound sack of beans. I only realized how tiring and time consuming this work is when I tried it myself.

The men mostly work as unskilled laborers in factories where they receive the legal minimum wage of fifty dollars a month, or as coffee-bag carriers in the warehouses. (The faster you can run with a sack the more you earn.) Or they sell fruit, sweets and roasted peanuts on the street.

The racial mixture is unimaginable, although in the favela the majority is black. One sees Negroid kinky hair in blond editions, or Blacks with slanted Mongoloid eyes, or Aryan blue eyes. Besides these hybrids, there are also the more or less "racially pure" Spanish, Hungarian, Italian, Russian and German favelados — the jetsam of various immigration waves. And they really get along with each other. What they told us in Germany is true: how friendly, obliging and, despite their misery, how happy Brazilians are! During our rounds through the favela we are always received with a smile, a cafezinho is offered (and drunk, despite the axioms learned about "tropical hygiene"). When you take a child, usually covered with terra roxa (red earth) and full of sores, into your arms, contact is quickly established. We have yet to see a mistrusting or closed face.

Londrina has about 120,000 inhabitants. The city stands (or falls) with coffee. Thirty-five years ago, we are repeatedly told with pride, it was all jungle here, which is hard to imagine when you look down at miles of coffee trees from one of the city's skyscrapers. The jungle was so mercilessly cleared away that the climate has changed in the last decades — there is no longer a regularly occurring rainfall and the earth threatens to erode. The mato (jungle) seems inexhaustible, but all that remains of it are little jungle-islands. It seems that every country must live out its own experience with soil exploitation — just as today's youth refuses to learn from the mistakes of the older generation. Eucalyptus trees are planted for reforestation. They grow quickly but exhaust the earth's alkaline content even more.

Londrina, September 18, 1965

The visits seem never to end. High society rushes to the favela with Brazilian beginner's zeal. Favela social work is the current craze. My head reels from so many new faces bubbling with torrents of Brazilian sounds. I am so confused by all this that my brain cells can no longer differentiate between Portuguese, French. Serbo-Croatian and Russian.

A comical side of our life is the constant shuttling between the poorest, shabbiest part of Londrina and the city's prominence. Suddenly it's "to the mayor!" and we hastily wipe the red dust from our shoes and the red ring from under our fingernails (*po,* dust, is the number one subject during embarrassed silences instead of the weather), try to cover up fleabites, rip off the favela clothes and rush to the prefectura (city-hall).

We hardly arrive home with our faces stiff from smiling when the next visitor is announced: a German family which is "developing" in Bolivia. They no sooner leave than two nuns arrive who are in turn replaced by the business manager of Fuganti's, Paraná's Macys.

The following is a song about a child from a Rio favela who died because "there is no telephone in the favela to call a doctor and no car to fetch him".

Acender as Velas

(Light the Candles)

O doutor chegou tarde demais
porque no morro
não tem automovél pra subir
Não tem telefone pra chamar
e não tem beleza pra se ver
e a gente morre
sem querer morrer.

(The doctor comes too late because there is no car to come up to the favela, there is no telephone to call him, there is no beauty to see, and the people die without wanting to die.)

*

O menino está morrendo! The child is dying. Maria came running to fetch us. We went. It was already dead, lying on a wide board alongside the other sleeping children. Why didn't the mother go to the Santa Casa clinic as I had urged her to? The child died of dehydration. Dysentery and the heat deprive the body of so much liquid that it dries out. They sit there crying and do nothing, call us when it is too late. Were the poor in Germany ever so apathetic? Are apathy and thoughtlessness the results of misery (which would disappear with better living conditions), or are they characteristics of these people?

Está morto!

You suddenly feel empty, helpless, stupid, knowing nothing. What can you do? I snap off my flashlight, a definitive sound, like an exclamation point behind the *morto*.

Here you are closer to life than would ever be possible in Europe. Birth, death, marriage, sickness, crippling, idiocy — you're right in the middle of it and not shut off by walls from all the vital, essential human events as in Europe where sickness is hidden behind hospital walls, madness within a sanitarium, birth behind maternity ward walls.

*

At a birthday party for a one-year-old Syrian boy I studied Londrina's haute-volée. The party took place in the living room and on the balcony. Suddenly I realized that I hadn't previously noticed the strict separation of sexes. I speak with a man on the gentlemen's balcony — for shame! The ladies sit stiffly in the living room like hens on a perch wearing powder and mascara masks, praising the birthday child who is plump and overfed, a little Farouk. With much effort they are able to coax a smile from the fat dumpling face. The child isn't treated as a human being but as a curiosity for the grown-ups to dance around.

The children of wealthy parents, spoiled and pampered, are in stark contrast to those others who will not even be born because their potential mothers are too weak and under-nourished.

*

During the night Dona Antonia sends for us. She has had a miscarriage. The third in her twenty-five years. The long shadows the petroleum lamp throws on the walls make everything seem even more wretched than it is.

E dura a vida da casada. A married woman's life is hard. Nevertheless, the women of Brazil, rich or poor, black or white, yearn for only one thing: to marry as soon as possible, despite their daily experience that drudgery begins with marriage – especially for the poor, of course.

Their lives are determined by the great rhythms of life – birth, marriage, motherhood – to which they are harnessed as though under a compulsion they must obey. A compulsion which gives their lives a certain structure, but no freedom to move outside this pre-ordained course. Life exhausts itself in *namorar, casar, criar* (fall in love, marry, bear and raise children).

I recently experienced a similar apathy and resignation in a dream. I lay stretched out on the earth (red earth!) and was about to be burned. I covered myself with paper so the fire would ignite more quickly. Adolf and Kaspar stood to my left and right and watched, unmoving. I said goodbye to them and lay down again with my arms stretched out wide and my face towards the sky. No fear, no desire to be saved, resigned, as though a will stronger than mine had decided.

While we are on the subject of dreams, here is another of my Brazilian ones. I am on a jungle river, probably a tributary of the Amazon. Hanging plants dip low to the shallow, turbid, lazily flowing water. I know that dangerous Indians live nearby. Then a huge, wild-looking, bearded man emerges from a cave. Quickly I hide among the hanging plants. He disappears into the cave. Shortly thereafter a half-civilized Indian emerges and just as quickly disappears. Then an Indian splendidly dressed in brocade appears — he seems to shine — with a child in his arms. He shows it to me and speaks calmly and peacefully to me. I think: these are the three phases of human development — the caveman, the normal, average man and the royal man, shining from within.

Londrina, September 28, 1965

We were invited to a children's party at the home of a black family. Their hut always seemed somewhat mysterious after some children told us that the Holy Ghost puts up there. Recently we heard, at night, loud tom-toms, African jungle drums in their monotonous singsong. Curiosity overcame my indolence and I went there. Through the window I saw women dressed in long white gowns dancing in a semi-trance. In a monotonous chant, gradually increasing in volume, they cried, Domini! Domini! It was African Sarawa Cult, a mish-mash of Catholic belief and African hedonist exorcism through which sickness is apparently cured (white Sarawa) and spells are cast (black Sarawa).

*

Now to the children's party. I was prepared for a birthday party but not for what awaited me there. As the daughter of the house led me into the shack I heard a wild drumming and smelled a penetrating odor of wine, incense and other indefinable things (mostly blood as I later learned).

The first thing I discerned in the semi-darkness was a black woman dressed all in red kneeling in the middle of the narrow, crowded room. She held a convulsively twitching chicken fast while a fat black woman hung with pearls and chains (apparently the high priestess, she looked weird with one eye half-closed and the other goggling fearfully) cut the chicken's throat, caught the blood in a bowl, mixed it with oil, wine and honey and drew a cross on the other woman's forehead and throat with it. The one in red then drank the horrible brew and immediately went into ecstatic convulsions, similar to those of the slaughtered chicken, fell down, sprang into the air, danced wildly and finally threw herself onto the floor and rolled her eyes. Then another went into the circle, knelt, another chicken was sacrificed and so on, some fifteen times in my presence.

The atmosphere was uncannily thick, somehow stimulating and oppressive at the same time. It was like being in deepest Africa, although by no means only blacks participated. At intervals the drums stopped beating, the priestess rang a delicate bell and all was still. She said something about Jesus Christ and Domini (I had the impression she felt duty-bound to introduce a Christian element) and at once the singing, dancing and twitching continued. All this in a tiny, dim, candle-lit room crammed with sweating people and many children who delightedly clapped their hands and sang along and who I drew around me as a protective wall. Everyone was very attentive to me, held my bag, secured a good place for me to see, fanned fresh *(sic)* air in my direction. I was invited for the evening session and, being most curious, I didn't let the opportunity pass.

The atmosphere was completely different: calm and solemn. The initiates, the *filhas de santos,* also children, were dressed in blossom-white gowns trimmed with lace. They formed a circle around a white tablecloth spread on the floor. A child put candles and flowers on it, then six plates. Bahia food was brought. Six children were allowed to eat of it, representing all the children in the world, for the ceremony was an exorcism of the spirits who can harm children. This part was most solemn, only to be transformed suddenly into violent drumming and dancing.

But I didn't have the impression that the people thus carried away — and it was real, not faked — were any happier for it. Their faces were distorted with pain, sudden cramps shook their bodies, they put the backs of their hands on their spines as though they had motors there that called forth the ecstasy through cramps and writhing. The Sarawa priestess told me afterwards that the descending spirit occupies the lower vertebrae, literally possessing the person.

It was somehow nice when a nine-year-old child sprang into the circle, danced delicately, jumped for joy into the air and took my hand and placed it on an old woman's wrinkled face. She was the only one whose facial expression was calm and happy.

Then I was called aside. I expected the worst. I was to try the Bahia food. Manioca meal mixed with some green stuff and a mountain of meat that threatened to stick in my throat: the chicken which I had seen twitching several hours earlier. The thought of the flowing blood and the memory of the penetrating odor so nauseated me that the physical exertion of forcing it down brought tears to my eyes.

Londrina, 1 October

The stream of visitors has ceased. It is raining. The *terra-roxa* dust, which normally covers the land, furniture and people like a cloud, has been transformed into clay-like, slippery sludge. We are as good as cut off from the outside world; no automobile dares to penetrate this mud. It began last night with an electrical storm. This morning we viewed the mess: water in the kitchen and living room.

Yesterday evening we sat on the stairs with a record player. Right away we were surrounded by a flock of children with whom we danced the *Hava Naguila,* laughed and "politicized". On Sunday the governor will be elected from two candidates. Even the children are ardent supporters of one or the other. Suddenly a twelve-year-old boy stood on the fence and gave a classical election speech. It was hilarious, especially when he graciously acknowledged our enthusiastic applause. It is the age when they never tire of asking such things as: Is there a *Castelo Branco* (the president) in Germany too? Is there war in Germany now? Are there blacks in Germany too? etc.

Londrina, October 9

When I look out the window I see a wedding tent. Cido's eldest sister is getting married. It will be the favela wedding of the year. The bride seems to belong to one of the best families. She even owns a radio-phonograph, which stands as a showpiece on a podium in the tent. On the porch are three rococo chairs. A special sign of wealth is that she lives in a stone house. Her father is a piece-worker who carries coffee sacks. The groom is an industrious electrician who lives in one of the new wooden houses. They have been preparing the bride's house for days now: painting, hammering, sawing, even the eternal lamp over the front door has been polished. It is the event. Often more money is spent on a wedding than the family's meager budget can stand. The girls of the favela make themselves beautiful. Their hairdos are veritable towers.

The wedding became a real festival, very gay for us but a torment for the bride and groom who only danced once and otherwise could only let themselves be admired by their relatives, many of whom had come from far away. The day was sweltering like a greenhouse, so I could only pity the bride in her tight-fitting dress and long white gloves. We had never been in such demand — by the children. A flock of them constantly hung onto us: *Danca comigo* (dance with me.) Finally we organized a dance line.

*

Since our paramedic once cured a boy's earache, more and more mothers come to us with their sick children. The word spread like lightning that there is a *medico* here. Most of the children have dysentery, probably caused by the impure water, and parasites. Schistosomiasis, caused by a parasite which spends the days in the intestines and nights in the liver and penetrates the intestinal wall each time, leads to serious liver damage. There is still no cure for Chagas disease, caused by the bite of an insect. One dies a long-drawn-out death. Now and then the government launches a campaign against parasites, but as long as the greater part of the population lives in houses without running water and toilets, they are useless. The people are always infected anew. Bloated bellies, lack of appetite, listlessness and apathy are the results. Many parts of the favela are incubators of pestilence. City sewers empty into the favela and the filth pours into a ditch and oozes alongside the water spring. During Pablo Pimentel's election campaign the sewers were lengthened by ten yards. Most likely the remaining pipes will have to wait for the next election. The stench when the west wind blows is bestial. The men wash themselves in the spring and the women do their laundry there. They also wash the laundry of the wealthy. If they only knew what kind of water is used!

*

This afternoon we watched a fight over twenty cruzeiros that a woman underpaid the iceman. Cooking-pots, clumps of earth and finally knives were used. The word *briga* (fight) brings everyone running like nothing else. Jos, the fight addict, gave this one a miss though; It was only an unworthy women's battle.

*

A letter from the Vila da Boa Esperanca (Town of Good Hope) Here is a loose translation:

Senhorita Ruti, (me!)

By means of this poorly written letter I come to ask if, through goodness and kindness, you could accept this little girl in the school. She doesn't go to school, has no mother and lives with her sister. She would like to learn embroidery. I can't come myself because I am about to give birth. And if possible could you send milk for two children until my husband is released from the hospital. He has been there a long time. I am without work and ill. If you can do anything I thank you in advance.

Londrina, October 12

Yesterday we delivered our first favela child. All day it was unbearably hot until a thunderstorm finally broke in the evening. We were outside enjoying the patter of raindrops when the excited father came running up. Armed with a midwife kit, a bottle of alcohol, rubber gloves, towels and a flashlight, we tramped hurriedly through the mud, equally excited. The room was very dark, the bed full of lumps, rain dripped through the roof, you could hardly hear your own words over the thunder. We didn't know how to say "push" in Brazilian, the dictionary apparently being incompetent in such cases. We therefore kept calling for *mais forca,* (more force) and finally the baby came. We were deliriously happy when it began to scream. The afterbirth was carefully laid aside and afterwards the mother buried it, for the child's protection.

A delivery in the Santa Casa, a Catholic hospital, costs about seven dollars, half a month's wages for a housemaid. So they go there only in emergencies and otherwise trust in the help of an experienced mother.

Londrina, October 14

This evening I was again with the old Sarawa priestess, Dona Jacinta. She is of imposing appearance, vital, strong, tolerant and unwavering. One can imagine that she would be honored in heathen Africa as a symbol of the Earth Mother. You feel well in her presence, she exudes calmness.

She led me into her Sarawa-room. On one side are wooden benches, in the opposite corner stands her altar with its countless holy figures. Many gods have Christian as well as heathen names. For example St. George is Ogún, the god of war in the African religion. St. Michael corresponds to Xangó, the god of thunder and lightning. Yemanjá, the sea-goddess, is the Virgin Mary. Exú is the Devil and Oxalá, the god of life and fertility, corresponds to Jesus and the Holy Spirit.

Dona Jacinta offered to read the cards for me. From a pocket in her wide gown she took out a deck of well-thumbed cards on which I caught fleeting glimpses of plants, houses, the moon and stars. She laid them down on the table with a slow gesture and crossed herself and the cards. I had to cut them (No, with the left hand), and she began.

You have many protective gods, especially the sun. Soon you will make an important decision and, later on, not live in Germany. You will have a very troubled life, put much in order, much in disorder, *minha filha*.

When I told her that I often have headaches, she offered to "push my head right". So I will soon put myself under her care. She has a thriving medical practice, even people from the wealthy neighborhoods visit her. I asked her how long she had been doing this work.

Minha Filha, I began in Bahia. I lived in the country where my parents had a tiny piece of land to grow sugarcane. I was strong, wild and unruly (*braba).* I loved to ride wild horses all day long. Now and then I had a *namorado* (boyfriend). Suddenly I became very ill. A doctor treated me but he couldn't help. Then someone told me, "Go to the *Macumbeiro*! I went and the spirit came over me and shook off the illness. But the most important thing was that my nature changed. I became gentle (*mansa*), tolerant, calm. Octal ordered me to work, so I became a *Macumbeira*."

And what does the Catholic Church say to this?

The Church does not like it. But what can she do against it? There will always be Sarawa in the favela. The poor receive comfort and support from me which the impersonal machinery of the Catholic Church cannot give them. I bless each one personally, whereas the Catholic priest only does mass blessings. All find in me an open ear for their troubles, while the Catholic Church is a church for the rich only. I am a Catholic myself. One can do both. Sarawa is a way to experience faith physically. Each should come to God in the way He is most visible. The sea-goddess Yemanjá and the Virgin Mary, the spirit Xangó and St. Hieronymous: are they not the same gods who have descended to earth in different forms? Just as Catholics have their saints we also have them, often Black and Indian martyrs from the slavery time. Only God knows the truth, men must be tolerant.

Londrina, Oct. 26

We have just returned from a Fazenda, a real cattle ranch, the house airily built, the birds flying in one side and out the other. The eye ranges over the extensive hilly land and the cleared jungle with burnt-out tree stumps. We met the owner, a former agriculture minister and Prefect of Londrina, as he was inoculating his cattle against a skin disease. The *Dona da casa* brought us creamy milk, finally undiluted with water. She greeted us cordially, but apparently goes through Brazil with her eyes closed, because we had to tell her about favelas in detail as she has yet to see one.

One can hardly imagine how rich these people are. Frei Nereu told us recently that a rancher he knows earned $160,000 this year alone — while there are favela children who have never played with a doll. Brazilians also think almost exclusively in terms of these extreme contrasts. They often don't know how they should classify us. I realized this when the son of the owner of the Funganti department store, made uncertain by our living in the favela and at the same time frequenting the country club, asked: Are you rich or poor?

Londrina, Nov. 6

Four days leave from the favela! A jeep from the prefecture picked us up and we drove over hard-packed red earth roads to a storage lake in the middle of the jungle where the prefecture owns a holiday house for city employees and "other important persons".

The weather was cool, sunny, clear air like in the mountains, wonderful for hiking, walking and physical exertion. In the morning we walked on narrow paths hacked through the jungle to a huge waterfall. In the afternoon I went off alone. It's somehow uncanny the cracking of twigs by unseen animals in the underbrush, the birds' warning cries becoming increasingly shrill as you draw nearer. You feel lost amid this exuberant growth of upward striving, thorny brush, bamboo cane swaying in the wind, ninety feet high *pinhieros* (pines) and coconut palms, especially when the midday heat weighs so crushingly on the earth. Once we got up at 4 a.m. and explored the lake shore and its side-streams in a boat. They were often so narrow that the jungle closed in again behind us, over us a steep wall of green. Steering the boat was an artistic feat that won me the title "King of Helmsmen". We navigated thus for almost seven hours. Meanwhile hunger drove us to land and luckily I recognized a sugar-cane field from a distance; chewing sugar cane and quite full we went on.

Another time a ranch owner's son, an ex-boy scout, took us out. He was an interesting mixture of Portuguese, African and Brazilian Indian blood (his facial characteristics seemed pure southern India). He led us through once cleared but now heavily overgrown jungle and showed us Indian medicinal herbs against rheumatism, colds, boils.

*

I often visit the black Sarawa lady which, unfortunately, usually includes food. Can you imagine how much gagging you have to do to get dry manioca meal down? Her healing practice is apparently flourishing. Recently an alcoholic of German descent from Rio Grande do Sul went to her to be cured. Dona Jacinta has a *caixa postal* (post office box) to receive letters of thanks, although she can't read.

*

This evening we were elegant again. An invitation to the opening of an antique furniture shop. The problem of how to get from the dripping, muddy favela to the city was solved in the classic manner: the prefect happened to be visiting and he drove us in. How unnatural you act when you want to be elegant. We had to laugh at the affected fussing and twittering of the heavily powdered and dazzlingly painted ladies (lilac tinted hair to match a lilac dress), the fashionably pursed lips, the bare traces of smiles. We moved about in the crowd and now and then retreated to a corner to laugh our heads off. The German pastor's reproachful look (raised eyebrow, severe lines around his mouth) is worth mentioning, and his words: But I've never seen you in my church. *Deus me livre* (God forbid)

Londrina, Christmas 1965

We were invited to spend Christmas with a Brazilian family from Guarpava (South Paraná). We went via Apucarana, Ponta Grossa. The asphalt ends there, and the route continues over the terra roxa, "roads" so bumpy, muddy and full of holes that the bus often listed like a ship; then came another strip of asphalt; our speed seemed that of an airplane on the runway. The monotonous landscape is relieved in Paranoia by pastureland with scattered cows and occasional jungle.

After a fourteen hour drive we reached Guarapava. How rich our hosts were we couldn't have imagined. When we learned through snatches of conversation that half the city (electricity and water works, fertilizer factory, sawmill, cattle and pig raising) belongs to them we put aside our humbleness and abandoned ourselves to gluttony. We paid no attention to ordinary stomach-fillers such as rice and potatoes; only fruit, vegetables, nuts, cake and meat, meat, meat did we eat. Meals were taken in a special wooden building, a dining-house, so to speak, in which the *churrasco*, (roast meat) was cooked on spits over an open fire. The spits with half a pig, goats and oxen were stuck into the wooden table at which we were all seated and each cut off as much as he wanted. What a treat for our stomachs so used to rice and beans!

We spent one afternoon at the German colony Entre rios. The landscape was transformed with a stroke — waving wheat fields, orderly juicy green pastures with black and white cows — a piece of Germany. The contrast with the barely cultivated land we were used to was so great that we began to vehemently debate about why Brazilians don't manage to do the same. I think that the Brazilian fazendeiro's relationship to the earth is different from a German's. The German farmer cherishes and cultivates his land, which becomes the embodiment of his home. The fazendeiro is more an administrator of property, from which he exacts the greatest profit with the least effort, than a farmer. The intensive cultivation of a small piece of land doesn't interest him. He operates an extensive cattle business or plants one crop over a huge area until the land is exhausted (sugarcane, tobacco, coffee). Historically this is understandable. The Portuguese came as adventurers and merchants and not as land-hungry farmers. Their strength lay in exploring the interior, not in cultivating the discovered. Nor did the nomadic Indian tribes contribute to the creation of the farming ethic. They lived from hunting and fishing, burned out clearings here and there in the jungle in order to plant manioca, corn and tobacco, then abandoned the exhausted land. The present-day jungle-burning and the lack of fertilizer is reminiscent of those methods.

But back to the German colonists. The majority of them came from Banat (Yugoslavia), the so-called Danube Germans. After the Second World War they fled and the Swiss foreign aid organizations gave them a few acres of land in Brazil, some cows and a little money. They started with practically nothing, planted wheat (rare in Brazil) and many have become so rich that they are overwhelmed by their steadily growing lands and income. These Danube Germans hold Brazilian citizenship but speak faltering Portuguese and are very anxious to preserve the heritage of their forefathers.

As with so many German immigrants they identify with a Germany which no longer exists, sing folksongs which we would call sentimental and talk about a Germany in which it is impossible to be free. The Germany of the nineteenth century and the world depression have been spiritually mummified here.

Londrina, January 1966

Recently I had an interesting conversation with the GDS (German Development Service). As I was originally supposed to be working here as a teacher but found upon arrival that there was already a school with six teachers, I suggested that we organize a kindergarten and a sewing circle. "But that isn't social work," was the answer. Now, however, it has been recognized as social work and I am even to be allowed to take a three-week kindergarten course in Gramado (Rio Grande do sul). The GDS decisions are unfathomable. "Impenetrable like the GDS" has already become a slogan.

Rio Grande do Sul is well suited to Europeans due to its temperate climate and having been mostly colonized by Germans — and, to a lesser extent, Italians and Poles. German or Platt dialect is mostly spoken, except in the big cities. It is a far cry from the real Brazil; no black faces, no openhearted sloppiness, no Brazilian *giria* (slang). Instead "Cultivate the German heritage" is the motto. Children, blue-eyed and blonder than in Germany, typical German farms with cackling hens on dunghills and carefully cultivated beets, apple and pear trees instead of mamão and abacate, wine instead of cafezinho.

Yesterday we went on a great excursion. After walking five miles we came to a waterfall surrounded by pine trees. Unfortunately, the place had already been "opened" to tourism – cars and transistor radios were all over the place. To be sure, we almost forgot this when we climbed down a sixty-yard steep slope through the jungle, scrub, prickles and lianas. Half crawling and with courageously suppressed fear of tree-snakes, we made our way to the waterfall. We saw no snakes, only two onças, tiger-cats, who glared at us from a branch, then quickly disappeared.

Londrina, February 1966

Events overlap: a trip to Mato Grosso, the opening of the kindergarten, a thief in the house. Let's start with the thief. At six o'clock this morning I heard someone moving about and thought it suspicious because on Saturdays everybody sleeps longer. I investigated and found Helmut wandering around the kitchen and dining-room. He jumped down my throat furiously in my half-awake state: Whose idea was this joke? What joke? He told me about his clothes being scattered about, the suitcase found chewed up by goats in the garden, and his radio that had disappeared. He thought we had hidden his things in order to inaugurate his moving into the new room. The affair was cleared up when I found traces of red earth on the easy-chair and windowsill as well as a clear footprint and fresh terra roxa on the stoop — the thief was clean enough to wipe his shoes before entering. A *ladrão* (robber) had honored us with his presence during the night.

Helmut, in good detective form, found more footprints and measured the length of the stride, from which he determined that they were made by a man with a 35-inch stride. We were told later that there are *maconha* cigarettes here, the smoke of which can temporarily weaken the ability to react, to the extent that a scoundrel can take something out of your pocket with complete peace of mind. Helmut, lulled by the *maconha* smoke, slept through the robbery. Also, the open window must have been too great a temptation for the thief.

In defense of Brazilians and the favela, I must say that until now nothing had been stolen from us despite the house door being unlocked day and night. Shoes and laundry remain on the porch during the day and we are often absent for days at a time. When the favela people want to steal they probably do so from the rich in town where, however, the houses are guarded at night.

Now to Mato Grosso. The trip goes under this name, although we barely touched its outer edge — Tres Lagos and the satellite city of Pilotos. Pilotos is a city for the workers who are building two dams on the Paraná River which are to supply São Paulo and Paraná with electricity. It will be one of the world's most important dam complexes. The work rhythm corresponds to its importance. Everything is well-organized, clean, expedient, clear and "technical". The modern, aspiring side of Brazil comes to light here. The workers are well treated, they earn more than usual, at least $100 monthly with free housing, inexpensive food and free medical care. We saw no one in rags, no beggars or rubbish lying about. Early in the morning we saw men raking leaves, mowing the grass, repairing defective lights. Everyone has his job, everything fits.

From Pilotos we went to Guararápes in the State of São Paulo. The parents-in-law of Manuelo, a carpenter from our favela with whom we were traveling, live there. As though it were the most natural thing in the world, we were fed and the family squeezed together so we could also sleep there.

We experienced the desolation of a medium-sized city in the interior of Brazil, and the life of a Brazilian family which, although it is beyond the anxiety about its daily bread, is completely untouched by culture — a not very happy in-between stage, as they have left childish simplicity (most favelados) behind them but haven't yet discovered thinking.

I almost forgot the funniest part. As I jumped out of bed early in the morning raring to go and to see everything, I realized that my right eye was stuck shut, only a tiny slit remaining open. During the day this also closed and when I awoke the next morning both eyes were so swollen that I had to grope blindly about. I, who had set out to see Brazil, could barely make out the coffee cup in front of me. Kaspar said I should go to a doctor. Luckily, we had the idea to buy sunglasses, after which the swelling went down to the extent that I could see again — a la Japanese. During the third night I got a clue to the cause of this strange swelling. I woke up with a dreadful itching, put on the light and saw a horde of bedbugs hurriedly disappear into their hiding-places. I fell into a true scratching ecstasy, controlled myself for a few seconds, then went at it again in full frenzy until, exhausted, I let the beasts have their way with me. Apparently they had also bitten me on the eyelids.

*

And now to the kindergarten! I have two groups, one from eight to eleven o'clock, the other from one to four. I have at my disposal four balls, matchsticks, some homemade dolls, jump-ropes and all kinds of miscellaneous stuff like coconut shells, rags, crayons, paper, etc. What makes the work difficult is that the children are especially jumpy and lack concentration, never want to occupy themselves with one thing for more than five minutes. Most of them didn't even know what toys were. Another problem is that they have so little sense of community. They want to pick up as many toys as possible and, from fear that another will take them away, hold on to them compulsively instead of playing with them. My back is no sooner turned than the toys are fought over, sometimes quite violently. With my squeaky voice trying to be thunderous, I restore order. Sometimes I think that I am too strict. After all, it's only too understandable that they are so greedy. But at some point they must learn to do things in community.

Discipline is unknown to them and they don't even obey their own parents. To form a circle or a line is practically impossible. When I have the last ones in order, the first ones are already dancing out of line. They simply cannot wait.

Another difficulty is that children of the same age are in such different stages of development. Some are in the crawling stage, others toddling, some draw people with their arms stuck onto their heads. They are all five to six years old but very different in their physical development. The black children look to be the strongest and the blonde, light-skinned ones seem to have the least resistance to the climate and illness. Most of the children look undernourished. They are regularly given rice and beans for lunch but lack protein and vitamins. The food here is very poor in mineral salts and in general is less nutritious than in Europe. This may be why they mature too early under the tropical sun and don't have time to draw strength from the earth. It seems to me that the apathy and debility of many Brazilians can be traced to this century-old vitamin deficient, carbohydrate-based diet. In the kindergarten, spontaneous outbreaks of unalloyed joy of being are followed by hours of indifference and sleepiness. Recently a little girl said with true self-knowledge: "Today I'm especially lazy." She hangs over the table and can't be moved, not even to put a crayon in her hand.

That's the negative side, which, as is well known, is so much easier to relate. How shall I describe that they are dear and affectionate? They bring me flowers, they share with me their only sucked-on candy, want to give me their hamster. They fan me with admirable endurance when it gets too stuffy in the kindergarten.

Today I again noted how little family life there is in the favela. During the mid-day break I was at Darcy's, my keenest morning pupil. The family is very orderly, the father works for the prefecture as a street-sweeper and therefore belongs to the favela's privileged class, because he has a regular income and will receive a small pension later. Darcy sat in a corner with a plate of rice and beans on her lap and ate her lunch. Mirinha, the younger sister, squatted on the stoop and picked obstinately at her food. No table, at which the family could be together, at least for lunch. At that moment the table became the symbol of family life for me. Usually one doesn't even think about it, but here in Brazil, and especially in the favela, it becomes increasingly clear to me how important it is that children have a proper space in which to pass their young lives. And a daily program with regular mealtimes, during which the family is together, belongs to this. In Germany the home is the center for the family; here everything is aimed away from the home. Even the sick would rather hang around a street corner than stay in bed at home. Getting up early at a certain hour certainly belongs to this regular daily program, and children are sent to bed at a certain hour. Here the children are often out on the street until midnight before they go to sleep — often in a family bed — and are so tired the next morning that they have no desire to go to school.

May 1966

Today is Mother's Day. Apparently it is celebrated much more here than in Germany. The school celebrates with cookies and lemonade, the prefecture distributes meat and noodles in the favela. Like the *churrascada* for the prefecture employees on May Day, this distribution in the favela seems so patriarchal to me. It's nice of them, somehow human, to think of the poor, but it is not enough when, with a sincerely friendly smile, you give presents to minimum-wage earners. You should rather give them the opportunity to buy meat and noodles for themselves, to struggle and to stand on their own feet. In my opinion, the most important thing is educational reform, and not only in a general sense (schools for all), but in a more profound sense (better school programs).

Yes, person to person Brazilians are generous and willing to help the poor. But the same people who give Frei Nereu a check for housing in the favela refuse to cooperate with decisive steps which would bring about fundamental changes (land reform, educational reform, street construction, reduction in coffee planting).

Every day I see Dona Dita walking in the midday heat with a load of freshly washed laundry balanced on her head. And an hour later she goes in the opposite direction with a bundle of dirty laundry under her arm. She works for some rich city families in order to earn school money for her son. It is admirable with what perseverance she washes in the stream hour after hour in order to give her son a high school education. She has discovered that you can only escape poverty through learning, learning and more learning.

But even when they have been to high school and have learned a trade, it is difficult for the poor to get a good job without having connections. More so if you are black. How stupid it is to characterize blacks as inferior and lazy. Brazil wouldn't even exist without the blacks. They worked like animals on the sugar plantations of Bahia and Pernambuco and in the mines of Minas Gerais and in this way kept the Brazilian economy viable. Furthermore, it was the intermixing of the Portuguese masters with their black slaves which — purely numerically — made the settlement and development of Brazil possible.

It wasn't only their strong arms, their labor-power, that they brought to Brazil, but also their abilities, their craftsmanship, their artistic sensitivity and their experience with tropical agriculture. They were far superior in agriculture and cattle-raising to the Indios and Portuguese. Also their food habits were less one-sided. Many plants, such as beans and bananas, were brought in by the blacks. Even cattle: the goats and sheep were imported from Africa.

The Sudanese, of Islamic religion, brought an especially active element to Brazil. They organized the slaves, gathered runaways and led them to the jungle where they organized their own settlements, the so-called *quilombos,* which prospered and offered proof of the Blacks' ability, especially in agriculture. They read the Koran in Arabic and thus it happened that in the early Portuguese colonization period there were fewer illiterates in the slave-huts than in their masters' mansions. The slaves were more cultured than their masters!

However, the reverse is now the case: the blacks are neglected and barely educated. That's why it is so important that a black woman like Dona Dita goes to so much trouble to send her son the high school.

What would Brazil be without blacks, without the contagious laughter of a Didi, the African rhythms of so many songs and dances, without the African cults, without the calm composure and motherliness of many black women, or the childish devotion of a Tereza? It is all a necessary counterweight to the somewhat melancholic, reserved character of the Indios.

Londrina, June 1966

This is a time of intense activity in the kindergarten. The school vacation period has begun and the children come in droves to do needlework, even the boys. So, with barely a pause for breath, I am busy teaching them how to manipulate the needles, stitch and undo the stitches again, unravel thread. Some also learn to knit.

After my vacation in July, I might start an arithmetic class. Mental arithmetic or, for example, how to construct a cube with certain dimensions, is not taught in the marginal schools. They don't know how to draw a three-inch line with a ruler. Very few vendors know how to multiply. In secondary school, however, they learn more mathematics than in Germany.'

*

God protect us from missionaries. A missionary has been in the favela since yesterday scaring people into church with loud, croaking music. No method is too dumb to lure the people to church: German and American military music, Mozart's A Little Night Music, The River Kwai March, The Bells ring out Sweetly pour over the huts in ear-splitting waves from loudspeakers. No sooner is mass over than canvassing for the next event begins: meetings with married women and widows, then for single girls, then come the fathers and widowers. (They shouldn't beget so many children, the priest tells them – but how?!) Marriages and baptisms are diligently performed, but in heaven's name not for illegitimate children, who were conceived in sin. The church considers such details un-Christian. But it seems to be Christian when a Catholic priest says that we should only distribute medicine in our favela and send the other sick people home.

Sometimes the children can make me quite angry. I noticed just in time that Darcy was throwing away his leftover sugar after the milk-break. *Não 'tou fome mais não*. He's full, he says. And tomorrow? I don't know about tomorrow.

No one would guess that this child comes from a slum, that his parents emigrated from the hunger-stricken north to find work on the coffee plantations in Paraná. The same children who are wasteful with sugar in the morning scramble crying for a few grains of rice that have fallen from a donkey-cart in the afternoon; or share one sweet among five of them.

The favela children, despite knowing hunger, have as little concept of the value of things as the rich. How often do they say: my father lost his job and we have nothing to eat. In spite of this, neither the children nor their parents have a concept of saving or provision and planning for the future. *Se Deus quiser*, if God wills, everything will be all right. Is this fatalism and living only for today an unchangeable basic characteristic, or a mental attitude developed over the centuries which can be changed through education, by awakening their slumbering capacities by means of training in thinking? Education by experience is apparently not sufficient.

But nothing will be achieved if the schools stay the way they are: schools for parrots who are bored to death memorizing the names of rivers and mountain ranges which aren't even shown to them on a map; of kings and explorers whose origins and aims remain unknown. Instead of motivating the children, they suffocate their desire to learn, their natural curiosity and joy of discovery through monotonous boredom.

It would be good if they could work together in groups: crafts, reading fairy tales and myths, exploration trips, sports to learn fairness, to learn to differentiate between beauty and kitsch by means of art appreciation. The children should be given problems to solve and objectives to be attained, so they will realize that in later life objectives must be set and that thinking precedes acting.

But who will give the favela children such schools of thinking? The politicians and the rich have no wish to stimulate the spirit of criticism and reflection, for this criticism would eventually be directed against them. And the poor do not possess the means. It's beyond their strength. And it would result in the "revolution from below".

1966

Today I received a letter from Brigitte, a school friend, in which she writes about the affluence ecstasy in Germany. I wonder why we are trying to elevate the favelas to the middle-class when the members of the latter are so desolate, mediocre, satiated, limited in interest to their stomachs, beds, automobiles and television.

Probably I have no right to ask this, coming as I do from the middle-class, because I don't know, don't really know what it's like to live in a leaking, wind-bent hut, and to have a stomach which contains more worms than food. And the ascent of the favelados to the middle-class — apart from the fact that it may be inevitable, the question being when and how — would probably be good if only because of the few people who aren't satisfied with a full stomach, but who use their heads and seek a real meaning in life.

Londrina, August 1966

The knitting bug has invaded the favela. The children teach their sisters and brothers and their mothers. Often you see them with their knitting on street corners and in the playground teaching each other. I didn't know where to get enough wool. Luckily, I am now able to buy leftovers cheaply at Fuganti's department store.

I want to see if I can arrange an exhibition of the children's work, perhaps even a bazaar to sell it. It's about time for the rich of the city to realize that the favela children can also accomplish something, if only given the chance. A few girls have begun to knit for this purpose, but it is still somewhat difficult. I tremble with every fallen stitch. Also the risk that I may be stuck until an advanced old age with Christmas ornaments, baby clothes, tablecloths, baskets, etc., gives pause for thought. Maybe their childish enthusiasm will fizzle out as suddenly as it came, for this present eagerness can hardly long endure. Last week I started to knit bigger things with some of the children and thought they would be kept busy for the next two weeks. But the caps were ready in two days and I had to think of something else.

Virginia's father just appeared, drunk again. The kitchen door opened and a brown hand laid a pair of socks on the dresser. I went onto the kitchen porch and saw him washing our towels and hang them carefully out to dry. He only said *boa tarde,* good afternoon, and carried on, as though it were the most natural thing in the world for him to be washing our towels on Sunday. When he could find nothing else to wash he thanked me and left. Surely this was his way of thanking me for the sweater I gave his daughter. He probably had to sell his horse, on which he always galloped past our dining-room window. To compensate he came today in a fire-red shirt. He lives in the very last hut of the favela, which is almost invisible because of the cacti climbing over it. His six-year-old daughter was burned with boiling water when she was three. The wound is still open.

Londrina, August 1966

It is uncomfortably cold. The Brazilians, especially the blacks, are quite hardened to it and freeze less than we. Recently I saw a black man sitting in front of his hut naked to the waist when the temperature was just below freezing. I shivered just looking at him. I woke up today and looked out the window: everything white! hoarfrost. It froze overnight. You can imagine the panic of the coffee planters. The first coffee buds are dead, the leaves hang black and limp on the trees; a pitiful sight. Conversation-piece number 1: the burnt coffee. Strangely enough they say burnt instead of frozen. Probably because it is not the frost itself that causes the damage, but the morning sun shining on the iced-over leaves. This year's harvest has just been brought in. The damage is therefore to next year's crop, 50-60% loss, according to the newspapers.

If it weren't for the workers, many of whom are being laid off and therefore must bear the brunt of the loss, it would be the best and cheapest way to get rid of the coffee. Instead of burning it after years of storage, it is burned already on the tree, so it doesn't have to be picked, cleaned, transported or stored. Over thirty thousand sacks are stored, while at the most fourteen thousand sacks are exported yearly. The fazendeiros, wringing their hands, wait for rain, so that the second buds may appear. Coffee blossoms three times. Therefore black (over-ripe), red (ripe) and green (unripe) beans hang simultaneously on the same plant. Ripe and unripe beans are "picked" at the same time, that is, knocked from the tree with a stick and gleaned from the ground. That's the reason for the poor quality of Brazilian coffee. We wonder why the planters haven't yet realized that there are more important crops than coffee so they could pull out at least the unproductive trees in order to plant rice, beans and wheat. Beans are imported from Mexico in exchange for valuable hard currency. The state now gives subsidies for every plucked out unproductive coffee tree and only gives credit for so-called "white agriculture" (rice, wheat, soybeans, etc. and cattle), which causes the coffee aristocracy to cry like stuck pigs. What they must put up with, and how unthankful is the state, especially since they bring in the hard currency in the first place.

Although the planters claim that their workers are protected, they are laid off *en masse* and stream into the city. The prefecture courtyard looks like a refugee camp. The empty coffee warehouses on the periphery of the city serve as emergency shelters. Now and then beggars come to the favela looking for something to eat. In their eyes the people in the favela are lucky, because they at least have a roof over their heads.

Yesterday I was at a German fazenda (farm) and spoke with the workers. A Russian woman works there who had been carried off by German soldiers in 1943, met a Pole in a concentration camp whom she eventually married, but had to emigrate as a displaced person after the war and arrived here with nothing. She has been working for the German fazenda owners, mostly in the kitchen, for twelve years. Her husband, who earns $150 per month, is the administrator of the farm. When he is ill he earns nothing. His son earns 30 cents an hour. With a ten-hour workday, he just about earns the *salario minimo*. He is always on duty, even when the *senhor* calls for him at night. I asked him if they are helped in case of sickness, if anyone cares for the workers' children, if the young girls are given the opportunity to learn something. Nothing! But many fazenda owners of German descent preach to us about humanity and sacrifice: One must really do something for the poor, who after all are so adept and willing to work. I asked the Russian lady if this doesn't make her furious.

No, they are quite human, at least they speak to us.

The same fazendeiros who do nothing for their own workers jump on the aid for development bandwagon as soon as they smell an advantage for their social prestige. Why is it that the same person who deducts the cost of rent, firewood and the use of the football field from his workers' meager wages is the same person who builds a clinic for the poor in the city? The reason: one happens in silence, the other in public view accompanied by the applause of the press and the acclaim of *sociedade*. It almost seems as if money for development is made available in order to enhance the prestige of a rich minority. How sensible!

Londrina, October 1966

During the past few weeks we have done a lot of work on the kindergarten with the boys of the favela, whitewashed the building, painted the chairs and tables, put in windowpanes, planted flowers and dug a pit for high and long-jumping. When the kindergarten, together with surroundings, stood ready in its new splendor, self-made, so to speak, we were all very proud. It is quite different if a kindergarten is placed ready-made into its surroundings, or if it is just a shell which the children beautify by their own efforts and make their own. It is infuriating how German technicians from the GDS are used to nails boards together to make wooden houses and to excavate ditches, instead of having them teach the masses of unemployed youths in the favela to do their own work. It's really a pity! They are cooperative, adroit, interested, not lazy, but at an age when they should be preparing themselves for a trade, they do absolutely nothing. They no longer go to school, they have outgrown the work they did as ten-year-olds (shoe-shine boys, scrap paper collectors) and they don't find other work. After the coffee froze almost all minors were laid off to make room for the unemployed agricultural workers, so they accustom themselves to sweet idleness. They aren't bored, because there is always a group hanging around for fun.

Training courses or trade schools which would take the young people off the streets – that would be true development and would really benefit the poor. There are very few such GDS projects however. It makes no sense for Adolf and Kaspar to be making small houses when any Brazilian carpenter could do it just as well. Could ... if the GDS people weren't around to take the work away from them. Strangest of all is that the GDS doesn't understand the absurdity. *Cabeça dura demais* — pigheaded. (The GDS have since learned from such experiences.)

*

With respect to my exhibition, I waver hourly between great enthusiasm and thinking that it will be completely impossible. We have made tablecloths with matching napkins using hem and cross-stitches. The abstract patterns and stitch counting are very difficult for some children; the boys usually do it better than the girls, which makes them very proud. Weaving with bast is easier because the work process is clearer. They also now understand that you cannot just select any color, that colors often clash. It is certainly good for them not to see only manufactured junk around them, but also pretty things which they can make. Native crafts which exist in countries that have ancient cultures don't exist here, except for the bone-lace of Bahia. The handicrafts of the original Indian inhabitants disappeared along with their culture as a result of the collision with European culture. The Portuguese masters, plantation owners, didn't respect handicrafts, so an artisan class never developed. The lack of this tradition is making itself felt now during the industrialization process. A factory in a country in which the carpenter's trade, with apprentice and master carpenters, didn't exist in pre-industrial times results – at least at the present stage – in work of inferior quality. Our sloppily joined closets and beds that fall apart are prime examples.

Londrina, November 1966

In general, life in the favela is peaceful and calm. But now and then this smooth surface cracks under the pressure of poverty or passion. Recently a woman lay in wait on a street corner for a girl from our favela and killed her with a kitchen knife because she was living with the woman's husband. Then she went directly to the police and said, 'Lock me up,' I want a rest from life. Now both she and her husband are in jail and their five children have been distributed among relatives. People help each other because state welfare is ineffective. At best the state would put the children in jail with their parents. Several children twelve to thirteen years old have been interned in Londrina's jail for years because they were once caught stealing.

Or recently: the father of Irany, one of my kindergarten children, took his revolver out of its box and wanted to kill his wife and twelve children. Irany had the presence of mind to run out of the house with his bullets – to the kindergarten! The father was fed up with being a night-watchman and a laborer during the day, all to barely feed his family. The next day he left them.

The Londrina jail isn't a pleasant place to pass the time. Twenty to thirty prisoners are jammed into tiny cells where they all sleep on a few thin mattresses, with a single bucket serving as the toilet. The walls are covered with graffiti depicting their wishful thinking. A rich person wouldn't last a day there. I can only imagine that the rich buy their freedom, or that there are also first-class jails. Many criminals are released so they can care for their families; they must report weekly to the police.

There are fewer drunks than one would expect, considering how cheap *pinga* (sugarcane liquor) is. But when they do get drunk they go all out. A few days ago we were playing, about forty children and adults, on the street in the fresh evening air, when a group of boys being chased by a drunk armed with a brick came running toward us. Screaming, everyone tried to get into the nearest house, with the drunk after them. There was total panic. Forty people trying to get through a tiny doorway at the same time. I grabbed a two-year old and stood in the shade of a tree waiting for them to come out. The woman of the house dropped the egg she was about to fry. Men in this condition are so dangerous because they are almost always carrying a knife. The police were called.

In Brazil crime is elementary and spontaneous, conceived in a passionate, uncontrolled instant and, above all, perpetrated against a certain individual. A murder is committed for a specific motive (jealousy, insult, etc.) and involves a certain person and no other. Murderer and victim are related by personal contact. Not like in Germany and other so-called civilized countries where unknown people are murdered, where lack of social contact engenders anonymous aggression, which is directed against defenseless people as revenge against society in general. Murder in Brazil is (except for political murder committed by professional assassins, *capangas*), strange at it sounds, more "human". As long as you have no personal enemies you are safer in a favela than in a European metropolis (1).

*

The longer I live together with the favela people, the clearer it becomes to me that the Brazilian people, especially the poorer classes, are uprooted, and at many levels. Even outwardly, in respect of origins. Brazil was discovered, explored and colonized by the Portuguese. Later immigrants arrived from Germany, Italy, Poland, Russia, Syria and, increasingly, Japan. And, of course, the involuntary immigrants. Thousands of blacks were abducted to work on the sugar plantations, were torn from their homes like weeds from the earth. From Africa they brought with them their Gods, their Sarawa-cult, their ritual songs. So Brazil's roots are in Europe on one hand and Africa on the other. Until the First World War the center of gravity was the northeast, Bahia and Minas Gerais. With the decline of the sugar monoculture and the economic center's shift to the south (São Paulo, Paraná), many lost their homes for the second time. Thousands migrated south seeking work on the sugar plantations and the newly developing industries. Most landed in favelas. They aren't driven from their homes for political reasons, but by hunger, drought, unemployment and the government's reluctance to energetically tackle the problems of the northeast. It is difficult to imagine the mobility of the poor. In times of drought, vague rumors that work is available in other parts of the country are sufficient to mobilize vast armies of people, on foot, or by train or truck. Industrial centers such as São Paulo, Belo Horizonte and Recife attract them like magnets. This is also why nostalgia for *minha terra, minha namorada* (my land, my loved-one) is the theme of so many folksongs and pop hits.

This mobility leads to a second uprooting. Despite their lack of freedom and their poverty, the slaves lived in relative security because of the landowners' patriarchal attitude, at least in the 18/19 centuries. After the freeing of the slaves the poverty remained, but the security was gone. The ex-slaves became the industrial and agricultural proletariat, to be fired at any time, continually seeking employment. Industrialization and mechanization have a negative effect on the poor. It is true that new jobs are created — but at what of wage level? Profits are for the rich. And isn't it true that capital influx from the "first world" only serves to intensify this tendency?

Theocratic thinking and patriarchal attitudes and their related agrarian system were replaced by industrialization, accompanied by its way of thinking and its social order. People no longer live in the stable framework of a tribe or clan which dictates the laws of life. They no longer find support in myths, art, folksongs and dances. They have forgotten their intuitive knowledge and natural healing methods. There are only vestiges of these to be seen. The

Sarawa cult, mixed with Catholicism and the worship of saints, is only partially understood. Due to the invasion of technology in their lives, the traditional commitment to their Gods has been lost, their ancient culture has become unintelligible to them, without a substitute existing for what has been lost. The knowledge which is passed on from generation to generation about, for instance, education or work methods, is lost or ignored, but there are too few schools to replace that knowledge with another which corresponds to the necessities of the times. Another example: Sarawa is decadent, but there is no church which gives the poor a new religious understanding. Religious instruction is limited to memorizing prayers and church hymns.

Thus the poor oscillate between two worlds, separated from one and not yet accepted in the other. They suffer spiritual as well as physical hunger.

Londrina, December 1966

We are preparing for Christmas. We intend to have a big celebration for all the favela children. A meeting takes place every Saturday and there is an abundance of things to fix and to make – hundreds of paper stars for a sky-tent, a small fence to separate the audience from the "actors", a wardrobe to change in, etc. Otalino is "chief artisan", Cido is "*Maitre de Plaisir*", he rehearses verses, dances and songs. It is a true trial of patience. Someone is always absent from rehearsals. They don't feel like it, or have to help their mothers, or they just sit apathetically in the corner (which is understandable, as the kindergarten is like an oven in the afternoon), and after a half-hour most of them want to dance and sing according to their own fantasy. Then I think as, dripping with sweat, I cry *silencio* at children who lose all control when music is playing, that I am ripe for the GDS medal. But it is well known that for that you have to be where the medals are awarded, not where they are earned.

As I was thinking about how to make a Christmas crib scene, my mother's *Weg zur Krippe* (The Way to the Crib) arrived. We found it so beautiful that we started cutting out with great enthusiasm till late in the afternoon and with growling stomachs, for the children decided it would be a waste to break for lunch. We also have a Christmas tree, a small araucaria, the symbol of Paraná. Costumes for the Queen of the celebration, the kings, Indians, dancers, doormen, curtain-openers, waitresses as well as the Christmas tree decorations are all finished. Now we are baking a mountain of cornmeal cookies for us and the audience; the only thing lacking is cold and snow. It's 90 degrees outside and the red earth reflects back the shimmering heat.

Londrina, January 1967

The parcel with the work material is here. I rushed to the post office and found a half-shredded parcel. With the worst presentiment I ran down the hill to the favela, feeling it all over. In my mind I could see the customs official's wife with the pearls around her neck, but *graças a Deus* my fears were unfounded: everything has arrived. Opening it was pure joy, together with Tereza, Cido, Otalino and other children. They all experienced the arrival and opening of a parcel for the first time. Solemnly they handed each little package to me, which I opened, and they stood around watching in amazement, oh oh-ing. They were all thrilled with the pearls and wanted to start stringing them immediately.

We began the day before yesterday and today there are hardly any pearls left. The first night we sat working until one o'clock in the morning in my room and at eight we were at work again. About 30 strings of pearls are now ready, some of them really ripe for display. The time has come to have the bazaar, but where?

*

We have begun weaving. But our minds are mainly on corn. We used the corn harvest for a corn festival. Together with Zeca, Otalino, and Cido, I went to a fazenda to pick up three large sacks. We met at 6 a.m., when it was still dark, in order to arrive there early. Lunch consisted exclusively of corn, roasted in a fire. In the afternoon we really got going though. We tried out various Brazilian (or rather Indian) specialties: one husked the corn, another ground it fine, still another pressed it through a cloth. It sprayed in all directions and the dark faces were sprinkled white. Another formed bags from the corn husks in which the corn meal was placed and then cooked in hot water. The result is called *pamonha*, a kind of corn cake. For dessert me made *curral,* corn pudding. The only thing lacking was corn whiskey, but even without it we were intoxicated by corn. Soon we will be walking around in corn slippers and will lay the fruit in corn bowls, then the remaining husks will be dried out and used for handicrafts.

*

A characteristic of the kindergarten day is the children's unrestrained chatter. Listening, I learn quite a bit about their way of life and their feelings. Dalva came running to me today: I am so ugly, *feia mesmo* (really ugly). Why was I born so black, I'll have to marry someone just as black and then my children will be just as ugly and black as me. She is 16 years old, absolutely not ugly, very clean and correctly dressed and works as an *empregada* (maid) in the city. To her great regret, her skin is dark brown, her hair is frizzled and her nose is somewhat wide. Her efforts to bleach her skin with a thick layer of rice powder and to straighten her hair are touching, but unsuccessful.

*

In Germany the people lie in the sun to become brown, I tell them. The children are skeptical.

You seem to think that black and ugly are one and the same. Whites can be just as ugly as blacks can be beautiful.

*

Zeca, thirteen years old, a lot of black with some Indian and Portuguese blood, says: I would much prefer to have straight hair. When I am collecting old paper and find a nylon stocking, I put it over my head to control the frizzles.

Twelve-year-old Maria Jos says she would never marry a black, because 'my mother says that life is hard enough as it is and the only thing we have left is our light skin.'

In Brazil white seems to be the ideal of beauty. Advertising models, beauty queens, movie stars are all white. At official functions, in the clubs and universities, on the fazendas and in the government: all pale-faces. The reigning color in the favelas, however, is brown-black.

The average Brazilian associates white with such words as pretty, rich, clever, initiative. The word "black" indicates characteristics such as lazy, ugly and childish. These crass value comparisons lead directly to Brazil's racial prejudices and latent social confrontations.

You often hear that Brazil is the land of racial equality. It is true that you can see white, brown and black children playing together in the slums and going together to school; a young black dates a light-brown girl. Blacks and whites squeeze into the same bus and sit on the same park bench. Upon closer examination however, this harmonious surface is shot through with cracks. There is no racial hatred like in the United States and South Africa, but that doesn't mean you can deny the political and social racial discrimination. It would not occur to a Brazilian to feel physically disgusted by blacks, but the white ruling class would certainly oppose any black who tried to enter their exclusive clubs or have an important position in a bank, university or in the government. They would consider it infiltration and a great *faux pas* because it would amount to the entrance of a socially unfit person into a realm in which, according to the unspoken social code, he did not belong. If the black keeps to the place assigned to him by the rich since the times of slavery, that is, in the miserable huts of the plantations and the favelas; if he works in "his" professions — laborer, street-sweeper, etc. or, at the most, mechanic or chauffeur; if he goes to the assigned schools (elementary schools, there are no blacks to speak of in the universities), he is treated kindly and with true Brazilian courtesy. The danger that he will work his way up from the serving to the ruling class is next to non-existent, for it is terribly difficult in Brazil to go from low to high, even for the light-skinned.

But if some energetic and talented person tries to overcome the social barriers, obstacles are put in his way, especially if he is black. It is relatively easy for a white who eventually rises to a position in administration or in a bank to become integrated; you can't see his favela origins in his skin color. For a black, however, all defenses are well prepared. When a personnel manager must choose between a white, brown and black employee, the white comes first, then the brown and last of all the black. Once I spoke with Antonio about the race problem. He works at the prefecture, his mother is black, his father white. He believes that as a black he is judged more critically at work than his white colleagues.

This example of Antonio indicates the possible solution to the racial question in Brazil: Blacks and whites intermix. The blacks become lighter, the whites darker; both find themselves to be *moreno*, brown-skinned. Thus the problem would be resolved – on the surface. But the question really lies deeply embedded in Brazil's great social problem: the difference between rich and poor. *Os problemas são inumeros!*

Londrina, February 1967

Time flies. It's almost July, when my work here will be at an end.

My birthday was the occasion for a three-day celebration. It enriched me with a porcelain penguin of considerable size, two small porcelain dogs of various breeds and several bowls and dishes. On the previous day the wood-burning stove was inspected for serviceability, we gathered wood in a forest and vegetables on abandoned farms. We cooked, roasted, baked, one cake-pan after the other was shoved into the oven (over 100 children and adults had to be provided for), *pipoca* (popcorn) puffed, many tins of *mamão marmalade* (a kind of tree melon) prepared, while we drank cafezinho — it was really gemütlich. I was only allowed to watch, not lift a hand. If I wanted to intervene, the work was immediately snatched from my hand. Gelsa baked a twelve-story birthday cake! And best of all, the children earned the necessary funds with their knitting. In the evening we continued the party in Cido's house. His father's boss donated a barrel of beer to commemorate my "self-sacrificing" work.

*

On Sunday the play "Little Red Riding Hood" was performed, twice, because not everyone fit into the kindergarten at once. Also extemporized skits about Brazilian comical figures in which the contrast between country bumpkins and city people lightly touched by civilization were characterized. The city folk, even the poorest of the favelas, consider themselves to be on a higher plane. And, in fact, most favelados are really a step higher on the social ladder. They have schools, aren't so at the mercy of illness or dependent on the coffee monoculture.

Londrina, April 1967

There was finally an article in *Folha de Londrina* (Londrina newspaper) with the elegant headline: I. *Exposição de Artisanato da Vila de Fraternidade* about the voluntarios, that is, social development workers: our bazaar was opened. Last month (during Lent, when we were supposed to be calm, diligent and not playful), we worked like maniacs and when I desperately needed money for more material, we took courage and went public with our handmade products. Now we sit every afternoon and evening in the Engineers' club, which was kindly put at our disposal, selling our necklaces, bracelets, wallets, bookmarks, our embroidered and knitted articles. Between sales we play quartet (in German!), dance the twist, paint cloth and paper. It is a lot of fun. In the evening Otalino brings our royal supper: rice and beans. We sit in a circle around the pot. Everyone helps himself.

Although the exposition is well attended, you can see that most of the visitors make no attempt to understand what such an accomplishment means to favela children. Children who until a few months ago never had a needle in their hands, who no one had ever helped until recently; who, though enthusiastic, have difficulty with sustained work, and are now experiencing how High Society comes to admire what they have accomplished. For the children it is a wonderful experience. For the rich it is, unfortunately, just another way to spend their free time.

While we were preparing the bazaar and exposition, hordes of powdered and painted "society ladies" came fluttering around to see the children at work. It is strange how little contact they have with the lower classes and how insecure they are even with the children. Made somewhat uncomfortable by the closeness of the room, the numerous shabbily dressed children and the smell of poverty, they don't have more to say than *que bonitinho* (oh, how nice). With many promises to return with work material, they disappear never to be seen again.

There seem to be two Brazils. The one that Europeans know: white population, American style skyscrapers, Catholicism, in short, a tropical Europe. Then the other Brazil: colored, living in poverty, with a culture and religion which don't derive only from European Christianity, but also from African and Indian tribal cultures. And both parts feel Brazilian. The gap between the upper and lower classes isn't only that of the unequal division of wealth. The contrast is more profound than that of rich and poor. Two different worlds seem to exist alongside each other, without touching, without mutual understanding.

Even the origin of the upper and lower classes is different. In general, the upper class is composed of the descendants of Portuguese colonialists and later European immigrants. The lower class largely consists of blacks and mixtures of Black, Indian and European. Europeans and European consciousness opposed to Afro-Indian origin and Afro-Indian consciousness. The former is immersed in the development of the intellect and will to freedom, while the latter don't yet seem to be able to utilize to the full their intellect and reason (which doesn't mean that they are stupid!). They are in the process of emerging from an existence devoid of history, unburdened by questions of where to? why? where from? Mostly their lives are unorganized, without orientation (Where am I in the past, present and future? What is my place in society? Is this place just, changeable, or ordained by God?).

Modern thinking and mechanization have uprooted these people and they have lost their culture through contact with Europeans. Therefore the argument that they have always been poor and why should they suddenly be different, is not valid. They already suffer the negative effects of industrialization; it is only just that they also enjoy some of the blessings of civilization.

Londrina, June 1967

After not having rained for three months – one literally sank ankle-deep in fine red dust and passing cars covered the houses with clouds of dust – the daily processions praying for rain finally worked: it is pouring ceaselessly, and the soft dust has changed to slippery mud in a matter of hours.

As July and our departure date is not far off, a good-bye atmosphere is gradually being felt, as well as a kind of last-minute panic. Our heads are full of ideas, only time is lacking. Some children want to learn to crochet, we want to organize an exhibition and a trip to a nearby river, I want to enroll some boys in the *senai*-school (trade school), others in the *escoteiros,* the Boy Scouts.

Even the Boy Scout movement is for wealthy children. There also only white faces. By favela standards the uniform alone costs a fortune. Despite their poverty, Otalino, Zeca and João have been accepted. I was glad that they introduced Brazil's brown element there. Such enthusiasm has never been seen among the boys of the favela. Whenever our new Scouts return from their tents or meetings they are immediately surrounded by a crowd of the curious, to whom they must relate their experiences in detail.

We are rehearsing the quadrilha, a folk-dance that will be performed during the St. John's season, on the São João, São Pedro and Sant' Antonio holidays. A children's wedding is also part of a real quadrilha. Tereza as the bride has been talking for months about this, the happiest day of her nine-year-old life. Her bridegroom takes his happiness more calmly — he is, after all, only eight. The wedding is performed by a thirteen-year-old priest in the "church", an empty house which we have decorated with an altar, pictures of saints and flowers. The wedding dance and dinner follow, and in the evening you sit around the fire roasting mandioca-roots and sweet potatoes, pine-kernels and *churrasquinho,* pieces of meat on a spit. The whole favela is invited. You can imagine the crowd and the congestion.

Santos, August 2, 1967

I'm going home! It's hard to believe. I'm sitting here in the port of Santos on the same bench as two years ago, while Kaspar is looking after the tickets. One day walking around São Paulo, one day walking around Santos and today, we hope, *se Deus quiser,* we sail for Genoa.

Maybe I'll come back soon. Dona Lina, the president of a Women's assistance association who obtained the space for our exhibition, has had for years the idea to organize work-at-home so that women may earn something extra by selling homemade articles. Many work in the city as maids or do laundry for the rich, but this involves the disadvantage that they must work regular hours and therefore leave their children alone. Something similar has already been done with success in São Paulo: One favela weaves, for example, another crochets, a third sews and a fourth knits (on a knitting machine bought on credit and paid off monthly with the proceeds of the work). A senhora from sociedade is responsible for a certain favela, teaches the women how to do the work and then organizes the sale in a São Paulo shopping center. Dona Lina has something similar in mind for Londrina and as I know at least one of the favelas better than the Londrina rich do, and as I already began something in this direction with our bazaar-exhibition, she thinks I should help her to tackle this initiative.

Thank God the farewell from the Vila is over. The whole gang brought me to the train. The station has probably never seen so much shouting, hooting, viva calls and running after the departing train. Today I leave Brazilian soil and on the 20th of August arrive in Italy.

THE CORAL-COLORED SERPENT

Once upon a time there was a coral-colored serpent and a little black girl. She lived in the middle of a dense jungle. The trees grew so high and the undergrowth was so thick that the way had to be hacked out with a bush-knife, after which the jungle closed in again. The strength of the sun and the sap of the earth were so strong that every trampled blade of grass and every cut-off branch grew back almost immediately. Wild animals, tigers, serpents, armadillos, monkeys and parrots inhabited the jungle; crocodiles lounged lazily in a wide muddy stream that wandered slowly to the sea.

Talinha, the black child, lived in this jungle. Her mother had died at her birth. As the angel descended to carry her mother to heaven, she spread her wings over the new-born child, which made her invisible to human eyes. Even her father could no longer see his daughter. Sad because he lost his wife and daughter on the same day, he left his house and the jungle for good in order to live in a place where there were more people. Talinha, small and defenseless against the threatening jungle, stayed behind.

As the sun disappeared behind the treetops the animals appeared, surrounding the plaited hammock in which Talinha slept. When she began to cry because she was hungry and cold, a mighty growling and murmuring went through the animal world: how can we help the child? After long deliberations, the onca, the tiger-cat, said: I will raise her, give her milk to drink and warm her with my fur. I will show her which plants are poisonous and which are edible and which have curative powers. And I will explain to her how the strength of the sun and the moon are transmitted to the plants and the animals.

Thus Talinha grew up among the animals of the jungle. She jumped over streams, frolicked with the cubs, rode on the backs of the young onças, swung with the monkeys from tree to tree. The only things the animal mother could not teach her were to walk upright and to speak. She grew to be a pretty young girl with brilliant eyes and a softly expressive mouth.

But she changed during her thirteenth year. She became thin and sad and her arms hung limply at her sides. All her high spirits and joy of living were gone. A meeting of the animals was called again and they deliberated long on what they should do. Finally they all agreed: the coral-snake must help.

The coral-colored serpent lived lonely and secluded behind the mountain. Three monkeys were appointed to bring her. Swinging from tree to tree, they soon reached their destination. "Cobra, cobra, come out, Talinha is ill!" The serpent slithered quickly out of her hideout and began her journey. It was high time, for Talinha lay completely exhausted in her hammock. As the coral-snake looked at Talinha with her glowing, powerful eyes, suddenly thunder and lightning raged through the bush and a cloud descended on the serpent and completely enveloped her. Then the cloud vanished and in the place of the serpent stood a young prince in a coral-colored, royal cloak. He said to Talinha: You have redeemed me from the enchantment. An evil magician transformed me into a serpent, so that I had always to creep along the earth. Now I can stand upright and have recuperated my speech. I can be human again.

Talinha suddenly understood her illness: she was born a human being but was not yet able to be one, for she lacked speech and an upright posture. The prince's words warmed her heart and filled her with joy. She spoke the first words of her life: And you, my Prince, have redeemed me and made me a human being. You have given me speech. Only now have I been really born.

They were so happy about the gift of speech that they decided to wander through the land and tell fairy tales. They were the first storytellers.

SOCIAL DEVELOPMENT AID - A SUMMING UP

A talk by Francisco Julião, leader of farm workers and lawyer of the northeast:

> *... I speak to the forgotten and to the abandoned in the jungles of the amazon and on the Babacú-settlements in Maranhão, I speak to the workers in the palm-tree forests of Ceará, in the sugarcane fields of the northeast, in the coffee plantations in the state of Bahia and in the far south. I call the rice planters at São Francisco, the men who grow mate-tea and the men of the pampas. They are all hungry. They are all poor. They are all exploited by the landowners. They are all slaves. They can't offer resistance to their misery because they are illiterate, because each knows only his own misery, because they are afraid. Therefore I appeal to them to unite like bundles of firewood and march for their rights. For when the masses unite they are so strong that not even the landowners can withstand their might ...*

Development aid works on the premise that the problem of the poor in developing countries can be resolved by giving them food, perhaps also by building schools and hospitals. But the problem also lies in the fact that the lower classes are considered by the rulers to be objects and do not participate in the decisions about their lives.

And that isn't automatically achieved by giving the poor something to eat. Perhaps that's why communism is so appealing to many: it not only promises them bread, but also participation in government.

Suppose development aid achieves the following: agricultural counseling, construction of dams and irrigation projects, fertilizer, etc., an increase in production which would alleviate nutrition deficiency; industrialization and, with technical help, the creation of employment for people in distressed areas; trade and other schools which would prepare them for life in an industrialized country; controlling the population explosion through education.

Good, let us suppose that the poor gradually ease into a middle-class situation and lead lives that are relatively secure. Then we would no longer see people in rags as opposed to the privileged governing upper-class, but better dressed, moderately prosperous citizens. But the problem that they would still be without equal rights would remain. Once having escaped from dire poverty, would they accept being treated as children by a small clique of privileged people, to not have any influence on the political, economic and cultural life of their country? Not being fully occupied with earning their daily bread, would they be willing and able to revolt against this domination? Or would they feel so satisfied with their modest prosperity that they would not want to risk it by engaging in a revolt with unknown consequences?

The Londrina students believed a well-fed favelado does not rebel, that only one who is hungry is willing to risk everything because he has nothing to lose. Therefore for them development aid only delays the inevitable social revolution. Gifts soothe the consciences of the rich and dampen the poor people's wish to revolt. Nevertheless, the students think that a push from outside is needed (the students themselves) because the poor, having to occupy themselves almost exclusively with obtaining food and clothing, and the feeling, ingrained for centuries, that they are objects and not the acting subjects of their own lives, do not even think of rebelling. There are only occasional, quickly ignited and just as quickly dampened, disturbances when the droughts in the northeast impel them to plunder shops in the cities.

Is the Brazilian situation revolutionary? Objectively yes, subjectively no. The objective conditions for revolt are present: land distribution, accumulation of property and capital in the hands of few; wages which only guarantee a minimum existence (or not even). Education monopoly: Universities are almost exclusively attended by the wealthy; most farm workers have no schooling at all; the primary schools in the peripheries of the cities are inferior in the extreme; there are hardly any trade schools for workers. Political, economic and cultural power is concentrated in the hands of a minority.

However, the subjective conditions, except for small beginnings by intellectuals and students, are not yet present. The awareness of the necessity for change and the certainty of change being possible are lacking. The people are not yet conscious of the injustice and even if they were they would see no possibility for change. The following conversation with Dona Maria from our favela will illustrate this. We were coming out of a department store in which only the wealthy shop and I asked her, 'Doesn't it infuriate you to see how well some people live, who carry home baskets full of goods, who own apartment buildings and fazendas, while you can consider yourself lucky to have a job in order to eat rice and beans and have a wooden hut to live in?' 'No, I'm not angry. After all, the wealthy worked to get what they have. And my patrão, where I work now, is very nice and gives me a present now and then.'

The answer is typical. She is neither angry nor envious because she doesn't see the connection. That her employer gives her used clothing because she can't afford them with her $25 monthly salary is, for her, cause for thankfulness, not for hate. She doesn't think about class differences, but sees the individual human being: here herself, there her employer, who treats her well and is occasionally generous.

The few on whom it has gradually dawned that the rich are rich at the cost of the poor shrug their shoulders and are resigned: what can a poor person do against the power of the rich? In the face of an injustice he acts as an individual, never in a group. He may quit his job, for example, but doesn't go on strike.

In my opinion, the favelado's situation is the following: As long as he has a roof over his head and he and his family don't starve, he is in equilibrium. Once one side of the scale is tipped more than usual due to circumstances beyond his control, the balance between life's burden and his subjective abilities is disturbed. The burden grows — through illness, loss of work — but the ability to bear these additional burdens is the same as before. He has neither outer reserves (savings), nor inner reserves (solid training in his trade). Additional burdens have him peering into the abyss on the edge of which he previously balanced. At this critical point the tendency is to fall. According to disposition, the reaction to misfortune varies. Either he unloads by drinking – like Virginia's father, who traded his horse and wagon, his means of existence, for pinga; by aggression and fury – like Irany's father, who took out his pistol and, in desperation, tried to kill his family; in apathy – like Otalino's mother, who, ill with schistomosis and completely worn out at 36 years of age, gave up. In all three cases the human being is no longer master of his problem, but the problem is master of the human being.

Or: On the scale of subjective reality there is such a strong vitality that it cannot be broken by any misfortune. Like Careca's mother. Her husband is operated on and can no longer work, she is expecting her tenth child. Despite the daily uncertainty as to how this family is to be fed, she is happy and full of the joy of living. She masters the situation in her own way.

Or again: he accepts the help of a third party who can increase the subjective ability and outer possibilities so that the increased burden of life becomes bearable. This is the starting point for all social work: stimulate the individual's own strength, create educational possibilities, supply new work, prepare social legislation, etc. This is partly a task that a simple social worker can take over, but it is mostly a duty of the state, which must first create the basis for a comprehensive social security system which embraces all classes.

The most appropriate moment to intervene is when this balance between the burdens of life and the ability to meet them is disturbed. Now, when his life's symmetry is destroyed by an unbearable burden, he is shocked, angry, indignant, also more open for something new. Anger and indignation provide an impetus that can have a positive effect as long as it is channeled into group action. A gathering force must arise which moves people and encourages them to act in groups and which first thinks about the situation. Such lines of force, which transform a multitude of individuals into a group which is capable of acting, could be drawn by social workers. Emotional indignation must be followed by a situation analysis and an investigation into the causes. For example: Why am I unemployed? Why are my children always ill? Here the individual realizes that he is not alone with his problems. Previously each complained for himself without noticing that everyone around him struggles with the same difficulties. This is the first step to the awareness that: We in the favela are all in the same boat.

The social healing process that corresponds to this first step is the formation of practical working groups. Their themes are supplied by the foregoing situation analysis. For example: Why are my children ill? Because they have worms, etc. The result would be an information campaign about the contamination of water, the continual repetition of infections through parasites, viruses, etc.

Courses for children and adults could be organized, work-at-home promoted, youth groups with theater, sports, etc., founded, help with schoolwork and much more. Tasks would be tackled which pertain to the favela as a whole. Besides mastering specific problems, the favela should grow together and the self-respect of the individual as well as of the favela as a whole would thereby be strengthened. The feeling of inferiority in respect to the wealthy would be gradually reduced.

At least in my field, work with children, I have tried to act according to these principles: not to be too accommodating, but to free their latent forces; to formulate a task that they already have the unconscious wish to perform and for which a working group is now formed; to encourage their creativity and then show the results in public at an exhibition. The profit from the exhibition is then returned to the community and not to individuals, which would only stimulate their egotism.

It sounds banal. But in practice social work usually proceeds from the patriarchal principle. If the wealthy or the government have guilty consciences, they give the favelados something, for example, they build a modern laundry in a slum, which then shines there like an alien body. Then they wonder why it's not cared for and that after a week all the faucets have disappeared. Their conclusion is that it's a waste of loving kindness to worry about the poor. Such installations must grow from within, be wanted by the favelados and, if possible, be made with their help. Giving makes no sense, it spoils the poor and weakens their own will to act even more.

Once a community has been formed from individuals, when they are proud of what they have accomplished and have the feeling of being worth something, then you can go one step further: raise their indignation to a higher plane. Gradually they realize that countless favelas exist, in Londrina, in Paraná, in Brazil, in the world. They begin to see that their own poverty is immersed in a sea of poverty. Their indignation becomes an indignation for the generality. *Poor of all nations, unite!* And the super-personal indignation which arises from an analysis of the social situation expands to the deeper causes of poverty. Why does this gap between rich and poor exist? Why can't my children have a higher education? Why are my wages so low? etc.

Thus we integrate poverty into the whole social-political structure of the country and the world and begin to understand something about the oppression practiced by the ruling oligarchies on the unfranchised masses. A Dona Maria would then probably not remain so calm when viewing the riches of her *patroa*. And each one would no longer feel powerless and alone at the mercy of the wealthy but would sense the strength that comes from the thousands who bear the same poverty.

How will this awareness manifest itself? As soon as the favelado no longer accepts his poverty as ordained by God, as soon as he realizes that change is necessary and also possible, then something must happen. The subjective conditions for transforming the social structures have been created. One can imagine that the poor would receive help from outside. For example, targeted development aid which would enable them to improve their lives. Schools and hospitals would be built, employment created, agriculture modernized, etc. By paralyzing the factories, public transportation and commerce through non-violent resistance, massive pressure would be exerted on the government.

Help from outside would go hand in hand with domestic assistance from government offices; and development aid would only be granted when the poor people's own efforts can be verified. The state would probably initiate partial reforms. Strikes would force the rulers to make life easier, by wage increases, school construction, cheaper medicines. But these are merely concessions, which would not resolve the problem in its entirety. It is not only that the favela people live on a bare existence minimum, but also that they are treated unequally.

The objective is that they become the subject of their own lives and the life of their country; that they participate in the country's political life, that they be represented in congress and in the government. Will the ruling power-groups voluntarily give up their key positions?

African Sarawa Cult

Sarawa is a widely disseminated religious cult in Brazil, a spiritist movement with Afro-Indian roots mixed with Catholicism and even Islamic elements. It is hard to imagine a Sarawa without having heard the wild, hours-long, stimulating yet monotone drumming through the night, and without having seen the participants falling into convulsive ecstasy as though shaken by a powerful invisible hand. It is questionable whether the word human can be used to describe these volitionless, wildly dancing creatures. They seem rather to be vessels into which a god or a spirit has been poured, who acts and romps and uses the mouth of an earthly being as his instrument, giving advice and answering questions which are asked via the medium. Human means to be able to say "I", to use your head. But the overwhelming impression one gets at a Sarawa is 'away with the head, away with thinking and consciousness'. The I is extinguished in order to make room for a supernatural being.

It is not a redeeming experience, rather a burden. The face is contorted with pain. Cramped and twitching, the possessed one lays the backs of her hands on her spine as though she felt pain there. At the moment when her own consciousness has been completely overcome through the penetration of the spirit into the volitionless human sheath, the filha de santo hands the priestess a cigar or a pipe and a glass of pinga, from which she drinks first and then passes to the other participants. Now is the time to ask her — or rather her spirit — for advice and help. It is also the moment that she cures illnesses.

It is very easy for such truths to degenerate into superstition, however. For example, when the macumbeiro transfers the illness to a fetish which he lays at a crossroads, hoping that someone will step on it and absorb the illness. This magical technique belongs in the realm of black Sarawa . Where you see the remains of a slaughtered black hen and a burnt candle, you can be sure that black Sarawa was at work. The favela is full of stories about magically acquired sickness, people suddenly dying and unexpected loss of work. These stories are told with such conviction that I believe them myself.

On the other hand, a sarawa-healer lives on the other side of this I-development. Her spiritual experience is not expressed in such an abstract form as body vs. spirit. Body and spirit still form a unity, so that the spiritual-religious can be physically experienced and, with the help of the body and certain materials taken from nature (honey, blood, oils), the spiritual world can be brought down to the human level.

DIARY 1970-1975

November 24, 1970

In view of the Brazilian coast. Another day and the ocean journey will be over. We are really carefree here on the ship, our Brazilian duties receding more every day instead of approaching. Since Las Palmas we have had beautiful weather, sunny and warm. We lay all day on deck, the ocean's vastness ahead, the mild wind over us and the officers' gaze on us. They observe our every movement with binoculars from the bridge. The poor fellows aren't allowed to come down and mix with the common folk.

December 1970

Well, here I am in the Waldorf School in São Paulo. In this bustle of cars, people, buildings, super-markets, banks, buses, in this contrast between big and small, poor and rich, under-developed and over-developed. Luckily I live outside the skyscraper zone, about a half-hour bus ride from downtown, in an attractive residential area with many trees and flowers. It's a bit cooler here than in the city and, above all, there is a very precious commodity: air. In the city after walking around for a few hours one is as black as a coal-carrier. A city of six million (1981: thirteen million) inhabitants without an underground railway system. Transportation in the city consists of buses and cars. One bus after the other, rattling, squeaking, emitting a black sticky cloud of smoke. A crazy town!

A new building seems to be finished every hour. If you haven't been in the city for two months, when you go back whole streets have changed. You look in vain for some building because it has already been torn down. Entire rows of houses disappear overnight in order to make way for a widened street. You can waste hours looking for something because it isn't in its usual place.

In order for a normal mortal like me without a car and living in Santo Amaro to send a telegram, three hours are needed what??? with traveling by bus and waiting. Everyone is in a hurry, working and running — and in this heat. Nevertheless, much of it is unproductive because the people paralyze each other, more so than in, for example, Paris. The skyline looks imposing and nice from a distance. Less pleasant is to have an elevated highway running by two yards from your third-floor living-room window.

The Waldorf School is situated in a beautiful, quiet residential area. The teachers are nice, not like the ones you see in many schools who have seen better days. The school makes an inspiring impression and one can surely feel good here. I will take over the third grade of mostly German, German-descended and also Dutch children.

This Brazil is very different from my social-worker time in Londrina. For the first time it is really clear to me how wide the gulf is between the Brazilians who have a roof over their heads, enough to eat and can send their children to a decent school, and those who live from day to day in a favela and often have no way to prepare themselves or their children for a trade or profession — not only in respect of the distribution of wealth, but also in respect of consciousness. Here they speak a grammatically pure Portuguese, don't much like the dark-skinned, in fact fear them, and cannot empathize with someone who has made the jump from being an agricultural laborer in a drought area into the confusing diversity of a modern city of millions. I am often angry at this lack of understanding. Comments such as: "She married a Black; I almost fainted." Or: "The Blacks must know their place," (that is, in humble jobs, in the favela, in mud). Or the lack of understanding about student movements (all bandits). It all drives me crazy.

In Londrina I lived very un-European and closely allied with simple people. It is good that I now have the opportunity to get to know the other side of Brazil. But in general this "white" side of Brazil seems to be the tip of an iceberg which peeks out over the surface while the essential part remains hidden. For me the real, alive and vigorous Brazil is that of the favela, of the country people, the Brazil of Dona Jacinta, the Sarawa priestess; of the laborers who pick coffee and plant corn; of the fishermen who bring their fish to market on the littoral; of the workers who, year after year, must make the same monotonous movements.

It is now much clearer to me how huge a country Brazil is, in which many forces are still in formation or must be awakened, in which the most diverse peoples — from Indians and blacks to Europeans and Japanese — contribute to making Brazilians a people, a nation. Like in Greece, where migrations had to take place in order to form the Greek people and make their culture possible. I don't really consider Brazil as being a nation yet, in spite of their great national pride. You can buy posters everywhere stating: *Brazil — love me or leave me, Brazil — confide in me,* or *God is Brazilian!*

But in reality there are thousands of Brazils, which are often fundamentally different from each other and in quite different stages of human development. What does an agricultural laborer of African descent – who is practically his employer's slave and has to live on the roots he digs up during droughts – have in common with an industrialist of European descent in São Paulo, whose life is completely dominated by technology? What do they have in common? Only that they are both human beings.

I believe that the students are almost the only ones who perceive something of the profound differences in the Brazilian people and try to find ways of coming into contact with the other classes and to break down the invisible barriers between them. To overcome the gulf between rich and poor, between life in the city and on the land, between people who are educated in schools and those whose only education derives from their mean daily lives and perhaps also Sarawa ; also the gap in white understanding of the blacks. I believe that the students at least attempt all this when they go on vacation to the Mato Grosso or to the northeast to work there with the simple people and explain some things to them.

May 1971

I survived the first week of school. The mutual teacher-pupil sizing-up has taken place to the satisfaction of both sides — I like the children, they like me ... but, what a job to teach them some order and discipline. They are a wild bunch of lively nine-year-olds who have a lot to offer but are very disorderly and have little consideration for the others. The boys especially are bursting with energy. I immediately steered this energy in the right direction: gardening. It was a pleasure to watch them remove the yard-high weeds with hoes, spades and rakes.

A black Brazilian recently passed behind the gardening plot on his donkey-drawn cart collecting old paper, bottles, etc. My pupils were frightened and came running to me. There will be a lot to do to teach the children that these people are also human beings.

The image of Brazil that the wealthy and the German-Brazilians and probably many Waldorf teachers and parents have must be fundamentally different from mine. Somehow one always unconsciously feels threatened here in São Paulo. By the people who are poorer or by the *jeunesse dorée*, for they also mug people and steal money and cars. Threatened by so many speeding cars, from which one is always fleeing. The bars on the windows, broken glass on the walls, watch-dogs in every house (recently one bit me on the calf and left a large blue bruise), the whistling of the night-watchmen – and if you include the runny-nosed children hanging around the streets and the women sleeping on the sidewalks (typical comment: She'd rather sleep there than in her bed!), then you feel on one hand fear of the brutality and unpredictability of the people and, on the other hand, a feeling of superiority arises. Sometime when I have more time I must ask the teachers what is done to awaken an understanding of the poor classes. In Londrina, in the interior in general, everything is calmer, quieter, more human, and you feel safer and freer.

October 1971

The Spring holidays were reserved for my long overdue visit to the *Vila da Fraternidade* in Londrina/Paraná. For four years *saudade*-letters have been going back and forth, and now the legendary figure — *a Rute do Jardim*, Ute of the kindergarten — will appear in flesh and blood. On the one hand I am looking forward to it; on the other I am thinking: will they be disappointed when the real me stands before them, after having become idealized with time?

I packed two huge suitcases with all the presents accumulated over four years in Germany as well as in São Paulo, bought my ticket, not for the bus but for a narrow-gauge railway, second class (I wanted to arrive as I had left Londrina then) and was seen off by Katerina. I remember clearly the feeling I had as I rode four years ago through the gloomy, endless outskirts of São Paulo and imagined how queer it must be for people loaded down with belongings and a dozen children coming from the northeast and hurled into such a confusingly enormous city and then having to adapt to an industrialized society. The first stop for most of them is the bus or train station, in which they find themselves among the crowd wrapped in rags or lying on newspapers. The second stop for many is a favela or sleeping places under bridges and underpasses.

I thought of this again as I rode slowly for over an hour through the city's outskirts. I took out my sleeping-bag, for it's still quite cool at night, and was thankful that the seats aren't still made of wood as they were in 1967. After a fifteen-hour ride though, I was so stiff that I could barely lift myself from the seat. I dozed and was woken around midnight by an excited argument. Although the light isn't turned off at night, a male passenger was bold enough to touch his neighbor's thigh in an unchaste manner, whereupon the incensed woman began to shriek. Two parties formed immediately, one in defense of the woman, the other for the man. Each inveighed loudly against the other, getting hotter and hotter.

More and more passengers came up, not wanting to miss the show. Suddenly there was respectful silence: *autoridade* approached in the person of the conductor. Very serious, he listened to the witnesses, wrote down addresses and finally handed down his decision: the lecher had to leave the train. He was pushed out into the pitch-dark night at the next god-forsaken stop. He stood on the platform cursing the departing train. The next train would come on the following day. The discussion continued for a long time. An old man spoke important words about the seriousness of the situation, which had a comical effect, especially as his eyeglasses were tied over his ear with a black shoelace.

I dozed again until sunrise. With great composure the train left the miles behind it, winding its way through the fields, stopping every twenty miles or so. It seemed to me that there was less coffee planted than previously and more useful things: beans, rice, corn, manioca, etc. Perhaps the government's measures to eliminate unproductive coffee-plants was having effect after all. The train went so slowly and in so many loops that it seemed to want to greet each field personally. A trip like that is so nice because you can look at the landscape calmly without having to worry about traffic, you take part in the general conversation and drink a cafezinho now and then.

Finally, at about eight o'clock in the morning, we came to the Paranápanema River, which separates the states of São Paulo and Paraná. Happy cries went through the train: Paraná, Paraná! Three more hours and I would be going past the Vila da Fraternidade and pulling into the station accompanied by the familiar toots. I found it especially exciting and moving this time, as though the train was announcing my return to the whole city with its tooting.

I walked through the streets as though I had never left. Still the same shops, the music store where we bought the records for the quadrilha, the wool shop where we bought our cheap wool. Only the store selling Sarawa supplies, herbs and saints, was new. Then the end of the asphalt, down on the *terra roxa* through the red-light district, a right turn at the corner, past some wooden houses, then left down the hill and there was the Vila da Fraternidade with "our" house standing before me.

I knocked at Gelsa's house and Uranio, who used to clean our school, saw me at the same moment. He has grown but is as funny as ever. He recognized me immediately. *Ah, é a ut ! Demorou mas finalmente chegou!* (Ah, it's Ute. It took a long time but finally she came.) An *abraço*, an embrace, and I was pushed into the store where a crowd of people stood around and Gelsa's mother was behind the counter. Gelsa came running with her two-year-old Marcelo. *Abraços.*

On the surface a lot has changed. The old barracks and the wooden shed as well as the abandoned bus in which an Indian family lived have all disappeared. There are many new houses with electricity and running water and the streets are partly paved. A health-center of the Prefecture operates in our old house. They do the same kind of work as during the development aid times: fighting the parasitic diseases, stool-examinations, etc., only with more people. Even my work with children has found its successors. Three, sometime four women from the prefecture care for some children. Their efforts, however, seems to be limited to letting the children play on their own with wooden blocks and then pushing the blocks together again with a huge broom — at least as far as I could determine during the week I was there. Smartly dressed young ladies, they mostly stand around watching the children.

Seu Esau was doing the same from a place in the shade — in front of our ex-bicycle shed — playing "lady" with great intensity, with one eye watching the children on swings. He hasn't changed a bit, the same help-seeking look, an eternal imitator of the higher placed. It is all quite bureaucratic, orderly and risk-free, but without life and enthusiasm. The main thing is that at the end of the day the list is ready and entered in a thick book that reports on the activities of the *recreacionistas,* play-time supervisors. It looked something like this: ball-playing — aims at coordinating the limbs and encourages sociability; building-blocks — encourages the imagination and equilibrium, etc, etc. And every day the same trash and the same warmed-over words. My skin crawled when I saw children who were too young for me to know them, but who knew my name from hearing it. A thousand things could be done with them, such as sawing their own building-blocks, weaving on simple wooden frames, making games, etc., all that we used to do with the children and what I have learned in the meantime. (Since 1975 things have improved somewhat; at least there are now sports.)

I had the feeling that this house, with all its employees, was like an island in the Vila without any radiation streaming out to the other inhabitants. No one really knew who these people were, what they were doing and what their names were. It's strange to think that they are Brazilians and we were the foreigners. Kaspar, Adolfo, Ute, Otto have become unforgettable names. The entire Vila still vibrates with us. *A vila ficou chata depois que vocês sairam,* it has become dull since you left. I was amazed at how deeply those two years are anchored in the children; nothing, but absolutely nothing have they forgotten. Tereza, Otalino, Vena and all the others could repeat word for word what I had once said on some occasion or other. They remembered every detail of the festivals, the outings, the sports-festival, the exhibition, the secret visits to

Koch-Weser's Fazenda, our raids on the abandoned fruit-farms, the wood gathering for the São João festival. All of it still lived in them, as though it had been yesterday and not four years ago. And whenever we reveled in nostalgia, it ended with the final words: *mas agora é chato, não tem quadrilha, não tem brincadeiras,* (it's so dull now, there is no quadrilha, there are no games).

For those children, who now mostly work as housemaids or in factories, those two years were a kind of golden childhood, full of the joy of life and crackling with the spirit of adventure. Now they must work, swallow their mistress's insolence for a wage of 20 to 40 dollars a month, or get up at five in the morning and fill honey bottles till seven in the evening, or whatever other spirit-killing work they can get. But no one is there now to undertake something occasionally with them, organize a festival or encourage them in some other way.

Despite the separation which, for children, is a long time, we haven't become strangers to each other. They are as open and willing as ever to tell me about their *namorados, noivos* (lovers, boy-friends) etc., as they once were to report on their childish experiences. Most are already engaged or on the verge of marriage. Even little Dirce, whom I left as a spindly nine-year-old, who has shot up but is even more spindly and angular, proudly told me of her forthcoming marriage.

I used my time to visit everybody. I sat in the same chairs in the same houses only with larger families now, sipped coffee like before, listened to what had happened in the meantime, and felt very good. But how much coffee I had to drink! And how often I ate beans and rice! Sometimes I ate lunch three times and dinner twice, always beans and rice. *Come a comida da casa,* eat here at home — I couldn't refuse. The first two days everyone said I was much thinner (and prettier!) than four years ago. At the end of my stay they said I had gotten fat in Germany. In reality this was the result of the six-day stuffing in the Vila da Fraternidade.

Has life become better? I asked. *Que nada, ficou do mesmo jeito.* No, not at all, it's all the same. Or, nothing much has changed, the Vila looks better, no more favela, but there is still not work for everyone, at least not regular work. A maid still doesn't earn more than $20 a month, the legal minimum wage is

$75. Sack-carriers earn by sack carried and earn up to $400 depending on how fast they can run, but only when there are sacks to carry. Gelsa's husband was without work and dragged himself around the house somewhat embarrassed. Otalino, as a car painter, earns a kingly wage: almost $250, regularly, every month. He told me proudly about his trade and, cavalier-like, lost no opportunity to spoil *me*.

But life has changed, one just doesn't notice it amidst the daily monotony. After a four-year absence the difference was immediately apparent to me: many children stream into the city and attend high school, many more have finished primary school with a *diploma*. The older siblings were left back sometime during their school time and finally dropped out in order to earn some money. Their younger brothers and sisters live in more orderly homes, do their homework on clean tables and finish school faster. I was happy for each one who told me he had learned a trade. And I was sad for each one of whom I heard that he had gone back to the land, to the *roca* (planted land), where there usually are no schools. In practice this means that at least another generation will pass before there is any kind of chance in life. Cido and his family also returned to the land.

In these four years Cido has an odyssey behind him. Unfortunately I wasn't able to see him, although he was advised by radio that I was finally back in Brazil. Shortly after I left Londrina in 1967, Cido's family also moved, trading their house for a bar near Londrina. That didn't work, so they traded the bar for a combi, packed their worldly goods and went to São Paulo. It must have been horrible: where to go in that monster-city with a family of ten? Seu Pedro, the father, was underway from morning till night in the combi transporting goods from one end of the city to the other. After three months they packed their things again and drove north, to Pernambuco, from where they had migrated twenty years before. They had relatives there (even a son who had been left behind with his grandparents because he was too small to withstand the strain of the journey to Paraná). The relatives had a piece of land from which now, suddenly, ten more people had to be fed. I think it was this idea of a piece of land in his own homeland which decided Cido's father to turn his back on the "wealthy" south — *saudade da minha terra*. Gelsa told me how the whole family appeared again one day in Londrina looking so gaunt and miserable that they were hardly recognizable. From Londrina they continued to Faxinal, about 100 miles farther, where they traded the combi for a piece of land in Marumbi, the end of the world.

I will visit them for Christmas.

Dona Jacinta, the sarawa-healer, glows with composure and peace, as always. You feel calm just being near her. You sit on a rickety chair in front of her house, say something now and then, listen, make automatic slow movements. Haste gives way. And I believed her as a matter of course when she said that she had been sure of seeing me again. *"E o destino"*. So I went from house to house accompanied by Tereza who, just as before, never left my side. It is still somehow nice in the Vila, but the atmosphere that prevailed before, when something interesting was always being prepared, is absent.

On Sunday I had to leave. I was so tired that I slept through almost the whole ten-hour bus ride to São Paulo, but I was glad to have finally been in Londrina again.

Londrina, 16 January 1972

Up and away to *Marumbi!*

I rode the whole night in the bus. Luckily, Daiggers brought my two impossibly large suitcases to the station. In Apucarana I made the usual connection with the *Viação Londrinense*, the Londrina bus company, famed for its busses breaking down after a few miles, which is exactly what happened. We all got out and sat at the side of the road waiting for the replacement bus. We were covered with dust by the time it arrived in a cloud of red dust an hour later. It got as far as Faxinal before giving up the ghost.

Thank God I was only going that far, where a jeep was waiting to take me and my voluminous luggage the remaining fifteen miles to Cido's adobe hut. It flew over rocks and holes, at one point getting stuck in one, and had to be pulled out. When I finally arrived, children and dogs came running and jumping all over me. They were all happy that I had really come again. I was given something to eat right away: a cucumber, saved especially for me, rice, beans and a piece of smoked bacon. And everyone talked, talked, talked, the children about how they had counted the days to my arrival, how they listened to the sound of every jeep; I, about how I had run around São Paulo inquiring about schools and work and how I told everyone about their life at the *sitio* (home on the land) and that everybody gave me things for them: dresses, shoes, shirts, suits, school-books, notebooks, pencils, sweets and a chocolate Santa Claus which was divided into twenty parts so all could have a taste.

The overweight suitcase was suspensefully unpacked to the accompaniment of much laughter. Ivan the Great's trousers came up to Seu Pedro's neck. His shoes were too big of course, but they are bound to the feet with laces and thus offer protection against snakes during field work. The new frying pan was consecrated with pancakes filled with strawberry jam donated by my Yugoslavian pupil.

17 January 1972

Rise and shine! We all creep out of our beds and gather on the bench in front of the hearth waiting for coffee and roasted corncobs. First water must be brought up from below where it trickles through the mud; not clear spring-water, but an opaque brew, probably infected will all kinds of viruses. Some of it is put over the fire to make coffee, the rest is for brushing our teeth. The sun is already quite hot and no one feels much like working, but there's no alternative: we must go out to the fields and pick weeds. I put on a straw hat, pick up a hoe and put long sleeves over my bare arms in order to protect my noble white skin from the brutal Brazilian sun. A rice field that had been weeded just two weeks ago waited with a thick new growth. Hoe, hoe, hoe — interspersed with conversation. Cido and Zéca had participated in a church youth meeting and were very enthusiastic. We talked about it. How should they love their parents? How should they love their country? Hoe, hoe, hoe! Why are you against nationalism? Hoe, hoe, hoe! Who was Hitler? etc. etc. As the heat increases the conversation dies out. I push my hat around hoping to lessen the impact of the heat on my head and see only weeds before me and — as in a dream — a nice pitcher of cool clear spring-water and a basket of juicy oranges. Then Maricela appears with a pot of not exactly clear but at least thirst-quenching water. Finally it was eleven o'clock and we shuffled back for lunch: rice, beans, a piece of pork and a vegetable treat for *Ruti,* (Ute) — pumpkin.

Another drink of water and back to work. The air shimmers with heat and the work is hard. The damned tree-stumps are all over, charred and full of holes and sometimes snakes. And this gently clinging grass *capim colonial,* which only comes out after three or four blows. When you see a mass of *capim* ahead, you feel like despairing. Luckily Zéca comes to my aid and pulls out the more resistant bushels.

In the evening I am completely exhausted and even a bath in the river doesn't have its usual healing effect. I sit lazily at the dinner table (how good that one can do that here) and don't have the least desire to teach anything. But duty calls. Inexorably Evaristo makes the sign for class: he writes with his finger on his left palm. *Então vamo,* let's go! We last until ten o'clock. One after the other we creep into bed.

18 January

A terrible rainstorm. The kitchen swam, the earthen floor turned to mud. In the "living-room" the rain streamed through the door and window and washed over the bean harvest stored there. While Evaristo was busy covering the smoke-holes on the roof with a tarpaulin, Cido was straining heroically in a race with the rain to push out the water that had entered through the door. The situation was serious (because of the beans which might rot), but also fun. Protected from the dripping water by straw hats, we all fought against the superiority of the streaming water, wading and slipping over the gradually dissolving earth floor. The mother, however, stood earnestly at the hearth trying to keep the fire going despite the rain pouring on it. She called us to order, saying that we should pray that the house isn't swept away by the storm, something which she had already experienced. No one knew what God had in store for us.

You really feel more at the mercy of nature and the elements here than elsewhere. A sincere reverence and faith go hand in hand with superstitious acts. For example, you shouldn't look in a mirror after dinner because you might see yourself distorted and remain so. Or a cigarette may not be lit from a candle.

20 January

Seu Manuel and family invited the neighbors to a Saint Sebastian celebration. As every year, Cido said the rosary with everyone who came by horse, donkey or by foot. He gave a kind of catechism class for the children. There were at least a hundred people, but all of them got some coffee and home-made bread. Later pigs and other presents, such as eggs, rice, corn, etc., were sold at auction. Seu Pedro did it very well and with humor. Then the long way home in the dark, stumbling over tree-stumps, springing over streams. No one really wanted to be first in this goose-march; the end of the line wasn't much loved either. Ghost stories were told. The forest over there is enchanted. Zéca rode through it once and his horse suddenly shied, listened to the forest, and wasn't to be moved from the spot. In the still darkness, with the moonlight stabbing out over the scudding clouds, the unexplainable noises — it all seemed really uncanny.

21 January 1972

Practiced arithmetic with Marili and Marinalva while we sorted beans, that endless mass that is needed for a family of fourteen for lunch and supper. Zéca rode to town, a welcome change from the boredom of weeding. He brought a sack of wheat to be ground at the mill and he had to buy coffee, toothpaste and sugar as well as bring a birthday card to the post office for Papa. There he was asked to whom he is writing in Germany, whether it's to the "good" Germany and if he has a girlfriend there, etc.

In the afternoon I harvested a sack of green corn in order to make *curral* (corn pudding). But how was I to carry the heavy sack home? With great effort I got it onto my head where it pricked me and almost fell over. The pressure was terrible and I ran as fast as I could to get it over with as soon as possible. It felt as though my head was getting flatter and my neck was being pushed into my shoulders. Relieved, I let the sack fall at the door of the house. Then I grated the corncobs for two hours, stirred the pudding for a half-hour under clouds of steam, only to see how the magnificent result vanished in five minutes into fourteen mouths.

At five o'clock Zéca returned from Faxinal, carrier of news from the "world" and of new provisions. The children came running from the field and gathered around the sack, from which he took coffee, sugar and a sweet for everyone. This sweet tasted better than any I have ever had.

After bathing I rode Gringo, the horse, to his pasture. Zéca: Now after riding twenty miles he should get special feed, not only this dry grass. It makes me sad.

After supper we refreshed our memories of the Londrina times five years ago. How Paulo Manteiga (Butter-Paul) climbed up the *abacate*-tree and was attacked by African wasps; how Zéca hurt his head diving in the swamp; how Cido washed strangers' cars in the city, was ashamed to ask the owners for money and came home without having earned a cent. Finally Seu Pedro came in with a whip cut from a branch to enhance my authority as teacher. We quickly got our notebooks out and quiet reigned over the table, broken only by the murmuring of sums and calls for help: Oh, Ute, what do I do now? Zéca had to write a report on his first day in Marumbi — I almost died laughing. The evening passed quickly solving riddles and talking about ships, airplanes, travel and the wish to travel. It went on in bed over the separation-wicker between girls' and boys' "bedrooms" until the first snores were heard.

22 January

Today nobody could bring themselves to go out to work. The wood was wet so we couldn't make the fire at first. It took an eternity till the coffee woke some will to work in us. There was no bread. I made pancakes from flour. As I stood at the fire the rain fell on my head and a simmering drop of oil fell on the sick chicken who was trying to dry out on the oven.

Sunday, 23 January 1972

It rained till midday, perfect weather for teaching. Evaristo struggles with division, Jõãozinho learns to tell time, Cido writes a report, Marinalva, Maristela and Marili learn to write. Zéca went to Dedinho's to bring him the sneakers I got for him when I heard that he doesn't go anywhere because he has no shoes. As thanks he made a pile of drawings and wrote a poem about land-laborers and city people. He could also be doing something other than hoe weeds (not even his own, but those of his *patrão*). *Joias perdidas no mato,* Jewels lost in the jungle — as the banana seller said when he passed by with his mule. Pearls lost in the wilderness. In many of the huts are people with good heads for learning who don't use them because there are no schools.

In the afternoon we took advantage of the rain-freshened air for a family outing, hopping over puddles through fields of mud. On the way back I cautiously asked Seu Pedro if Zéca couldn't come to São Paulo with me now, before the harvest, in order to register for high school. Contradicting all Zéca's prophesies, he had no objection. When we got back I gave Zéca an essay to write: What would you do if your father said you could go to São Paulo? Everything which had been seething in him bubbled out in an hour's writing. When he finished I told him that he could go.

24 January

This morning the dirty drinking-water took its toll. My stomach twitched and rumbled terribly and I couldn't even think of coffee and beans. They gave me a horribly bitter drink and health was restored. Conversation about *benzedor,* people who heal by means of blessings, prayers and herb-teas followed this cure. The power of prayer is deeply ingrained in young and old alike. At night before sleeping they all sit on their beds and say their prayers. Through the dark huts you hear from all sides "*a benção, Mãe; a benção, pai*" — bless you, mother; bless you, father. This attitude, which transmits faith (though it's sometimes mixed with superstition) to the young, is what gives me the courage to risk life in the city – so full of thieves and temptations — for

Zéca and Cido. These children have substance and a solid inner life, which they hopefully will not lose even when they sometimes despair of the world and themselves.

27 January

We rose with the birds to go to Londrina. Soaking wet from the dew, Zéca and I reached the road, on which a car might pass that would take us to Faxinal. We had better luck than the last time, when we waited from eleven in the morning till three in the afternoon: an open combi picked us up very soon. We spoke about the play we intended to put on. One day Cido had come from the fields and announced, "I made up a story". I grabbed a pencil and paper and wrote while Cido dictated. No sooner had we finished than Zéca said, I have also invented a story, and a poem. A fruitful day!

Cido intends to write a play about his own life: the family move from Pernambuco in a pick-up truck filled with twenty people, some benches, suitcases, bundles and the gas oven, which had to be unloaded four times a day to cook coffee, rice and beans; his mother's fright as she woke one morning to find them all white and stiff — white from hoar-frost. Later the wretched beginnings in Marumbi, the monotonous life on the land with few diversions, such as the ant invasion. One morning after a heavy rainfall the house was swarming with ants; shelves, beds, walls, cases, there was nothing not covered with the black, excitedly crawling beasts. When the ants weren't gone by evening, the inhabitants turned the house over to them and slept on mattresses and sacks in the yard under the mamão-tree. The next day they were still the masters of the house. The second night out of doors. On the third night they left, all in the same direction.

Anyway, we rode on to Londrina in the rattling bus and considered who would play which roles, the costumes, etc. The choice of costumes was of course not large: the curtain, a tablecloth, Maria's wedding veil and my dress-jacket would have to bear with it.

In Londrina we ran from one place to another to get Zéca's documents in order: voting card, military service certificate and similar rubbish. The next day we returned to Marumbi.

29 January

Normally my morning chore was to pick up the milk from a fazenda two miles away. But since the milker disappeared Zéca went with me. The cows weren't exactly gentle. First we drove one to the milking place. The hind legs had to be tied together with its tail a good trick with the hind legs continuously kicking out. I held the calf that was struggling for milk away on a rope while Zéca pulled rapidly on the udders until a thin flow of milk streamed into the pail. The cow began to kick again and I, in fright, let the calf go, which greedily began to suck. The cow ran away with the calf after it, still sucking. Zéca and I ran after them and the whole procedure started again. When a quart of milk had been accumulated she deigned to let go with dung. The meager final result was a quart of milk and pants full of liquid cow-shit. I couldn't stop laughing. How easy it is in the city where you only have to go to the super-market!

Today I stuffed myself with corn. Breakfast consisted of *curral* (corn pudding), lunch *pamonha* (boiled corn wrapped in cornhusks) and in the evening one roasted corncob after the other. I feel like a corn depot. We spoke about war and the beginning of industry in Brazil. Seu Pedro told how the first automobile was received with fear and cries of joy in Batateira, his hometown, and how the unaccustomed honking accelerated his grandfather's death. The first airplane was seen as a flying monster. When Seu Pedro rode on the train he was celebrated as a hero in his town. And now, at least in the big cities, you can hardly escape with your life from the enormous amount of cars.

Sunday, 30 January

On the daily milk-march with Zéca through corn as high as a man's eye and tangled underbrush, I learned a lot about Brazil. He told me about flying snakes that used to exist in Pernambuco, and about the seven-headed monster in Juazeiro (North-Brazil) which was rendered harmless about fifty years ago by a priest's prayers. We also spoke of the wage earners in this area, their fear of the fazendeiros and their complete subordination. We arrived at the fazenda and fought with the cow, but with more success this time: two quarts.

During the afternoon I went to Arlindo's under a fiercely glowing sun to give him his part in the play. He's another boy who can only put his strength and reason into planting bananas. I had enough sun for one day. During the day it cooks your brains; in the evening it blinds you.

31 January

I was a bit weak today and couldn't bring myself to go out to the fields or teach the children. Probably it's the result of yesterday's over-exposure to the sun. It was evening before I recovered. At night we observed the stars, which you can see so clearly here compared to the city. They once saw a glowing sphere cross the sky; what could it have been? The mother told me in detail about their dog, who survived all their journeys to São Paulo and Pernambuco, only to die of a snakebite here. The goat, which was to have given milk as antidote, fell over in the dog's presence and died soon after. So strong is the power of snake poison, said Dona Maria.

1 February

Hot, hot, hot! The children are working in the jungle clearing a piece of land with bush-knives in order to plant beans there. You trudge into an opaque mass of branches, felled trees, ferns and prickly undergrowth and chop your way further into the *mato*. Later it is all burned and the planting is done on the ashes between burnt out tree-stumps. Zéca killed a *cascavel* (rattlesnake) with a brood of fifteen. Now I walk through chopped-down undergrowth with mixed feelings to bring the children the longed-for water jug. I have already fallen several times into strange holes in which snake families could still be living.

Today Dona maria told me how Evaristo came home one day from the *roca,* fell exhausted to the floor in the shade and said that he could hardly see anything. The *benzedor* was called. Prayers, faith in God and *Nossa Senhora da Aparecida* (Mary) and garlic compresses on the head and wrists did the job after three days. The boy looks so strong despite being full of parasites and viruses.

2 February

For unknown reasons everyone was nervous today. Everything went wrong. The milk wasn't picked up, land wasn't cleared because of yesterday's rainstorm; There were only beans and manioca-meal for lunch because there was no rice left. Afterwards we all had stomach pains and had to drink the horrible tasting bitter herb-tea. The lessons didn't go well either. The two youngest children, Rubens and Marcia, cried and were finally brought to the benzedor. The only decent thing we did was to make props for the play: crowns, hats, knives for the guards, etc. Things picked up around evening. Mario and the other Ukrainians came, later Dedinho and Odair, for rehearsal. At last we became the usual merry company. After rehearsal we played. Young and old jumped on each other's backs and laughed like crazy.

3 February

Rubens still had stomach pains, so I brought him to Odair's grandmother to be blessed. What an animal-friendly house! Pig in, goat out, among the usual plucked hens, shaggy dogs and cats, as well as geese, mosquitoes, stinging fly, etc.etc. I sat eating my corncake surrounded by two dogs and countless hens who counted the bites. Finally a hen jumped up onto the cake and took her portion.

5 February

As today is Saturday as well as the day of the theater performance and farewell party, the children stopped working at twelve o'clock. In the afternoon we made the stage out of bamboo with a straw roof. Jõãozinho was sent to borrow a large petroleum lamp – a two-hour walk. Cido got a threshing tarpaulin from the next hut to use as the curtain and Cido saddled the horse to distribute the last invitations over the mountain. He returned from this expedition at nine o'clock at night when the house and yard were already bursting full of expectant guests. The concept of time must still be developed, otherwise things won't work out very well in the industrial age in São Paulo. Cido was nervous and angry, yelled at Zéca, who, offended, refused to act, and it took all my powers of persuasion to appease their wounded honor.

After this behind-the-scenes skirmish, the play finally began and they were all better than ever, improvising, introducing new jokes; even the dog took part in the hunting scene. The smiling faces of the audience were visible in the dim light of the kerosene lamp. My temperamental revolt against the king's injustice, the battle with swords in the palace, the ending, when King Zéca proclaimed that now the poor as well as the rich would be happy, were all a great success.

After the theatre we danced until four in the morning.

6 February

Zéca packed his two pairs of pants, two shirts, toothbrush and towel. After yesterday's gaiety, the atmosphere is tense today. Departure time is near.

7 February

Tears, sobbing, wailing: Zéca is going with me to São Paulo. Nothing and nobody can hold him back. As we walked along the road with our suitcases he proudly told me of his plans for the future. "I'll show everyone that you can become something even though you're poor." Mario, the Ukrainian, rode after us to ask us to find his brother in São Paulo.

February 1972

I've been back from Marumbi for several days. Six weeks at the end of the world, far from the smog of São Paulo but also far from any chance to study. Nervously I prepare the zoology course for my fourth grade children and try to readjust myself to blonde hair and blue eyes.

Zéca is now the proud owner of four documents: health, trade and personal I.D., as well as a voting certificate. You go around here with a file full of documents, which you can only obtain by standing on line from four in the morning at different government offices. Today is his first day as a construction worker. He will go to high school at night. He is not to be envied. After a hard day's work he sits in school from eight to eleven at night being stuffed with sterile stuff: physics without experiments, geography without maps, etc. But for him it's the only way to a better future. I often help him with his schoolwork. Recently we tried to penetrate the mysteries of the consonant B. It isn't so easy to make a B; the schoolbooks provide exact instructions, which poor Zéca must memorize for the exam. Drab theory.

Marumbi, June 1972

Yes, I'm back in Marumbi, sitting in an adobe hut on the rice harvest, because the peanut harvest is being shelled on the only chair. What am I doing here in the middle of the school term? During the summer holidays I met a girl who has suffered from asthma for twelve years. I arranged for treatment in a São Paulo clinic, but she had to come immediately. I requested a leave of absence from the Waldorf School and traveled all night and a half a day to get here to the wilderness. It's more or less civilized until Faxinal, but then the dirt road becomes bumpier, ever narrower until finally it's no more than an almost overgrown path. It must have looked strange to the occasional *caboclos* (farmers) who rode by to see me briskly marching along in the morning sun with a knapsack full of warm clothes on my back. And then the surprise when I arrived, alone, and with the heavy knapsack, as though I wasn't afraid ...

A cup of roasted coffee tasted good. Gradually we came to the main reason for my visit. I was prepared for the possibility that Hilda's parents would be afraid to let her go to the big city. They have barely emerged from the last corner of the world. But Hilda decided to go immediately. For her anything is better than sitting here day after day waiting for her nightly attacks. Father and mother sat across from each other and simply couldn't decide.

The father said to the mother, You decide, as far as I'm concerned she can go.

The mother said to the father, You give the orders here.

And so it went for hours. With the patience of an angel I listened to it all. Hilda implored me, she even wanted to run away with me. When I was stiff from sitting so much I went to the nearby river where Dondoca was doing her wash. The parents were afraid that I was going away. Result: Hilda would go with me. Tomorrow she would pick me up at Cido's, where I was staying the night, and we would take the early bus to São Paulo. I had to be back in school.

The next morning I waited for her and when she didn't come I left with a lightened knapsack and mad with rage. Hilda's mother now had a *simpatia* against asthma, a feather and a brown powder, which she had got from the church and buried in the mud wall of her house.

July 1972

I'm moving again. As we must move out of the schoolhouse sometime anyway, I looked for an apartment or a house during the holidays and nearly fainted when I realized that the cost of renting a simple apartment is the same or more than I earn in a month. As a last resort I considered marrying some rich old slob. But I was saved from this fate by a teacher whose house had been broken into and looted and who generously offered it to me because he didn't want to set foot in it again.

I decided on the spot and in three hours we packed all the books, clothes and pictures, bought some furniture, rented a pickup and moved into our little house in *Vila das Beleza*. I'm ecstatic. This part of the city isn't nearly as fine and beautiful as the surroundings of the school. We have an extensive view, not of flowers and trees, but of eroded land. From the window you can see the Brazilian people in all their racial mixture and not only the eternal foreigners as is the case around the school.

End of July 1972

Life is certainly full of variety. Yesterday I had lunch with a German engineer at the Hilton Hotel where a waiter pushed a chair under me and today I sit on the stoop of a favela house and warm myself in the sun surrounded by a flock of children.

Zeca and I went to visit his family, who have moved back to Londrina. The bus broke down twice and it was icy cold. The coffee plants will surely freeze again. The knowledge that there are only two blankets for fourteen people at Zeca's didn't exactly warm me up. Finally the bus recovered and we arrived in Londrina around midnight. We ran to Zeca's house and knocked on the door. Everyone was asleep. The dog recognized us and woke up the house. Joyfully we were dragged to bed. They all hopped about and laughed. Soon we were sleepy and warmed ourselves according to the closer-closer principle. I was afraid I'd be assigned a single bed and have to freeze alone in it. But thank God I slept in the big double-bed wedged in between the children. I snuggled against Maristela's back.

Zeca's sisters and brothers haven't found work in Londrina. Only Cido works a few hours a day. We scoured the city looking for work. All for nothing. It drives you crazy. Everyone just hangs around. Those who can't hold out go to São Paulo.

Christmas 1972

Holidays! At least holidays from the Waldorf School. No sooner had I promoted my class into the fifth grade, put on a play, distributed report cards, etc, than I rushed off to Londrina. With two huge suitcases full of presents and used clothes and an unwieldy traveling bag, I stood before my door waiting to be picked up by a fifty-year-old bachelor. Like all bachelors he had his ticks, and only wanted to drive me as far as the city airport and not to the bus-station, which is farther. Luckily I was able to convince him to go by the Banco Mercantil, where Zéca works. Zéca had to help me drag the suitcases to the station. Two minutes before the departure time we arrived panting and laughing. We checked the baggage as I wanted to travel light. But the driver told me that, although this bus did go to Londrina, *mine* had already left and I should chase it in a taxi. I was furious as I saw the bus with my luggage, but without me, drive off.

Then I saw that it stopped for a red light and I ran after it, made imploring gestures to the driver until his heart finally softened and he opened the door and let me sit in front alongside him. *Graças a Deus!*

In Londrina Cido and I rehearsed a Christmas play with some children from my development aid times. It was a nice celebration. We also showed slides of the "good old Londrina times". I was doing again what I really wanted to do: work with the black-brown, curly-haired children.

The accumulated weariness from the school year didn't diminish, however. Sometimes it is so hot that every movement of the hand requires a special effort of will. It's also not possible to get a good night's sleep in the hut because of the mass of children. Their whispering doesn't stop before eleven o'clock. During the night the cockroaches rustle about and the rats gnaw at the ceiling. I am still not able to get used to these disgusting cockroaches. One fell on my head and I had to look for it in bed with the light from a match. Another time I woke up and found myself face to face with one of the beasts ...

At the end of January a group will come to São Paulo in order to learn a trade with me and to work: Cido, Zéca's brother; Dandoca, Zéca's cousin; Odair, Zéca's friend from Marumbi. Perhaps also nine-year-old Maristela, to attend the Waldorf School. A growing family. We'll see how long I hold out. In any case I'm happy with Zéca. You can see how he is growing, how the seeds fall on fertile ground and he absorbs the new and thinks about it, without scorning the old, without ignoring his roots.

January 1973

A few days ago I was a guest of Dona Irida, a Waldorf teacher who has a little house on the beach in Suarão, where I let my back get sunburned. I returned to São Paulo on the narrow-gauge train through the *Serra do Mar* around many curves and through twenty tunnels. The view is marvelous, real jungle with lianas, orchids, parasites that hang from the trees, and the constant view of the sea. The trip, which should take four hours, took six. At one station we stopped for an hour to repair a light. Then, with enthusiastic cries from the passengers, the train "sped" on. After fifteen minutes it stopped again. The train is derailed! A robbery! All kinds of rumors buzzed about, everyone got out. Let us pray, someone cried. In fact a freight-car had derailed, but as the train goes so slowly, nothing happened. The occupants of our ten cars were transferred to a train with three cars – a throng of children, baskets, enormous fishing rods and baggage. With a cry of triumph we crawled into the metropolis of São Paulo.

February 1973

I sit surrounded by four half and full illiterates. They are astounded that I always find the right key among the forty on the typewriter.

Our "commune" is doing quite well so far. Besides Zéca, Cido, Odair, Dandoca, and Maristela, the youngest, now live here with me. We almost died laughing today. Dandoca has no birth certificate, so we decided to obtain one so she can get work. We had to go to the civil registry with two witnesses in order to introduce her to the civilized world. The poor thing doesn't know anything about herself though, except her first name. Cido, Zéca and I tried to get some information out of her.

— What name would you like to have, Dandoca?

— I don't know?

— How old would you like to be? (She's about 22.)

— 20. No, better 18.

— When's your birthday?

— No idea.

— Well, we'll use mine: February 25th.

— That's all right.

— What's your father's name?

— Everyone calls him Ne.

— Ne! We can't put *that* on the application. We'll call him Manuel.

— And your mother?

— Josefa.

— Last name?

— No idea.

— We'll call her Josefa da Conceição.

Then she practiced writing her name. Finally we proudly went to the civil registry, which was closed by then. Tomorrow.

It is certainly a change to be part of a big family in a big city. São Paulo is confusing enough for us, but for someone who can't read it must be a nightmare, not able to read bus or street signs, nothing. What is the red light for? One must explain what a traffic light is, the meaning of red and green. But I am constantly surprised at how quickly they adapt to this new life.

And the moral support! When one of them is homesick, the other despairs of bureaucratic trickery and tells him that he will never get his documents and therefore will not be able to work. When I finish my pep-talk and try to encourage them, I also have to say that they should urinate *in* the toilet and not alongside it. But these educational tasks go smoothly and are accompanied by laughter. Playing with Maristela, teaching her German, teaching the boys arithmetic and Portuguese, drawing the alphabet with Dandoca; in the meantime preparing the Krishna legend and Botany for my Waldorf School class — and the day is over.

May 1973

School started two weeks ago. I have the fifth grade and Maristela is in the second. She has adapted well and learns easily with her great capacity for imitation. At this moment she is singing in English, "Good morning, good morning, good morning to you, how do you do?" She is blooming: drawing, handwork, eurythmy — she soaks them up like a dry sponge. Arithmetic less! Every evening I read a fairy tale to her. She asks a lot of questions, often profound ones that don't occur to adults anymore: Where do we come from? Will the world end some day? Where are God, the saints and the angels, etc. She likes animal stories best.

May 1973

Everything happens at once. At least a week ago I received a phone-call from the *Policia Feminina*. I had a bad fright until I realized that Hilda was at the bus station waiting for me. Hilda is the girl I wanted to bring here a year ago because she has suffered from asthma for twelve years. In the meanwhile it's thirteen years and with daily attacks. Now she lives here with us and I am trying to find out from every possible source what kind of treatment might help her. One says there is a new miracle injection, another that a concoction of garlic, spices, marjoram, cloves, cinnamon and honey will help. We've already prepared it. Every morning an egg with honey and iron pills against anemia; and two to three anti-asthma shots at night. I give the shots in my sleep (only good deeds can disturb my slumber). After an attack last Sunday I brought her to the hospital, where they gave her a ten-inch needle in the vein, after which her eyes rolled and she spit bile and called *Ute de céu* (Ute, for the love of God!) It was terrible, especially as a cripple lay in the last throes next to her and a young man was continually spitting. In the presence of this human suffering I prepared the history course for school: Buddha's life. I thought they would keep her in the hospital, but the doctor kept asking her if she felt better. So we rode back in the bus through stinking São Paulo.

June 1973

We went on a two-day outing with my class to a *sitio.* A Sitio is a piece of land with a simple house, some corn or manioca, some fruit trees. Here there is also a small reservoir, surrounded by a forest with wild bees, snakes, armadillos and an anteater. We picked the coldest night of the year, just below freezing. When we woke up everything was white with hoar-frost and white swaths of fog rose from the pond. Most of us slept in tents, but one girl swung in a hammock between two trees. I got up twice to see if she had frozen to death, but she snored away snug in her hammock. In the morning we danced ourselves warm with a quadrilha. Cido came with us and taught the pupils the dance. Then we hiked with bush-knives through the forest and over cleared fields. On the way back it was so warm that the children jumped into the water.

Maristela is doing wonderfully, she has many friends and is an ideal Waldorf pupil. Weekends other poor children from the neighborhood come by our house, and she teaches them everything she's learned. At the moment three of them are in the bathroom. Lessons under the shower! Afterwards she paints with them, as she has learned to do in the school. It's funny to walk into one of the stinking holes in which these children live and see that the only patch of color on the wall is a Waldorf picture. Maristela also reads them fairy tales and lectures about the detrimental effects of television!

June 1974

Thus the house has gradually filled up. We are now at the respectable total of nine. Soon there won't be an inch of space left on which someone isn't lying. Recently a mother from the school gave us three mattresses and three wool blankets. It was a great moment when we threw out the old dusty straw sacks and initiated the mattresses.

Some days I don't know where to jump next, being just stone-tired. The boys all work and go to hotel school in the evening. In order not to live entirely on sacrifice, I go regularly to an anthroposophical study group. We read "An

Outline of Occult Science" and I hope to have trod the path of knowledge at least so far in my life that I can develop the holy patience necessary to patiently "develop higher" the many people around me. Many habits are so strongly ingrained in them (urinate *alongside* the toilet, spit on the floor, sweep everything into the corner, etc.) that they can only be exorcised through continuous repetition.

My class, the sixth grade, and I decided to organize a Christmas party for poor children. We rehearsed a simple manger play in Portuguese. We worked for weeks making hand-made presents, in the school as well as at home: Some knitted dolls and animals, others made necklaces, some drew holy pictures. All baked Christmas cookies and put them in hand-painted cans. They went to so much trouble, as though they were making presents for their best friends. The Dutch family Ens put their sitio at our disposal and we spent the whole day there with the children: my pupils, their parents and the favela children, a total of about seventy. What luck that we have the Ens family! The festival was very nice. At eleven o'clock we met at the sitio, decorated the *real,* planted evergreen trees and played. My pupils had prepared some games such as sack-hopping, etc, with prizes. The ice was soon broken. The parents admired how Zéca and Cido played with the children.

Then came food, very important. We placed the meal on a huge table under a tree. But — a tropical rainstorm poured down and we all crowded into the house with our plates. At about five o'clock we got the theatre ready. The parents sat on chairs and tree-stumps as Cido emerged with the children from the dark. You could see their faces lit up by candles and torches. The crib scene also had a beautiful effect in this natural setting under the stars.

Just before the festival the class outing had taken place: a week in the Itatiaia mountains. I trained the children in my travel style: a lot of walking and simple fare. They accepted it all with good grace and are of the opinion that our outings are the best in the school. When the other classes rode up behind us and had caviar for lunch, they found it out of place and unworthy of a class outing.

24 March 1975

I would like to disappear, be free, wander in nature, sun, wind as in student days — the beach, waves, water, music, dancing, have a person who listens when I try to bear the problems of others. Where has my enthusiasm gone? I have the feeling that I am not giving the children in the school and at home what they need. My classes seem dry, without fire.

I have tied myself down too much, contrary to my need to be independent. But if you're always only independent, "free", at the end you become a tramp. Somehow everything has its time: the time for unattached wandering in the world and the time for commitment in order to accomplish something, and that involves restrictions and sacrificing certain things. But all that doesn't help: you have to commit yourself totally to the children as though they were your own, never only halfway.

May 1975

The family is growing: another child, Elizete, eleven years old. Her father disappeared years ago and left huge debts that her mother must pay off with great difficulty, so she couldn't afford to send her children to school any more. The solution? Dona Ute. I somehow managed to get a place for her in the Waldorf School, where the class is very full. Then Ruben's sister, Marcia, came. She's six years old and goes to the kindergarten.

We are quite conspicuous. Recently seven of us went to the dentist, and we filled up the waiting room. Five of us to the photographers and there was no room left for anyone else in the little shop. ("Are they all yours?"). Last week six of us at the doctor's ("Are you in charge of an orphanage?") We all took out our knitting and sewing needles in the waiting room and went to work (we had calculated a three-hour wait). Delighted cries ensued: *"Que bonitinho!" "Que maravilha!"*

Finally we were able to see the doctor. Basically they are all healthy, only Elizete has anemia. At the end the doctor said he had never seen such well-behaved children. They really are very nice among themselves and some families even compete to invite them as playmates for their own children.

The two older children, Maristela and Elizete, and very independent by Brazilian standards, travel alone by bus, go shopping, etc., which is a sensation here. They are also very solicitous and take good care of the smaller ones. Elizete and Marcia are the cleverest, Maristela and Rubens have hearts of gold, so respectful and participative, as is seldom seen in children. Recently I came home tired from the teachers' meeting; they all had a peeled orange in their hands. Rubens said: "Now we will all give a piece of our orange to Ute". We share everything. If one of them has a piece of cake from school he saves it in order to share it with the others. This is more important to me than any cleverness.

Once I came home from a rehearsal at the school. Smoke told me that the children had been cooking. They were all in theatre costumes, Rubens as a servant took my shoes off and put my tired feet into comfortable slippers. Then I was led into the living-room where a throne had been prepared; I sat on it and pillows were placed behind my back. The performance began: dancing, flute-playing, mime. Then they gave me a menu and finally the food. How nice!

October 1975

Outside someone was clapping. In Brazil, especially in the country, this is the way you announce yourself. I went to the gate. They were children from the favela. "Do you have something for us, dry bread or anything else?"

They go clapping from house to house and beg for something to eat. I gave them something, talked with them a while and asked where they lived. "Come visit us, we don't live far from here, in the favela Monte Azul."

One day I went with them to their huts. What miserable lives they lead in these drafty wooden huts perched on muddy slopes. Children, children and more children, but all friendly. They hang around, not knowing how to play.

The girls are tied to the household — washing clothes, fetching water, caring for the younger ones, etc. The boys are much freer, they play football or ride around in busses or go to the super-market to beg or guard cars. In reality these children have no childhood; they are miniature adults.

What to do?

I was reminded of an idea I had two years ago as I wrote my pupils' report cards. I saw Helmut before me, Gisela, Carla and many others. I considered: What could help Gisela to become self-aware? She would need the feeling that she also had something to give by using her handicraft abilities. To write reports on Carla became boring with the years because she was perfect in everything. What was she lacking? To open out to her fellow-human beings. And Helmut? He was too occupied with himself, thinking that only he had suffered in life. And so the idea developed in me that it would be beneficial for many pupils if they could teach something to other children who had not had the same opportunities that they had had.

But at that time the pupils were in the fifth grade, still too young. And I didn't know any favela children. But now I might risk trying to interest them in the idea. One morning, somewhat timidly, I proposed to them my idea for an *escolinha* (little school) for favela children. A rush of enthusiasm. They all had ideas: I can teach the children gymnastics, I knitting, I handicrafts, I can play with them. We'll collect clothing, crayons, old cloth, drawing paper. Yes, and where will all this take place? In my house, we can use the old shed in the yard. So it began.

Advent 1975

Christmas is almost upon us. I just finished wrapping the thirty presents for Christmas Eve. Marcia wished for a sleeping bag for her dwarf, which I crocheted for her. Then a hammock for the smallest doll and various things for the crib, which "disappeared" a couple of weeks ago and will re-appear embellished on Christmas Eve.

Yesterday was the last day of school. I will be happy if I see two good reports. Next year there will be four, as Marcia will go into first grade, Rubens in the second, Elizete and Maristela in the fifth. Therefore Maristela is the academically farthest advanced in their family, after Zéca. The fourth grade was the highest for the others, while some didn't go to school at all. She is as simple as always though and doesn't try to lord it over her sisters and brothers.

Rubens goes to school with an enthusiasm that delights his teachers. He is continually collecting stones or flowers, wrapping them as though they were the greatest treasures in the world, and giving them to the teachers. This regard for things and people, which is in him, is something very special.

December 1975

Here, life goes on as usual — fun, anger, celebrations, fighting the cockroaches, overflowing wash-baskets and ever more people who live, learn and work here.

You wanted a list of them. Here it is.

Williams, from Bolivia, 29, learning to be a waiter
Renato, from Chile, 26, learning to be a cook
Mario, from the Ukraine, 23, learning to be a waiter
Cido, from Paraná, 23, learning to be a cook
Odair, from Paraná, 20, learning to be a cook
Maria José, from Paraná, 19, learning to be a nurse
Jõão, from Paraná, 19, learning to be a waiter
Eliza, from Paraná, 14, learning to be a seamstress
Maristela. from Paraná, 12, Waldorf School
Elizete, from Paraná, 12, Waldorf School
Rubens, from Paraná, 7, Waldorf School
Marcia, from Paraná, 6, Waldorf Kindergarten

So we are fourteen altogether.

Zéca and Williams have just returned from Bolivia where Zéca traveled around for three months with our Bolivian and could satisfy to some extent his permanent thirst for travel. At dawn I heard voices outside my window. First Zéca marched in dressed in a poncho, then Williams and behind him a third one — a Chilean, Renato. They met during the days-long train ride from

Bolivia and, as they had only ten cruzeiros between them, they decided never to part. Thus he became the fourteenth inhabitant of the house and sleeps, in want of a better place, on a borrowed ping-pong table in the so-called *palacio*, the lumber-room that we had cleared for Williams, painted and put in an electric light. After only a week in Brazil this lucky chap already had a place to sleep, study and work. Zéca was able to get him admitted to the hotel school. When Renato gets up in the morning he must role his mattress up on a ball and cover it with a cloth, because in the afternoon twelve favela children stream into the same room. Twice a week pupils from the Waldorf School come and teach five to twelve year old children from the favela. They paint, sew, knit, play theatre, work with clay, garden, etc.

The pupils are thrilled. I went with a pupil to the favela recently. She brought baby clothes, milk and diapers with her and put on the diapers like an experienced mother. The children act much more naturally when they are in contact with the favela people.

THE DEVELOPMENT OF A DEVELOPMENT WORKER

I would like to describe how my idea of development aid, which led me to work for the German Development Service, was transformed through practice and finally gave rise to the following questions:

Is development aid meaningful in its present form?

Do we have any right to engage in the third world development process and these people's lives?

During the GDS training cycle, we were faced with the question: Why did you join the GDS? First there were the personal reasons: to get to know people from different social origins and with different cultural backgrounds; to master difficult situations with simple means and, well, desire for adventure. Alongside these personal motives are the more altruistic ones, which, however, are also egoistic in that they influence one's own personal development through the positive effect on others: to alleviate misery through the simple desire to help and from a certain shame at being well-fed whereas others go hungry. Behind this is a more or less clear picture of a world divided between rich and poor. Expressions like population explosion, hunger, educational deficiency, arise and finally culminate in the idea that only the industrially developed countries can bring about an improvement in the lives of two-thirds of humanity through capital investment (building up the infrastructure, industrialization), personal aid (sending experts etc.) and improving commercial relations (higher prices for raw material).

Armed with this knowledge, I enlisted in the GDS and was sent to Brazil a few months later where, aside from kindergarten work in a favela, I occupied myself trying to get boys and girls away from the deadening effects of hanging about the streets by giving them worthwhile tasks. Handicrafts, theatre, sports, folk-dancing, sales of their work in the wealthy part of the city, were able to give many children the feeling that they could accomplish something through their own efforts.

When you see someone who needs help, you jump in and help him without considering whether the help will have a lasting effect. This is what I did in the first months of my development aid work. But after a while you lift your head up from the daily details, look around and then adjust your contribution to development aid and the social conditions that made this help seem necessary, according to a broader view of the economic, social and cultural conditions of the country. You feel out of place in the presence of rich coffee plantations, modern skyscrapers and fully stocked, elegant shops. Is it really necessary that we come from Germany as volunteer development workers to a country that has so many people living in abundance? This caused the first crack in my faith in the value of development aid.

Nevertheless I still saw the value of working in a favela and directly helping the poor as far as possible — working with children, collecting old clothes, obtaining American powdered milk for mothers with small children, etc.

But I gradually realized that development aid, even when it actually reaches the poor, can be dangerous. The poor accustom themselves to receiving without contributing anything: when they're sick, and if they're lucky, they are given medicine; when they're cold they are given, God willing, clothing; if a child is undernourished the mother is given powdered milk, if she's lucky.

These two criteria — first: you get something without doing anything; second: only when chance wills it to be so, strengthen the passive "as God wills" attitude of the poor, which doesn't allow them to become active in determining their own destiny. It is the receptive, waiting attitude of a person who expects the good as well as the negative influences on his life to come from without, and not from inside himself. The wealthy corrupt the poor with their gifts and purely material help. Characteristics which are, in themselves, positive, such as cheerfulness despite poverty and little envy of the wealthy, are fatal in their effects. They coincide with the generosity of some of the wealthy, awake feelings of thankfulness in the poor and assuage the consciences of the rich, despite their privileges, which are obstacles to a just social order.

Through observing my social environment and the effect of development aid on the character of its recipients, I came to plant the question: Is it right to aspire to an evolutionary model for under-developed countries based on western standards, which, in the best of cases, can result in an improvement of living standards, but leaves the political and social structures unchanged? Or is it preferable to dispense with the immediate improvement of living conditions and substitute a revolution from below which would eliminate the present social forms and replace them with a new democratic social order?

What role can a development worker play under these conditions? Probably only in the field of education; all other forms of development aid are harmful to the recipients if they don't stimulate them to act on their own. Education in the sense of imparting information on a wide basis: get the children off the streets and into primary and trade schools. It must be kept in mind, however, that mechanical learning through memorizing can suffocate the natural desire to learn which is innate in every child, and that thinking and the critical observation of the environment should be promoted. Education also in the sense of consciousness-building: make clear to the oppressed how their favela existence is the inevitable result of the overall structure of the country. Education, furthermore, in the general human sense: restores a spiritual center to their lives.

The problem of a rich upper-class and poor land and slum dwellers is not only a problem of well-being. Material misery and nutritional deficiency are merely the most extreme forms of a gulf which goes much deeper. When Che Guevara said, "It's not a matter of how much meat one eats or how often one can go to the beach. It's a matter of the individual feeling richer and much more responsible *within.*"

I think he analyzed the problem on a much higher level than most official representatives of development aid. They take the position that poverty can only be eliminated if you give the poor something to eat. But the problem is also to change the fact that the lower classes are objects to those who govern and to allow them to participate in the decisions and the life of the country. Furthermore, their traditional world-conception, which corresponded to their way of life and supported them spiritually, having been torn away, it must be made possible for them to create an inner world which corresponds to an industrialized, technical society. All this will not be accomplished by giving the poor more to eat. Their need is not only physical, but also spiritual.

Poverty has always existed. But hunger, poverty and misery in a jungle village, where the people are supported by a spiritual background, is different from hunger, poverty and misery in a favela. The stomachs growl in both cases. But the spiritual situation of a black in a jungle village is different from that of a black in a favela. Together with civilization, cinema, TV, assembly-lines, the crowds and hectic activity of big cities — this technical world into which they have been thrown without being able to enjoy its amenities — their spiritual world has been taken from them, the myths and fairy tales, the beliefs, the instinct for correct nutrition, appropriate ways of raising children, medicinal plants. Substitutes have hardly been provided; efforts to eliminate illiteracy have a practical value, but do not create a new world of ideas. The devastating effects of the stolid learning of the ABCs, the memorizing of historical dates and Geography concepts in school can be best seen in the favela people. They are complete materialists. Their efforts, as soon as they have overcome the most basic misery, are directed towards obtaining civilization's material goods such as radio, TV, etc. For me development aid is real help only when it is oriented towards the *human being*. Here is an example from our favela.

It makes no sense to build playgrounds or public laundries if there is no group of people to teach the children, the mothers and, when possible, the fathers, to actively adapt themselves to life, to consciously absorb the phenomena of the environment together with all its injustice, and implant in them a new spiritual hunger. This can be done through practical work, for example, the building of a youth center with the children in which handicrafts, theatre and stories in which the world outside the favela is brought into view are undertaken; and always done in a way that enables the children to be introspectively active and carry responsibility themselves, and are confident that in *every* case one is responsive to them, even if it means running the risk of failure. Alongside the external arrangements (for example handicrafts which could be sold to help finance the youth center) the feeling must exist that something has been done through their own efforts. Will-power must be cultivated and a seed planted which can grow into the attitude that one's life can be changed through personal efforts and is not dependent on a destiny uninfluenced by personal acts.

There could be regular meeting with the adults about how to make the favela more worthy of its human inhabitants. Specific problems must be addressed which are tackled by knowledgeable workgroups. There are enough problems and questions to be dealt with: obtaining water, garbage disposal, additional earnings through work at home, regular school attendance for children, etc. The desire for improvement must come from within — it makes no sense, for example, to build a laundry when the favela people never desired one. During regular meetings, however, the wish for one could arise from within and then be realized. In approaching common problems in this way, the awareness would gradually arise that one is not alone with his problems, but that thousands are in the same situation. Democracy in miniature could be practiced. The favelados would be treated a *human beings*, as acting, feeling, thinking human beings — and not as objects.

A social worker can act as a catalyst. Not as leader, for that would be tutelage under another name, but as a person who give impulses but doesn't do what the other can do: partly stimulating, partly meeting them half-way.

Origins

Most favela dwellers come from the north, from Bahia, Pernambuco, Ceará, Minas Gerais. Many from still farther away. Most find it a thousand times better here than there, even if they must live in a favela. "Here at least we eat. There you plant in the scorching heat and then comes the harvest. You harvest, but the buyer pays a miserable sum." Or: "You plant, it doesn't rain, the crop is ruined." "We suffered there, and when the harvest brought nothing in I swore never to plant again; two days later we left with our belongings and children, a two-day bus trip." That's not so much though; most leave by train, which takes up to ten days, depending on the distance.

They usually leave their traditions and customs behind. Once in São Paulo they seldom dance the quadrilha, hardly any folksongs are sung; *bumba meu boi* (meu boi: "my ox", a kind of religious theatre and procession) or Folia dos Reis (a musical play about the Three Wise Men), are hardly ever performed. Many are ashamed of these things and think that in the city they must be "modern" and sing, dance and celebrate differently. That's why life in the favela, almost everywhere in the city in fact, is so barren and monotonously gray. But that's also why most of them still harbor a silent nostalgia for their "terra", and many want to go back when they're old to live in peace on their savings.

In the city they no longer orient themselves according to the goodness which emanates from the people, but according to the civilization of the wealthy as they see proclaimed on television, etc. — with disastrous results.

Education

Officially, there are eight years of compulsory education. But many children, especially girls, don't go to school at all because their parents don't consider it necessary, and they do more work in the home than the boys, who grow up much freer and hardly help at all. When they do go to school they are often absent and are handicapped by the fact that their parents can't help them with their homework. Furthermore, they have not had adequate nutrition or stimulation since the time of birth. They are usually left back in the first year, drag themselves through school life, and give up at the third or fourth grade. Completing four years of school is already something special and makes life easier, because then there are various trade courses which they can take: for girls hairdresser, manicurist, seamstress, nurse's assistant; for boys: mechanic, waiter, cook, etc.

Earnings

Most favela people earn the salário mínimo (the legal minimum wage) — about $100 per month. The family income is increased by what some children earn by shining shoes, washing cars or delivering women's shopping home in carts from the markets. This isn't much, but sometimes they earn in a day more than the father's daily wage. This is of course very tempting for them. They earn some money from which, according to character and inclination, they pass a larger or smaller amount to their homes and the rest they spend on chewing gum, sweets and similar stuff which they never got as small children. But the future is lost because they then either don't go to school anymore at all or only sporadically, reach only the second grade and never have a chance to learn a trade. This means that they, like their fathers, must do the heaviest and dirtiest work.

Food

Rice and beans, rice and beans, rice and beans, for lunch and supper. The beans are usually cooked in a pot, spiced with some garlic, and rice is added. Also *mistura* (mixture). This means everything else, for example meat and vegetables. The poorer ones divide a small piece of meat among the members of the family. Vegetables are hardly ever eaten and when they are it's mostly tomatoes and "leaves" (any kind of lettuce). But in general green is written in small letters. For example, if something better is cooked for Christmas, it consists of rice and beans, somewhat more meat (usually chicken), noodles with tomato sauce, "maionese", that is, potato salad with mayonnaise. Meals are monotonous and stereotyped. On the one hand it's practical, for the housewife's dilemma "What will I cook?" is absent. On the other hand this monotony has negative effects which go beyond the physical. At home I hardly ever cook beans and rice and "invent" new meals from leftovers. That's what I always tell the children, that cooking is an art and that they should invent something, even if it's not always successful.

In the north rice (which isn't native to Brazil, having established itself around 1810 with the opening of the harbors) is hardly eaten. Sweet potatoes, manioca, cará and other roots are preferred. A lot of manioca-meal is eaten with beans. (We call it sawdust because it's so dry and you have difficulty swallowing it at first.)

DIARY 1976-1980

7 September 1976. Brazil's Independence Day.

I first stepped on Brazilian soil eleven years ago. Surely I was more rested then after a 24-day ocean voyage than I am now. In any case, I am exhausted today and really feel the need for a rest. I must take a breath and objectively think about what I am to do during the next years of my life, whether I'll stay on the Waldorf School or not, what I can accomplish here, etc. Many who think altruistically say I should dedicate myself completely to the "poor". But how? I must earn money. Furthermore, I find that the wealthy children are often just as poor, when I consider the more difficult cases in my class.

November 1976

The school play is approaching with enormous strides. The performance of "Widukind" with my eighth grade is almost upon us. I am torn asunder between rehearsals, painting scenery, costume fittings and my housewifely duties. The children at home bear it calmly and often receive me with nice surprises. Besides all this are the normal classes, preparation for Christmas, etc.

Christmas 1976

Every year Waldorf schools perform the "Oberufer Christmas play". For the past three years I have been taking increasing numbers of favela children to see it. This time there were about forty. And how do you organize this bunch to get them all into the city buses? Well, it's not easy, but the mass isn't so amorphous either, for smaller groups develop naturally within the larger one, which is difficult to oversee as a whole. Older children care for younger ones, brothers and sisters watch out that they are all still there.

Before we depart I look to see if we are more or less presentable. They all gather in front of my gate. " Blow your nose." — "Go and wash your hands." — "Get the comb in the children's room and comb your hair and if it's still too stringy, put a kerchief over it."

A boy with whom I had only a nodding acquaintance came without shoes. I loaned him a pair of Ruben's. But they didn't fit, so he carried them in his hands and when we arrived at the school he placed them neatly at the entrance of the auditorium. Being so squeezed in was just too unusual for him. After all, the shepherds go barefoot in the Christmas play.

Finally we are ready to march. Divided into two groups, I push them into the first bus, then the second. "We'll meet at the Borba Gato bus stop." Except for the bigger ones, the children all pass through the turnstile without having to pay.

I march up the hill to the Waldorf School with this endless tail of children. In an orderly column we enter the auditorium. Many parents smile, touched; others look on somewhat shocked at this unexpected, unusual sight of poor, brown, black (but also white) children in this "white" setting. We sit in the first rows and they all beam at me. The play begins, the angel floats in.

"An angel!" Vitoria cries from the heart. She, who is so pitch-black and always pushed aside by the others, could hardly grasp the angel's brilliant white light. For most of them theater is reality.

We met Peter Schmidt of the Giroflex factory on the way back. "What is this mob of children?" I briefly described our work in the favela. "We'll come back to that again," he said. A historic phrase! For he really did come back to it, for which I am eternally grateful. He was the first to take our work seriously and promised to help. And not only promised. In 1977 we had a teacher paid by Giroflex. We were thus able to expand the favela work and the children could come every day. After a bad experience with a trained teacher, I employed Cido as youth supervisor, cooking teacher, etc. The children were thrilled. Cido is simply ideal in that he has imagination, ideas, likes to work, feels good with the children, is able to handle the large groups which stream to us during festivals. Furthermore, he was poor himself as a child and knows how it feels.

The number of children has grown enormously. Thank God Dona Regina and Dona Helena had pity on us. Dona Regina sews purses, pillowcases, blankets with the children from leftovers and tells them stories while doing so. Dona Helena knits with them – wallets, dwarf-dolls, sweaters. Both are desperate for more room. We are so cramped. Everything is done in the tiny children's room, which contains a three-tier bed, a closet and desk. Children swarm everywhere – on the bed, the floor, the desk. And the smell and the heat that develop after two hours of work! The smell improves somewhat when Cido is giving his cooking lessons at the same time. Meanwhile I help the children with their homework, clear a niche in the kitchen to prepare supper, listen to Ruben's multiplication tables practice, do rhythmic clapping with Marcia, etc.

Space! Space! Space is what we need!

July 1977

I've just returned from Guarajú, the beach serving the São Paulo upper crust. Dr. Gudrun of the anthroposophical clinic lent us her holiday house for a week. Us, that is, me and fourteen children from the favela as well as Maristela, Marcia and Rubens. As the children entered the house they were stunned for a moment, then broke out in cries of joy, ran through all the rooms and just couldn't believe that it would belong to them for a week. The same thing happened when we went to the sea: first apprehension looking at the infinite expanse of water, then they skipped in screaming for happiness. So much water all at once. Most of them knew only the miserable favela streamlet where they get their water. The week was a complete success: water, sun, an excess of room to play, rocks to climb, sand and castles and waterfalls to build. For once they were always clean, with full stomachs and occupied as children should be. I could teach them all the games I knew (ballgames, halma, memory, mikado, jumping, racing) During the mid-day break they read, drew or knitted. Most impressive was that *everything* was fun, even the things which don't usually inspire much enthusiasm like cooking and washing dishes. My main occupation at the sea was counting heads in the waves. What a fright when one wasn't visible behind the waves!

September 1977

Perhaps Evaristo Gazzotti, one of the most important landowners in this district, will lend us a piece of land. My house is already full of used building materials: windows, doors, toilets, sinks, beams, etc. If it comes through, we want to build a youth center. Sometimes, when I have a headache for example, and I think of all I would like to do and if I will be able to do it and persevere, it all seems terribly murky. At my age men are at their best but women are already going downhill. And when everything depends on one person it's very shaky. My situation recently became clear to me when we were with Everisto Gazzotti. Dr. Gazzotti behind his immense leather-trimmed desk; Peter Schmidt, owner of the Giroflex factory; Mr. Blaich, the imposing Waldorf School personality; Cido and Zéca — but the nucleus of it all was my own humble self.

If the Gazzotti land doesn't come through, we must think of something else. My house is simply too small to accommodate forty children every day. When, like now, it has rained for a week and everything is damp, the wash doesn't dry, the children bring in mud which sticks everywhere and it rained into the shed in the back, I could literally go crazy. There's so much land in Brazil and not even a little piece for us. Something must happen in any case. Boxes, cases, sacks, suitcases full of Christmas presents are everywhere. The products of the children's work that they will give their parents for Christmas (35 sewn pillows, calendars, Christmas stars, etc.) and the used clothing for Londrina — it all winds up here. Where should we store the three sacks of oats, the two sacks of cookies, the five packets of chocolate pieces, the used clothing, the 15 pairs of sneakers, the 30 pajamas for outings, the five doors, three lattices, toilets, bidet, a truckload of wood??

October 1977

Gazzotti gave permission. We are allowed to build. To work!

Today is Sunday. We have just come from our plot of land. Last Sunday we demolished the ruins of the house that stood on it. It sounds easy, but when four people shake a house wall until it finally falls over, it becomes quite strenuous under the Brazilian sun. The roof-truss hung awry from one wall. We pushed against it with beams for a long time before it condescended to fall. Our men all helped, but also many favela children. We saved the serviceable bricks and carried them to the back corner of the plot in order to build a wall there. I must have stooped a thousand times today to carry six, seven or eight bricks, covered with sweat and red as a beet. The children carry everything on their heads, the small ones one brick, the older ones more, or whole beams.

The following Sunday we began to build the wall. I never realized that it's such an art to set one brick onto another. I, at least, had to reset them every time. Last night I dreamt of bricks and walls. Gazzotti, who visited us yesterday in order to measure the plot, couldn't get over his surprise at so much enthusiasm for work for which no profit is expected.

January 1978

Disappointment. Anger. Gazzotti, or his mother, reneged on their promise and we are again without land. I was already suspicious, as he has been postponing the signing our contract for two months.

Now I'm going to see if we can get a piece of land from the prefecture. Running around — heat — running around — waiting — heat — in this heat one is always in a better mood after a cool shower than after social work.

Excursion to Itatiaia

We've already had many outings with the favela children, of one day or of a week's duration, to the zoo and to the Butantan Snake Institute in São Paulo, and outside São Paulo to an orange fazenda, to the sitio Ens, to the reservoir, to the beach; but the most complicated outing was to the Itatiaia mountains, about 250 miles from São Paulo in the direction of Rio de Janeiro.

It began complicated. We wanted to go by train; Itatiaia has a train station but the trains don't stop there. However, from my school experience I knew that it's possible to get special permission from the Station-Master, who issues the corresponding instructions for the train to stop there. So I went to the main station and after asking around I finally found the right man and he promised me that the train would stop in Itatiaia.

We informed the parents what kind of trip it would be, with special emphasis on the fact that it would last a week. The mothers gave their permission, the fathers didn't, all the children wanted to come, even the five-year-olds. A lot of coming and going. But finally we had a group of fifteen children, boys and girls, between the ages of nine and fifteen.

Everyone was supposed to contribute food and they arrived with packages: rice, beans, cornmeal, sugar, salt, noodles. Cido and I went to buy the "rest": some meat, sausage, eggs, onions, potatoes, peas, flour, etc. Blaich gave us vegetables. We packed it all in two huge crates and some small boxes.

Second problem: how is all the baggage to get to the station? I called Seu Armando, who said he was willing to pick us up with his *perua* (Volkswagen minivan).

At six o'clock in the morning the first children arrived. Seu Armando was supposed to come at seven. We placed everything on the porch: crates and boxes of food, fifteen plastic bags containing the children's belongings, two suitcases of toys and games, pajamas for all, rainwear, books, handicrafts tools, an armchair — an excursion of gypsies! But how was it all to fit along with seventeen people in a minivan? I sent Cido and some of the children ahead in the city bus, the rest were packed into the van. "Kommt ein Wagen vollbeladen, voll mit Kind und Kegel!" (A wagon comes fully loaded, full of bag and baggage.)

After snaking our way through the morning traffic, we arrived at the train station about an hour later. Now the heavy baggage had to be carried to the train — we were soaked in sweat and exhausted after doing it. Everyone gaped at us, including the conductor. Just in case, I asked if the train would really stop in Itatiaia. "*Ninguém deu ordem.*": No one has given the order. In heaven's name, now we were in trouble. I wanted to see the Station Master, but he was still sleeping. Finally, at the last moment, the written order came. Relieved, we sat in the train, it departed, dragging itself slowly through the treeless suburbs: factories, favelas, desolate and seemingly without end.

Only after two hours ride did it become nicer as we came into the *Vale do Paraiba,* where green rice fields and vegetable gardens refreshed our eyes. What a relief to know that somewhere things are still planted.

The children made themselves at home: some knitted, some played, others ate oats. The trip took six hours and we arrived in Itatiaia at about one o'clock. The train entered the station whistling loudly, we jumped out with our baggage, waved and thanked them for the "extra service".

Third problem: we stood in the deserted station two miles away from the town and five miles from Matthias' house, which he had put at our disposal for the next five days. We put the children and the baggage under a generously shade-giving tree. Cido took care of the hungry children while I went down the long treeless road to the town to find a taxi there. After some bargaining, I found two which were willing to take us up the mountain. But what did we get ourselves into!? One of the drivers seemed to be more occupied contemplating his navel than with the numerous serpentine curves and chasms. I sweated blood as he sped so close to the chasms: the responsibility for the children and no insurance! *Tá louco*. You're crazy!

Suddenly a huge boulder stood before us. It was too much. I ordered the children out of the car. The driver's pleas didn't change my mind, we continued on foot. He met us at Matthias' house, safe and sound and defending himself in front of the other driver. Well, we finally reached our destination. The little house was very nice and we accommodated ourselves right away. Some began to cook and finally we sat at a long table, said grace and attacked the food.

The next day we went walking, quite far, bringing groans from the children — to the waterfall, Véu da Noiva, to Maromba and to Lago Azul, an ice-cold brook that bubbles down from a mountain and empties into a lake. We swam there and sprang into the freezing water. Little Solange was the bravest and at the end of the outing was given the title "*A mais corajosa da água fria*" (bravest in cold water). There was also a nice little museum with Itatiai's animal life. The insect section with wasp-combs that look like modern architecture astonished the children most.

In the evenings we played wink and mime, Poor Black Cat, and improvised a theatre. The nights were pitch black, without stars, so that you couldn't see a yard in front of you. The children almost died of fright when they had to step outside. Therefore we undertook night-marches or trials of courage. Only Zezê, Adivina and Solange were willing to walk down the mountain with me in the darkness.

Only when the children are with you like that 24 hours a day do you really get to know them. Especially their fear at night. Once I took one of the girls with me at night and we gave the boys a fright. They were already in bed and we knocked on the window from outside and made sinister noises. The giggling in the boys' room stopped abruptly, it was deathly still, then the whispers: *o fantasma,* the ghost, *fica quieto, é o cão, o bicho*: keep still, it's the monster, the devil! They trembled with fear and all eight jumped into Cido's bed, which luckily was only a mattress on the floor. Although they knew later that we were the ghost, they slept near Cido from then on and didn't want to extinguish the candle.

The two older boys wouldn't let the younger ones sleep one night and Cido sent them to the living-room. They didn't close their eyes once all night and whined. Oh, Ute, *deixe a gente dormir no quarto com os outros* — let us sleep in the room with the others. We remained firm however, for after all they're fifteen years old and shouldn't be frightened by some shadows of trees that fall into the room.

During the day Cido taught the children many new dishes and they often baked bread. Whoever worked and helped best, or voluntarily cleaned the toilet or carried the food basket, got a star.

On the last day we distributed prizes: the bravest in the dark, the bravest in cold water, the most helpful, the best cook, etc.

That night was New Years Eve. We played until midnight. In honor of the year 1978 there was churrasco — nine pounds of meat! At midnight we opened a bottle of champagne, the glass was solemnly passed around and all drank their sip of friendship.

Then we had to think about departure. The train would not stop in Itatiaia on the way back, so we had to rent a mini-van and go to Resende. With a smaller load than on arrival we left, saying good-by to the mountains of Itatiaia. At the station in Resende we had a fright. The train was due to arrive in an hour-and-a-half but, we were told, it was already full because of the holidays. I stayed stubbornly in line. It turned out that there were twelve seats free. We alone needed more than that. So I left the line and we stood with children, plastic sacks and our pot of food (a mixture of noodles and beans which gradually fermented due to the heat). The train arrived with people hanging out of the doors and windows. I gathered the children and, although we had no tickets yet, we stormed through the gate and pushed our way into the train. Fortunately it was the same train we took coming, with the same crew. They offered us a place in the baggage car, which made us deliriously happy. Thus we rode comfortably sprawled on the floor toward São Paulo. It was pouring rain when we got out. This time there was no helpful Armando to pick us up. We ran soaking wet and loaded down (like migrants from the Northeast) with sacks and pots through the streets of São Paulo past the high-rises, crossing the wide avenues. A sack fell, Zezê bent to pick it up and his trousers split. Now he had to hold them as well. But finally we were all jammed into the city bus on our way to Vila das Belezas and Monte Azul. They were all anxious to know how things were at home and looked forward to seeing their families.

Recently a "lady" asked me: "And don't they feel too strongly the difference between this and their homes?" No, for they are happy to see their mothers and sisters and brothers again. They like to travel, but they look forward to the return just as every child does, whether they're returning to a palace or to a miserable hut.

Mirani

Early this morning I went to the favela to inform Pedrinho that we would be going to Volkswagen today where he was to apply for the three-year training course. Dr. Sauer, the President of the local company, had given instructions that "Dona Ute's children" could also do this training, which is otherwise reserved for relatives of the factory workers.

I slid down the steep muddy path to Pedrinho's house, expertly avoiding a pile of shit which lay in the middle of the path. As I'm on vacation, more time is available, so I stopped to chat with Mirani, Pedrinho's mother. The training takes three years, I told her. And what will we do with Pedrinho when we go back to Bahia? Are you going to move soon? Yes, probably next year when my husband gets his invalid's pension. Well, then he can live with us, like the other boys from Paraná.

Bahia and pension were now the catchwords. She told me about her life. "I was born in the *roca*, the interior of Bahia. My mother didn't let me go to school. She said that girls only wanted to learn to read and write in order to send love letters to boys. I was stubborn though and learned it alone. Later I married my husband who brought six children into the marriage, who I raised."

Charming children, with a touch of Indio. "I always wanted to see São Paulo. Everyone talked about this wonder city. Then I became ill and we moved to São Paulo, because the doctors are better here. We had just enough money to pay the rent deposit and the first installments for two beds, a stove and a table. The room was abominable, it rained in, the neighbors were nasty to the children who I had to leave alone during the day because I went to work as a cleaning-woman".

"Then came the coldest winter I ever experienced. My lips were frozen blue. In the factory the other women asked me why I didn't put on a sweater. I said I wasn't cold, but my whole body was shivering".

"But I was so cold that I overcame my shame. 'I have no sweater, I've just come from the North.' The next day a woman brought me a flannel jacket. It was nice and warm, but as the children had nothing warm to wear I left it with them at home. Then some women workers got together and gave me five sweaters".

"One day I said to my husband, 'This can't go on. We're working to pay the rent and the installments and to buy rice and beans. I heard that one can live free on prefecture land' (I didn't yet know the word favela). Instead of continuing to pay rent, I got an advance from the firm, we bought old wood and found a small space in the favela Monte Azul. If we hadn't done that my children would still be in rags and we wouldn't have enough to eat".

"Two years later my husband was injured at work and declared unfit to work. His application for an invalid's pension is still pending in court. Since five years!" Adivina served us coffee. Nice.

"My husband would have given up long ago, but I kept at it. Why is there a court and justice? If we get the compensation, we will go back to Bahia and open a little store. I'm ashamed to live in the favela."

"You shouldn't be ashamed of that. You don't live here because you have committed a crime."

"No, but still ... The good and the bad live here together, but the worst thing is that we are all so crammed together and the children see and experience everything. At Christmas four murderers were arrested and the policeman cried: "Yes, just look, you women and children, last night these men killed fourteen people with razors and robbed them." And they began to beat the defenseless men. The mother screamed, 'Let them go, oh, my children!' You hear it all in the whole favela."

I thought of the jails: twenty in a small cell. Four beds which they fight over. The strong terrorize the weak. Now and then the police come, pull one out, whip him and then throw him back into the cell, whether he is guilty or not. Many vegetate there so many years they forget that they are human beings.

Two hours later I left, climbed up the muddy hill, passed by our youth center and went home. One must *do* something for these people. I only hope that Pedrinho can learn a trade at Volkswagen and lead a life worthy of a human being. And that he doesn't forget that he was also poor as a child and helps others to pull themselves up.

Easter 1978

We painted 120 eggs and hid them at the Sitio Ens yesterday. We drove out there in the morning, the borrowed minivan having to make two trips to bring all the children. It was great fun. It was boiling hot and the children jumped directly into the swimming pool, 35 children romping, squealing and screaming in the water with Cido and I watching from above like hawks that no one went under.

Then there was a good nourishing lunch, for which we gave thanks with many songs. The children became less fish-like, said good-day, no longer threw everything on the ground and, more important, had something to give. Mrs. Ens was very impressed by the Brazilian songs we sang. Afterwards we went for a walk, during which the eggs were hidden. Then the seeking, the joy of discovery!

A birthday at Solange's

Solange came by early this morning. She wandered around, helped a little with the cleaning, did some leather work with Dona Raimunda. You could see though, that she really wanted something else. Maybe our Godchild was ill or they had no money to buy food. Finally it came out: she wanted to invite us to Ademir's birthday party, who was three years old today. What she also wanted to say didn't come out though — that she wanted to bake the cake in our oven. At home they have only an open fire, upon which the cake was finally baked. A coal-black pot of dough was placed on a hot platter and on the lid, a piece of old tin, glowing coals. It was done four times until the four-tiered cake was finished. What a tiny, lop-sided cake it was, but it was decorated with much love by Solange and her oldest brother, Juracy. The birthday-child Ademir patiently watch the hours-long baking process from a "throne" until it was finished.

It was already dark when we finally lit a candle with the number 4 on it, which the boy had found somewhere. About twenty children were gathered to cut the tiny cake; some standing, some sitting on the only bed, all with glowing eyes. We sang *Parabens* (congratulations), "Happy Birthday" in English and finally "Hoch soll er leben". Everyone got a piece of cake and a sip of juice.

The mother said, "I'm ashamed that everything is so simple."

"But you shouldn't be ashamed, *comadre,* the children are all very happy. Many think that a party must be elaborate. But that's not necessary. Just look at how the Birthday-child is so proud to be the center of attraction. That's important for him — to break up the commonplace with little festivities." That put her at ease.

I think this shows that a home is not so much the house as the atmosphere which reigns in it — love, affection, togetherness, that makes life worthwhile. Children whose fathers have disappeared and whose mothers work are never in a hurry to get home. The smaller ones even point out their houses with pride when, for example, we ride by in a bus. The older ones realize *what* a house they have and that they live on the edge of society.

As I walked up the hill towards home, I thought how sad it is that such simple festivities have been lost in the city. On television and in advertisements they see how the wealthy celebrate and think that's the only way. I'll never forget the obtrusive, revolution-provoking and for Brazil insensible advertisement: Natal de rico , assim — Christmas for the rich, so — and a huge ham and bottle of champagne stared at the poor every day during the pre-Christmas season.

And what nice people they are: Solange, Juracy, Joceni, Sirlane, Ademir, Claudemir, the mother and the father. After all the festivals in the escolinha they bring their mother something — a piece of cake or a cookie saved for her.

When we went to the Represa Billings on a two-day excursion, I found a veritable hoard of bananas and bread, etc. under the pillow — para minha mãe, for my mother. Recently I gave Juracy three cruzeiros so he could take the bus to work. He had to clean up a garden. When he returned he gave me the money back: "I didn't need it, the driver let me ride free." Such honesty! I hope he doesn't lose it in the battle for every cruzeiro. He, thirteen years old, goes every night with a group of other boys to Brooklin, where there are a number of expensive restaurants. They guard and wash cars to earn their cruzeiros and often come home after midnight. Juracy gives all his earnings to his mother, in contrast to many others who buy cigarettes and sweets and only give a part of it home. In the morning he is of course often tired and skips school. That's how the vicious circle begins: they must earn money and therefore school is neglected. School is neglected so they don't learn a trade. They don't learn a trade and are therefore poorly paid and find it difficult to escape from life in the favela.

Something good radiates from these children.

Claudemir is mine and Cido's godchild. We watch his health as though it were our own. Now that he is over a year old we give Solange fruit and vegetables for him in the hope that he will develop in a manner which corresponds to his age and doesn't acquire that calm, apathetic expression that almost all the favela children have between one and four years of age. They can sit for hours in a corner or on a lap without doing anything, without playing or saying anything, patient, not participating.

The two children Dona Ella has taken in are completely different. They observe everything with a wide-awake look, play, laugh, cry, react normally. In contrast the favela children brood within themselves, without reacting to what comes to them from outside. Well, and that's what Claudemir looks like. Why is it so? No stimulation and, probably, despite our efforts, not enough vitamins; probably in his case lack of stimulation is more to blame — always the same grey walls of the tiny room in which family life takes place. No toys, no pictures, no color. But love, yes. Solange takes care of him, the boy rocks him, the mother feeds him, all in narrow confines and in the same bed.

When he arrived at the crawling stage there was no room to crawl. The approximately 5 by 5 feet space in the room (= house) not taken up by the only bed, the chair, the suitcases and the wood-burning stove, are dirty or dusty. The floor is of trampled earth which is always crumbling. So he hardly crawls and thereby misses an important stage of his development, as is the case with many Brazilian children. Now at fifteen months he angles around the edge of the bed a bit. It's touching how Solange and Sirlane support him from both sides so he can take a few steps — a picture of care and dedication.

Antonio

Another new child! When I came home from school he stood next to the wash basin with his pale triangular face and huge black eyes. Fourteen years old. I said hello and asked him in. His mother had already disappeared, happy to have gotten rid of him. The other children were already eating supper. "Come and eat, Antonio." "No, I want to wash my pants first."

Finally I talked him into it. He sat at the table, ate something and peered furtively from one to the other with his large eyes. After eating we played Mikado. Then Rubens and Marcia went to bed and I read them a fairy tale, hoping that Otacio, who has been here for a week, and Antonio would also listen. They did, and with great interest. How good, I thought, for in this way they can recuperate part of the spiritual formation they missed as small children. Later Antonio said that fairy tales are lies and nonsense, but he always wanted more. Then we prayed the Our Father. The two new ones said it with us, Antonio somewhat hesitatingly. Probably he had never really prayed before. How good that the small ones are here to help give the older, spiritually starved ones, nourishment. That way it's a matter of course and not at all forced. How can you bring a fourteen-year-old to absorb substance, to pray, to open himself to the beauty of the world, who until now wandered the streets at night, hung out in bars, smoked and often went home at dawn from some kind of party?

After a week he lost his timidity and anxiety. At table he dominated the conversation and we all laughed at his jokes and anecdotes, mostly having to do with how you can fool someone. Sometimes he had to be asked four times what he meant because we couldn't understand him with all his stuttering, mumbling and giria (slang). Later he prepared a lexicon for me with every new giria expression he used. I studied it, but the use of giria gradually died down. It was too much trouble for him to write down every word.

I'm getting to know him a bit better every day, especially Sundays when he's often home alone with me. Once we went to Mrs. Alps' who has adopted several babies. On the way back we waited a long time for the bus. He began to talk about himself and I hoped the bus wouldn't come too soon. It all bubbled out of him confused and humorously (gallows humor). When he was seven, he said, he lived with a family in Assia, Province of São Paulo.

"One day I left to look for my mother. I walked and walked, outside the city, just following my nose. Finally the police found me and brought me back to my foster family. Soon I was put with a different family."

"And your father?" "I don't remember much about my father. I can only see him beating my mother. When I was three or four he got sick and died. My brother thought he was only sleeping, but I knew he would never stand up again. I'll never forget that, not till the end of my life."

"And how was it in Londrina?" "Last year I lived with three different families. One woman in Londrina didn't even give me a bed; I slept on a mat on the porch."

I was shocked by his story and thought I must tell him that I would be his last "family". I must take away the fear of continually going from one to the other without a home and security.

"And with another foster family," he continued in his stuttering, merry manner, "I had to sleep in a tree."

"In a tree?" "Yes, on a branch that grew over the wall, that's where I slept. But don't tell anyone else."

"And what did you do the whole day?" "I went to school, made some money sometime at the market; mostly I just hung around. In one family I had to help slaughter oxen. I was pretty much a *malandro* (scoundrel), never obeyed, was always on the go, *bagunçar*, no one could stand me for long. Later on I lived with Dona Isaura. She was nice and good to me. But I did a lot of nonsense with her son, Luis. We stole things and the police caught us once. Luis was in jail for a day but I got away. So Dona Isaura's husband, Seu Mouzart, didn't want me around anymore. Just imagine, sometimes Dona Isaura secretly let me sleep in her house, and often she went looking for me to bring me something to eat."

I thought: "That woman has nothing herself, I give her used clothing, but she has pity for the boy and does what she can for him without talking about it."

"So I had to move on and came to a family where I had to help slaughter cattle. I was supposed to drive a knife into the steer's heart. I didn't want to do that, so they sent me away. I gathered my things in a plastic sack and then ... where to? The only one who didn't send me away was Dona Isaura. She gave me food and let me sleep in her house, but only when her husband was asleep and didn't notice. One day she told me about Dona Ute. And that's how I got here."

The bus finally came, we pushed our way in and the talk ended. I had to wait weeks before I learned more about his life. He didn't seem to miss his mother; in fact he gave the impression that she was a stranger to him. He talked more about Dona Isauara, wrote to her and wanted to visit her without fail during the July holidays. On Mothers Day he wrote a poem and gave it to me with the words: *"tenho dó da minha mãe"*. (I am worried about my mother)

As with all the children, I treated him on the basis of trust. But I soon realized that he consistently abused it. He lied, stole, and you never knew if he really went where he was supposed to go. I think he sold a pair of our shoes to buy cigarettes. He was always disappearing for a quarter, half or a full hour.

"Where were you?" At Daniel's, Leo's, playing football.

Once I saw him from the window bent over looking for something at the bus-stop. Cigarette butts, which he smoked in the bushes. Once we went to the theatre. He found a piece of half-eaten candy on the floor. He put it into his mouth and sucked it to the end. Another time he found a stepped-on pie on the way to school. His appetite is huge (his face is no longer triangular) as is his lack of self-control while eating. Seeing, taking and eating are all the same to him. Nothing is safe in the refrigerator.

"Antonio, more children live here. I bought these three avocados for seven people, and you have already eaten one." *"E a lei da sobrevivência."* — "That's the law of survival."

Once we were invited to Dona Barbara's to swim. Pears and apples lay temptingly on a dish.

"Give me the pears." "They're not mine." "Give me the pears." How can I give them to you when they're not mine?" Then he found a grapefruit. "I'll put the grapefruit on the plate and eat the pears."

Life has taught him many subterfuges. Where will this lack of self-control lead when his sexual appetites awaken? His body occupies him in many forms. Now that he feels at home here he passes wind from both ends with relish. I didn't find that so terrible, but finally it became so exaggerated that I threatened to give him an essay on the digestion system to write. After the next farting concert he had to write it after all.

He shot up in length and breadth. "I'm becoming a man," he announced at least ten times a day and counted the hairs in his armpits — 19, 20, 30! Finally he gave it up, but the problem worried him and, thank God, it was possible to talk about it because of his frank remarks.

His attitude towards women is appalling. Men are everything, women nothing. His head is full of theories and prejudices. Men are strong and courageous, etc., women weak and fearful.

"Who's stronger?" Boom! Maristela gave him a shove and he went flying onto the floor. Elizete took on Otacio. Both "men" lay on the floor and the women put their feet triumphantly on their chests.

"Courageous? Who will go to the farthest corner of the garden in the dark?" No one was very enthusiastic, but finally Maristela mastered herself and went. Thus we indisputably disproved a number of prejudices about masculine superiority. Now the boys are braver and sleep alone in the shed in the back, despite the cats having recently visited and stared at them with their glowing eyes. But how will such a boy treat his girlfriend and wife if he's never known love? And he is looking hard for it and will look for it soon in early love-affairs. Lei da sobrevivência! How can he be shown that there is also a lei do amor, when he has never known anything like it.

Once when he did something he shouldn't have, he wrote to me: "I don't want to leave. I like it here a lot." Probably because he senses that I like him. Sometimes he hangs on me like a small child on its mother. It's touching and disturbing at the same time. When I was ill he brought me huge sandwiches, pots of tea with "a little sugar" and looked constantly into my room to see how

I was. When Rubens came in, his whole being expressed care and consideration; Antonio was ungainly and wooden, as though he had never done anything good for someone.

Daily dialogue:

"Did you practice your typing?"
"No."
"Do it."
"Did you wash yourself?"
"No, tomorrow."
"Put your pajamas on, like a civilized person."
"I can't find them."
"Go get the blanket for the night."
"No, later."
"You'll disturb Rubens and Marcia then."
"What's that to me?"
"Wash the supper dishes."
"I'm not a slave!"
"Neither am I."
"What will I get for it?"
"Nothing. You've eaten."

Scraps of dialogue. Revolt. Keep calm. But alongside these negations there is also light. He paints a picture and is happy doing it. He reads a story and tells it to the others, puts a flower in the vase. Or asks: "I'm improving, aren't I?"

Then come the gloomy days again. "I'll dig my grave." Such thoughts are associated with self-pity. One evening I read the children a story, they said their prayers and went to bed. After a while Antonio got up, sobbing, and wrote and wrote and laid the letter on my night-table. "It's hard to live without a mother. I've lived in ten different houses."

What to do? Love him. Show him that he now has someone he can trust. Give him support and protection. Praise him when it's at all possible as counterweight to the many admonishments and to the consistency with which he must be handled. His days must have a rhythmic element. We get up at five-thirty, now without grumbling. Mornings he works with Otacio in the Waldorf School printing-workshop. From there they both go to the 'grupo escolar'. At five in the afternoon they come home, relax, eat, play and practice typing. Supper at seven o'clock. Then we usually sit in the living-room painting, rehearsing a play, doing handicrafts, playing, talking, reading, etc.

At eight I put Rubens and Marcia to bed, tell them a fairy tale, say their prayers with them. Then I usually read something to Otacio and Antonio. It's the hour when I'm alone with the boys and they ask questions.

"Are there black people in Germany?" "When was Germany discovered?" "What is methane gas?" "How are children born?", etc. They say their prayers, then I hear them talking and giggling for a while and soon they fall asleep."

Such a daily rhythm gives support. On weekends he is relaxed; we visit someone, go out to a sitio, go to a movie or theatre, to the hippie-market or something similar. His narrow view of the world and his hardened way of judging people must be broadened. Tell him about strange lands, watch folkdances, observe a flower, go to a museum, Terço — pray the rosary with Cido, see new scenery in the vacation colony or in Monteverde, meet other people, theatre, watch slides, read books, paint watercolors, draw geometric forms, make flowered Christmas cards for the bazaar, etc. One tries a thousand things. Does it help?

The most difficult thing is his mask: revolt and falsity. I realize gradually that goodness and trust are stupidity in his eyes. He doesn't understand because he isn't used to being treated with strictness and consistency and immediately afterwards with love. Once I gave him a thrashing so he'd understand that I refrain from hitting him not because of weakness, but because I want to educate him through love and trust. "Life is stupid", he said once. "You have to do so many stupid things in life."

Dancing, pinga, smoking, playing, football, girls, cars, music. That's life. How is he to be given the feeling that life can also be other things? Recently we watched slides of my travels. Aha, that's nice. I'll go with you to Germany next time." "Yes, you may, but first you have to learn a trade." "O.K., I'll do it."

Give him an objective. Enrich his view of the world. The world looked to him as follows: families with many children who, as soon as they are ten, eleven or fourteen earn some money to buy sweets and cigarettes and give something home; the red earth of Paraná, the dull classes in the grupos (state primary schools) with little respect for the teachers; bars, pinga, etc.

Therefore: like him, show him a path and help him to overcome the indifference and pessimism instilled in him by having been rejected.

May 1978

Here we're all healthy and lively, sometimes too lively. When all six children have attacks of liveliness at once you think you're in a madhouse.

Most likely I'll begin to build again — and finish this time, I hope. The prefecture is lending us a 1,400 square meter lot near the favela for the youth center. All that's lacking are money, workers, building materials and time to find them all.

When the youth center is finished we'll build an out-patient clinic in the favela. We'll find space to do it despite the terrible crowding there. With such plans I have little time to relax. And I'm already 40! If I were a man I'd be at the height of my creative powers.

June 1978.

An unexpected one-sentence letter came from a lawyer I know, Dr. Luchterhandt: if I can use 8,000 to 10,000 marks. This donation came like a gift from heaven. I wrote back — yes, I can use the money, I'll build a social center with it. Wonderful, now to work!

An architect from the school drew up a plan, Mr. Blaich worked out how much wood and so forth will be needed. I learned something about which I had no idea: how to build. During the July vacation I went to Paraná and, with the help of the former prefect, bought the wood. Buy materials, watch the construction, ask Mr. Blaich if it's being correctly built, buy cement again, look for used materials. Is the mason doing what he should?

September 1978

I went by the construction and saw the carpenter sawing something on the roof. The whole house shook. Something must be wrong. He assured me that it wouldn't fall down. I spoke to Mr. Blaich: No, that won't do. I thought I could entrust the construction to the tradesmen, but no, the more it advances the more I must watch them, like a lynx.

Another time I climbed up to the loft. We especially wanted a usable loft where one can move about without difficulty and where someone could eventually even live. What a disappointment! It was so low that you had to crawl around on hands and knees. OK, do it again. That's how it is with everything. But when everything is finished, or at least something like a house stands there, like now, I show it proudly to the visitors.

Francisco 1979:

The year began with a new boy from Paraná. How modest and awkward they are at first. He sits sideways at the table with the plate so far away that the way to his mouth is sown with rice and other food. The laborious path towards civilization begins: table manners, toilet use, cleaning up, etc.

You have to offer him every item of food, or he doesn't eat and then it seems to stick in his throat, so timidly does he sit there. As answers to carefully thought-out questions, all you get is a yes or a no. Like all newcomers he is extremely willing to work, but free time is that much more of a strain. They can't occupy themselves alone because they are never alone in their homes and normally free time there consists of football and television. We don't have a television here and Francisco can't always be playing football, if only because he doesn't know anyone here yet. He discovered the bicycle and enthusiastically practices equilibrium on it. When he sees me he becomes shy at once. When the other boys are around he is a bit braver and says something on his own now and then. It is strange how we so carefully feel each other out, neither knows the other, but this will soon be his home and I must like him and he must trust me. With the help of the other children and the daily rhythm of school and work, it will come relatively soon. Only the first days are so difficult.

Today is his third day in São Paulo. I was at the prefecture about the opening of the youth center. When I returned Francisco had just gotten home from work; he came up to me, took my package from me and smiled. The ice was broken. He talked the whole evening. Tomorrow we'll go to Volkswagen. Francisco, Otacio, Antonio and Pedro from the favela will take the selection test there. If all goes well, they will take the three-year course there and learn a trade.

Otacio and Pedro passed the test. They start the course in April.

Several months later: What in heaven's name am I to do with Francisco? He stands around, his finger on his nose, and looks on as the others play, study, work. He only does something when I force him to. Recently when I came home from the teachers meeting at seven-thirty, he was sitting calmly eating supper. But his carpentry course starts at seven o'clock. He doesn't know how to play. His only games are fighting and tests of strength. He works at a snail's pace. His underwear is almost falling apart and would if I didn't have pity on him and sew and patch it. Recently he urinated in a corner of his room (probably he was afraid to go outside) — and left it to dry all day until I noticed the stink ...

He seems like a bear, slow, awkward, good-natured (when he looks at me and his mouth slowly twists into a smile). But he also has a bear's strength, which sometimes erupts abruptly and out-of-control when someone angers him. When I ask him what Seu Paulo, the carpentry teacher, told them about his trip to Germany, he answers: "ele contou coisas." If you ask him what the doctor taught in his class, he answers: "Ele contou algumas coisas.", he told us some things. Then, however, he surprises us by bringing home relatively good grades from school. Is there any point in his staying here when you can't see any progress in five months?

The battle of Antonio seems to be won. Recently I asked who had left the bathroom in such disorder. I was looking more at Francisco. Antonio said: "I did." I couldn't believe my ears. Antonio knew I suspected Francisco. He repeated: "I did it." It was the first time he had told the truth and admitted to being guilty. I accepted it as normal. No praise. No fuss about something which should be normal.

And now he's always like that, tells the truth and excuses himself when he's done something wrong. Today he said: "I'm going to teach the mason to read and write. I feel sorry for him." And he left with a pencil and notebook. A victory: he's doing something for someone else.

January 1979

The construction is in its final stage! Today seven strong men, former Waldorf School pupils, began painting. It's a pretty picture to see someone working through all the windows and doors. I had difficulty convincing them to stop and eat lunch. Afterwards we loaded their jeep with the remaining suitcases, crates and sacks containing our things to be moved. But then there was no room for people (I thought). But the boys were unconcerned. They sat on the cases and Stefan, our Tarzan, squatted on the hood (bonnet) and we took off.

Today was a good day. A large group of volunteers, boys and men, came to fence in the land of the youth center, paint, transport furniture and other heavier work. It's similar to the "International Civilian Service Camps", this sense of solidarity, getting tired and dirty together and the good feeling in the evening of having accomplished something.

Soon we'll inaugurate the Youth Center and the new school life will begin! Kindergarten, courses (sewing, carpentry, cooking, knitting, typing). Also painting, theatre, festivals, excursions. And all filled with happy, serious, diversified life in the Escolinha!

February 1979

Today when I came home I found a nice mess: the children's and my rooms in the worst disorder with everything upset and upside-down ... my first thought was for the dollars donated for the youth center. Gone! I rushed to the police. In eight copies my name, my father's name (very important), were written down. Then I could leave. I asked if it wouldn't be a good idea if the police were to look at the scene of the crime. "Oh yeah, good idea." I should go to the investigation division on the first floor.

The process of writing down my name was repeated. "Can't you look for fingerprints?" "Oh yeah, good idea." I should go to the technical division. Finally we left the police station. I went to the bank to block the bank account just in case. In the meantime the police came and took fingerprints.

At home I looked around more carefully and realized that more was stolen than I thought, among other things the slides of Londrina. Only those of the Sarawa were left by the thief, probably from fear. They must have made him nervous. The worst part is that I suspect someone who used to live here. I am tempted to give it all up. That was also the comment of most of those who heard about it. Ungratefulness, that's all you get out of helping the poor, etc. Peppi, an Austrian mechanic said to Mr. Blaich: "I don't underhand why Dona Ute associates with these people."

Blaich: "It's her life's work."

Peppi: "Well, if she hasn't found any other yet.. maybe she should give it up though. But maybe she'll go to heaven."

Peppi told me of this conversation and I had to laugh. Then I asked him: "What's your life's work?" He squirmed, smiled and didn't quite know what to say. His hands were full of motor oil, he was repairing a car's motor. But he has earned a house, a sitio, a car ...

Mid-March 1979. Ambulatory Clinic

Today P.S., a factory owner who has often helped us, came by.

S.: "I would like to talk with you about the planned ambulatorium. I have other ideas about it".

U.: "Yes"?

S.: "Let's see if we can get it finished quickly. My workers can build the first rooms and then the favelados can do the rest".

U.: "Then they'll all wait for the second part to be built by others as well, and that's exactly what I don't want — that the favelados are always waiting for help from outside and don't help themselves. The ambulatorium should be a way to mobilize the people. I provide the materials, the wood from Volkswagen, etc., and they do the rest".

A skeptical grin. Maybe he's right, but I want to try.

U.: "There is simply no point in treating people — even if they're illiterate — as objects"

S.: "Yes, I'm sometimes paternalistic."

U: "I can't feel that way. I don't consider myself better than they are, on a higher plane, etc. I respect them as human beings — even if they're uneducated and have no trade. Maybe they drink and have been coarse and uncouth during their lives. Despite all that I respect their humanity, their innermost selves. And therefore I want to help them to help themselves. Their human dignity is better protected that way."

It's difficult to convince the donors and others who help. The next day It's difficult to mobilize the people from the favela!

Everything went well the last two Sundays. A large group of helpers came and we worked hard leveling the ground, planning, etc. But today: What an arduous job! At eight o'clock I went to the favela. Arnaldo, our "construction boss", was already gone. I waited and waited. Probably he got stuck in some bar. Finally I went to the construction site. Around eleven two workers came. My impatience wasn't justified, I thought. We prepared mortars and set up some bricks for the piles. The building is to stand on piles. Then a new problem: the plumbline. Arnaldo disappeared in order to get it — and didn't come back. The others waited for their "boss". It was ridiculous — he simply vanished. Meanwhile, in order not to sit around doing nothing, I recruited some boys to bring bricks in a wheelbarrow from the plot where we had once started to build. On the second trip the wheelbarrow broke. Finally Arnaldo appeared, somewhat tipsy, with the plumbline and an enormous amount of huge leaves which one apparently can eat.

So the day wasn't very successful. Putting into practice my idea of furthering the human dignity of the needy is often very trying.

> Money is always lacking, but the principal needs aren't alleviated with money alone. If a lot of money comes in the problem of distributing it remains. It is more important to convince the people that they must participate in the process of change. And that's harder than getting money.

A new heaven — a new earth.

31 March 1979

Almost every Saturday or Sunday something is going on in our Youth Center. Last Sunday the amateur theatre group from the Giroflex factory was here. How the children laughed! The hall was full of laughing faces.

Today we prayed the Via Sacra. It's touching to see how these boys and girls, who stand on the shadowy side of life, try to understand what Easter and Christ's suffering mean. Some adults always participate. They pray with fervor; they know what suffering is. But the children don't hold out long being serious and introspective. That doesn't matter. After the last Our Father during which all joined hands in a large circle, the tables and chairs were pushed aside lightning-quick, and they danced. And how they dance! With what rhythm and love of movement. I had to think of Hans Georg, one of my Waldorf School pupils, who once said: "They dance away the troubles from their hearts." Yes, this liberation which they find in dancing must be given them in other areas.

Perhaps in theatre or in work completed. I think that these children find a similar joy when they say to me at the carpentry course: "Here, Dona Ute, the chopping-block that I made." And I admire the smoothness of the wood which they sanded-papered with such patience and love, so that the beauty of the grain appears.

Or when, after a days-long struggle with knitting needles, a child shows me his finished cap, it's not only the joy of having the cap which now warms his head (or hides his frizzy hair), but it is also the joy of having overcome obstacles. As St. Exupéry said, "*C'est l'obstacle qui fait grandir l'Homme. Grandir l'Homme! Le besoin de naitre!*" (Man grows on obstacles. Let man grow! The need to be born!) That's exactly what I mean: not the visible thing — the knitted cap, the delicious cookies, the nicely planed table, the sewn skirt, the completed Social Center, etc. It is more important to me what changes all these things cause inside the people involved, what effect the processes of learning, personal renewal and pleasure in doing have in ennobling and transforming them. These things become instruments which form the person. More important than the improvement of outer conditions of life is the inner development of the child, the person, the helping person as well as he who is being helped. Of course a child must be given the outer conditions in order to develop. It must have proper nutrition in order that its body and brain are able to absorb things. It must have a table to paint and work on and to do homework. It must live with people who can open the world to it. But these aren't ends in themselves, rather are they foundations on which to develop into a real human being.

That's why I would like to organize occupational education (in case I am able to build more and specific workshops or promote trade apprenticeships) so that it's not so rigidly oriented towards a trade and future employment. I would like to enhance them through artistic activities; with a doctor's lectures that can show them what a human being is; through lectures and slides which can show the children what the world is like.

Several months later. — Something has been accomplished in this direction, but too little and provisional: besides the carpentry course, there are art and anthropology courses for young people in the evenings.

Sunday

Somehow I bring myself to go to the favela. We have been working on the outpatient-clinic since February, that is, we meet every Sunday and build a bit more. It goes like this: I go to our "compadre" Arnaldo, who is our construction boss, so to speak. Everything is calm. I of course want to start right away. But that's out of the question. Someone goes to buy bread. Then they notice that there's no sugar. A child runs to a bar and buys sugar. Finally the fire is lit, water is brought from the tap below and we drink coffee. Meanwhile I go to some shacks and ask if they have time to build. Well, it would be difficult to do anything today. One was sick, the other had to go to work, another wasn't in the mood, another had to visit a sick child. Finally one, Tonilda's father, came with me. I explained what could be done today. Then I went visiting parents. I have to fill out forms for every child that goes to the Youth Center to submit to the Children's Emergency Assistance in Duisburg, in the hope that we may receive help from them. I drank countless cafezinhos and ate four lunches. My belly was like to bursting. Then Dona Ana offered me a chicken-blood pudding.

I also announced that there would be a theatre performance in the Youth Center today. The anthroposophical clinic Tobias will perform the Tobias play.

At four o'clock I went to the "escolinha". Doctors, nurses, therapists, all were in costume waiting for the audience. Two or three children were already there. The rest were still in the favela, taking showers, in some cases still eating lunch. I tried to explain that they would all come, but not in a great hurry. "But it's already 4.15," an actor said. "We'll start anyway."

I was of two minds. On the one hand I wanted to explain that the favela children, and the adults, have little sense of time, and often have no clocks. On the other hand I would like to teach them that they must learn to be punctual.

Dr. Sonja told the legend. Meanwhile a troop of children poured into the hall. Then it was wonderful. The children listened attentively. A baby began to cry; the mother gave it her breast. At that moment Dona Flor, as an angel, floated on stage in eurythmy dress. An eurythmy performance and a nursing mother, Dona Flor and Lúcia, a single mother — what a contrast. I had to laugh to myself.

April 1979

Recently I went by the super-market Pão de Acucar. From behind the parked cars two dirt-crusted boys ran out and cried happily: "Oh, Dona Ute!" They were from the favela, two boys for whom I had never been able to do much because they were too used to bumming around looking for things in the garbage or trying to earn some money at the supermarkets or by begging. Sometimes they come to my house and were at the zoo and on excursions. But they could never make the jump to regular attendance at the escolinha, and therewith to life. Neither has a father, which means that the mothers work and they are left on their own. One of them, Arthur, is seriously disturbed in his development. He doesn't speak right and still wets the bed.

Neither has the strength of will to attend school regularly, although I tried to convince them to do so. The illusion of earning money and the temptation to spend some cruzeiros for sweets is too great. How can you convince an eight-year-old that it's better to give up the sweets now in order to have a better opportunity in life afterwards. Being an adult is too far away for them. Perhaps now that the evening courses are starting I can grab them and make something of them after all.

I went up to them and said hello. Ademir took some cruzeiro bills out of his pocket and gave me nine of them. He owed me ten cruzeiros. Surely this was the first time this had happened, that a street-boy gave a "lady" money and not, as is usual, the other way around. With that thought I went to the bus-stop. Maybe I shouldn't have taken the money but I found it right to do so. Ademir owed me something and now he paid it back: honest conduct between equals. Then I heard someone calling: O Ute! O Ute! I turned around and there he was again and gave me the outstanding cruzeiro in coins. He raced across the street like the wind, dodging speeding cars, and took up his post again at the super-market.

28 May 1979

Every Sunday I go to the favela where we are building an outpatient-clinic. This time Stefan, a former Waldorf School pupil, came along to help. Everyone ran down to see the "Huck da Favela." The rumor had it that he was so strong he could lift a side of a Volkswagen container by himself. Today the work went well, everybody sawing, nailing, planing. Meanwhile I did my house calls. For example to Joceni. He's eight but has an aversion to water and is always dirty and spattered with mud. He drinks too much coffee and is nervous and can't concentrate. Today he pleased me though. He took a large tin can, stretched a rubber-band around it which he raised on one side with a piece of wood and played on this primitive instrument all the songs he had learned in the escolinha — and with a concentration and skill of which I had never thought him capable.

June 1979

Today Rik and Gabi came to take pictures in the favela. First we went to Josenildo's grandmother's where we were served according to the old farmer's style: coffee, mandioca-roots and bread. I borrowed a hammer and a jimmy and we went to the clinic, where a lot of men were working. After I had almost given up the idea of the clinic as a community effort of the favelados, today the work was progressing nicely. Then we visited Vitória. The house (house! - it's about as big as a small kitchen) was full of smoke. Because it was so cold the mother lit a fire on the dirt floor. Three small children smeared with snot were chewing on a piece of white bread. Vitória just stood around, the mother sat crying by the fire.

"I'm going to move from here, my oldest son gives me no peace. He doesn't work and only comes home to hit us. Then he takes the few things I have and sells them." How can one help there?

"And your daughter?" "She lives with a man — she's probably already fed up." "Then at least send Vitória to the Youth Center so that she doesn't wind up the same way."

Desolation. Vitória! What a name in this misery.

We went on, to Roberto, the cripple, to the water-tap, etc. Two hours later I went by Vitória's house again. Her mother was on the way up to where the asphalt is. She had a bag in her hand with something to eat; the three-year-old looked on earnestly, the four-year-old said they would go to the police; Vitória was ashamed. The mother, drunk, stumbled around, asked Jesus for help, knelt in the mud, struck the earth with her fists, cursed her son, prayed again to Mary and Jesus. All the children in the neighboring shacks saw it, laughed, made remarks. The women tried to calm her down; a man derided her.

"Get the baby," she called to Vitória, "the last thing you'll have to do for me. Yes, I'm drunk. I'm leaving. I'll poison you, you damned son!"

What can one do? When I saw Roberto directly afterwards, I felt better. Here is the will to live. Roberto is twelve years old and has been lame almost his whole life. His parents lived in Mato Grosso, in an area where agriculture flourishes. But as their son was ill, one day his mother packed their belongings and left on the days-long trip to São Paulo in order to have him cured in the hospitals and in Aparecida do Norte, a welfare center.

The boy was in the hospital for eight months. His ability to move improved. Now he's with us in the escolinha. First he just looked, but soon he wanted to do everything there was to do. Once we made little cars; everyone sawed and hammered. I took a saw and a piece of wood and we sawed together. Then he had to sand it. It went fairly well. Once a truck came with bricks and all the children helped with unloading and piling them up. Roberto of course as well! What joy when he is treated as the other children are treated and can help. And at quadrilha dancing! I pushed and shoved him so (and supported him) that he finally danced the whole quadrilha through and from pure enthusiasm cried: *O que gostoso*!

The high point was when he was able to go with us to the lantern festival in the Waldorf School. Meanwhile several volunteers have taken him under their wing, doing physical exercises and instructing him. His mother is unbelievably cooperative and does all kinds of work. You can feel how thankful she is that her son can be with us. Recently something nice happened. Mrs. von Osteroht, a Waldorf School mother, wanted to see the outpatient clinic. Unfortunately I had no time to take her, so she went alone. A woman came along and cut out steps for her down the hill with an enxada. It was Roberto's mother. "I have experienced so much good that I could at least show thanks once," she said.

June 1979. São João Festival

We have been preparing for the São João festival for weeks. The boys are building the booths, the girls are cutting the banners, etc. All are making lanterns and rehearsing the quadrilha. The past few days have been of intense activity. Cido baked corncakes with his cooking pupils, made mamão-jam. I went to the market with Dona Edda to buy huge amounts of popcorn, peanuts, salt, juice, milk, chocolate, sausages, etc.

The festival began at three o'clock. Each group of children was responsible for a sales or games booth: bingo, quentão, pipoca, (hot cider, popcorn), rice pudding, sausage, ring-throwing, kick-the-can, and so on. Others took care of the bazaar (things prepared by the children and used clothing). The people streamed in. Dona Ute here, Cido there, Dona Ute, Cido — calls for help from all sides. We ran back and forth. So many people, adults and children!

It grew dark and we lit the lanterns. Just at that moment Roberto had his attack. He's lame and has cramp-like attacks now and then. He screamed and moaned, rolling his eyes. When he came to his first words were: I want to dance the quadrilha. I was afraid of that. During rehearsals I took him by the hand and we danced together. But he would be a disturbance during the real performance. His mother came and we were able to start the lantern parade. A line of glowing points snaking through the favela. Then we lit the bonfire with torches and recited the fire-poem. The children danced the quadrilha, then the adults and finally we all danced freely.

A beautiful festival.

July 1979

This year there are two vacation camps, one for the fourteen-year-olds and another for the little ones. I've just returned from the first. It was the strangest vacation camp I ever experienced. Besides the fourteen-year-olds, Roberto was there as well as Sac's wife with their month-old baby. A mixed group. If someone watched us leaving from the escolinha through the favela to the bus-stop, it would look quite unusual: Roberto storming ahead on his crutches, his head bent forward, his legs, which wouldn't go as fast as he would like, dragging and stumbling behind. His mother with her deep-set eyes following and calling paciencia, calma! The boys hopping happily along with their knapsacks, one of them constantly repeating the same song on a flute. Janete with her baby and crates with provisions in a mini-bus, Zeca at the wheel.

Everything went well at the sitio Ens. The children played, did household chores and there were ping-pong, swimming and hiking competitions. During the day I announced a bravery trial for the night. Yeees! We're not afraid. At nightfall they were less vociferous. And when it was completely dark it was only after much persuasion that we could convince a few to venture into the darkness. These children are terribly afraid of ghosts, animal-men, etc. Primeval fears and "modern" fears of thieves and robber bands. The Indian and African initiation rites were very wise in that they helped the young to overcome these fears.

In the evenings we played games, theatre, mime or read stories. Yesterday each one had to read a part from a book about whales. What stuttering, in heaven's name! One could really despair of such a weak school system. The next morning during gymnastics I despaired at seeing what stiff, weak bodies they have. This is what deficient nutrition, education and environment have done to these children. Their intellects haven't developed, their bodies are weak and their feelings are developed in one direction only: satisfaction from smoking, alcohol, television, sex without love. What happens in Mario when he looks for a fight at the slightest provocation, flies into a rage and swears revenge? His words are always of revolt.

Mario: "I'm going back to São Paulo." I: "Why?" "Because Ivanil annoys me." "What did he say?" "He insulted my mother." (That is, he said Mario was a son-of-a-bitch). "That's nonsense. You can be thankful that you are having such a good time here instead of always complaining. I also have a heart that has feelings and I'm not always happy with what you say."

Then he lay his head — we were at breakfast — on the table and remained still. Five minutes, ten minutes. What went on inside him?

Mario has been with us for two months. He is smart, sensitive, argumentative, doesn't go to school anymore because he had an argument with the teacher. Both parents work. He has probably never had a real home as the family has been moving from one place to another for years: Rio de Janeiro, Minas, Mato Grosso, São Paulo. Sometimes he lives with aunts, sometimes only with his father, or with his mother. His father seems nice, but exhausted from night-work. What does he need? What is he seeking?

Love. His little sister, Magda, is in our kindergarten. Mostly she is taciturn. At the São João festival we all stood around the fire. Mario behind his sister. The candle in Magda's candle went out. He relit it, bent over her and kissed her on the forehead. How much love lay in that gesture.

He only budges from the escolinha to eat. Mornings, afternoons, evenings, he's always there. Once he said: Here I will become a man.

A thirteen-year-old girl, Claudia, waits at a bus-stop in the city of São Paulo. Beside her stands a black woman. They are both shabbily dressed. You can see that the young woman lives in a favela, you can also smell it, for they often smell of smoke from their open fires. The child takes courage and speaks to the woman:

— Do you have children?

— Yes, two boys, the girls all died.

— Can you take me home with you?

— I can't. What would your mother say?

— My mother chased me away. I was in a home, but I ran away. Back to my mother. But she chased away me again. — Please take me with you.

The bus came, the woman got in, the child followed her. When the bus stopped, the child followed her to her miserable shack. Since then she lives there.

One day I noticed a girl at the sewing course whom I hadn't seen before. She seemed cramped and worked with a sour face. Several days later I saw Claudia again. She came up to me with joy in her eyes: "I'm going to learn something in the escolinha and make something of myself!"

July 1979

It's ice-cold today. It hasn't been a good day in the favela. Along with the biting cold there's a strong wind. This morning many women were occupied fixing their shacks, especially the roofs. I visited Dona Iraci, who went to the hospital a few days ago in order to give birth to her seventh child. It's a Sunday child. How good, I thought superstitiously. As Cido and I entered the shack it seemed empty despite so many children. Dona Iraci, the mother, wasn't there. The baby was overweight so both had to remain in the hospital. Solange, thirteen, was taking care of the household. She's completely overtaxed. Washing, cooking, taking care of the two smallest ones seemed to be all right, but the rest looked as though they had never been touched by water. But worse was the absence of the loving nucleus. The mother. They were all sad, Sirlane was crying. For the first time I understood the mothers' fear when they go to give birth: the fear of dying and leaving their children alone. And how awful for the families abandoned by the father when the mother has to work all day.

Like, for example, Iracema's family. I could hear her little brothers and sisters screaming from far off. Iracema, fourteen, has just given the baby its bottle. A mess of clean and unwashed clothes on the bed, breadcrumbs on the dirt floor, milk stains on the torn couch. Four small children jumping around and fighting, the thirteen-year-old boy hanging around. Itacema is trying to bring order into this chaos but has no authority over her brothers and sisters. Shirley screams piteously and shivers from the cold; she literally shakes.

"Put a sweater on," I say. Iracema looks in the pile of clothes for a sweater, finds only a dirty one. "I don't want that one," Shirley screams. She goes on shivering, screaming, whimpering: mae, mae.

What she really wants is her mother, not a sweater. She only sees her late at night and on Sundays. But then she's tired and, recently, often ill.

Iracema says: "I'm proud of my mother, she brings us through even though we don't have a father." Unfortunately she is expecting another child. "My mother is in her fifth month," Iracema says. "She wanted to get rid of it," she lets slip. "In the fifth month that's no longer possible. Right Dona Ute?" Jacira says. What information these children have at twelve years of age.

"Maybe she'll give it away." If not, this drudgery will start all over again for Iracema. At fourteen she has already brought up four babies. And because of this eternal housework she seldom comes to the escolinha in order to learn something whereby she can get a better job and help her mother. The wind rattles the walls, it's depressing, I want to leave. Then Diva comes in. She lost her mother two years ago, her father three years ago. She's been living with a man ten years her senior for a few months now. She's still a child. She smiles at me, happy as ever, childish as ever.

"Are you working?"

"No, but tomorrow I'm going to look for a job." She'd rather play house with dolls.

* * *

I always reserve a few days during the holidays to go to Paraná. In Londrina and Faxinal Dona Isaura's and Dona Zita's children, Otacio's mother, etc. expect me then. Often I don't feel like making the long bus-ride, but the children's disappointment would be too great. And when I see the happiness and affection of the children there I'm ashamed that it ever entered my head not to go.

I'm off, pack the suitcases, bags full of used clothes, school material, a woolen blanket. I go to the station like a loaded-down donkey. In Paraná it's harder to find cheap clothing than in São Paulo. And the head of the family earns even less there.

The deeper inland one goes the more "parado" (restrained) everything is. When you leave the lunatic asylum São Paulo (rush, stink, contaminated air, traffic din beginning at four in the morning, where you feel like a hunted rabbit crossing the streets) the peace and quiet of Londrina is a shock. There you don't get up until six o'clock, go to work on foot, come home for lunch, rest, then go back to work — that is, when you have work. The worst thing about cities like Londrina, which now has 300,000 inhabitants, is that there is too little work. It's very hard for parents who have children who could be working to see them unemployed, hanging around, unsatisfied because they would like to have better clothes, which they can't afford. Or when grown men must do work which is done by children in São Paulo. For example, I met Edney again. During my development worker time when he was ten years old, he went around selling peanuts from a basket. Now, twelve years later, he's married and has a child in his arms.

"What do you do?" I asked him. "I wash cars."

He must have noticed that I looked surprised. "Well, I can't find a proper job, but at least I earn my bread honestly. I'm not a bum.

"Of course. You don't have to be ashamed." But I thought: what is this man doing with his intelligence, his strength, his hopes for a fulfilled life?

Expectations from life? What do we expect from life? I believe that everyone has the desire to investigate the world, to know his surroundings, to know himself and the meaning of existence. Every person, at least every child; often this desire is suppressed, snuffed out by the brutality of life. But when this desire awakens and becomes more or less conscious, ideas and hopes are associated with it; the world and the possibilities of investigating it seem to be without limits. But one soon realizes that these possibilities are limited, as they are everywhere, by one's abilities and character. But then they are reduced even further — by education and upbringing, the family's social class, money and employment possibilities. So finally only one thing remains, and it's very narrow. As Dona Raimunda says: "You work in order to survive; more isn't possible. But at least we live and don't die of hunger," she adds thankfully.

She passed her childhood in the drought zone of Paraiba where life depends on one question: Will it rain this year or not? There it was simply a matter of survival; if you survived you were satisfied. Her children, who grew up in Paraná, are less grateful. They expect more from life than mere survival. Most leave for São Paulo as adolescents following the urge to earn money and be able to do what they are continually impelled to do by TV and ads: fashionable clothes like the singer so-and-so, television, transistor radios etc. São Paulo, seen with a halo, the magnet of Brazil.

Leda, who was the beauty of Vila da Fraternidade during my development worker time and one of my best pupils, yearns for those "golden years": *O, tempinho bom que não volta,* the good old day that never returns.

They look back instead of forward. And when they do look ahead, it's to São Paulo. When you see a bar, and there's one on every corner, it's bound to be full of boys and young men. They can't find work so they hang around there; someone always has a few cruzeiros for pinga or something similar. Drinking, smoking, *maconha* (marijuana) evenings at the corner, Baile sem vergonha (dance without shame), where a fight always breaks out and the police must be called. Do nothing, live for the moment, no future. Horrible. What will come of these young people who no longer live on the land, but in a city which has nothing to offer them.

It's no wonder that so many mothers don't know what to do with their sons and ask me to take them to São Paulo and "endireitar" (straighten them out!). Antonio, for example, would surely be in jail by now if he had gone on like he was a year ago in Londrina. He's not bad, just weak.

Faxinal is even more desolate. It has about 10,000 inhabitants and consists largely of warehouses for agricultural products from the region: beans, rice, tobacco, soybeans, etc. There's even less employment than in Londrina and the people are shamelessly exploited. And they don't even have the advantages of the country, the beauty and strength that streams from nature.

Mid 1979

The schoolteachers have been on strike for two months, bus drivers for three days. A city of twelve million people without public transportation! Some walk, others just stand around. The streets are clogged with traffic. It took us two hours to get to school. Conversation theme number 1: How to get from home to work. Our school guard left home at 3 a.m. and arrived at the school at 8 a.m. — a five-hour walk, and what a walk. The pedestrian has no rights here, he flees from the cars like a shooed-away hen, has to jump over dead dogs, holes, wooden beams, broken water mains, animal droppings. It must look like a lunatic asylum from an airplane: everyone looks out for himself trying to get through the traffic chaos.

Worst are the school strikes. Thousands of children on the streets, the boys hang out in bars, completely forget their duties and get into trouble. There are too many children in the escolinha. The morning children also come in the afternoon and vice versa. Furthermore there's a swarm of unregistered children who look in the windows and sit on the fence. We're sorry for them, but they're a disturbance.

You can understand the teachers who are fighting for better working conditions and more pay. But what are the consequences of this lack of responsibility for thousands of children? They can be as lazy as they like, without direction or duties; and when school starts again it takes a long time to re-establish the necessary equilibrium and rhythm.

Second building phase: July-August 1979

— The kindergarten in a separate house

— A carpentry workshop;

— A veranda on the "main building";

— An outpatient clinic (open on week-ends since February).

August 1979

Feverish activity! The ambulatorio (outpatient clinic) is to be inaugurated in a week's time. Painting, putting in the windows, nailing down the last floorboards, painting and installing the doors; Zeca, Arnaldo, Manuel help, as well as the children, Antonio, Francisco and a Swiss volunteer. The cleaning up and installation: closets, chairs, desk, medicine, beds — all brought from the escolinha to the ambulatorio on the heads of the boys of the favela. And the cleaning! The children sweep, carry water, wash, scrub. Dona Inez waxes the raw floorboards. She's very competent, mother of five children, toothless and therefore looks to be 55 years old although she's surely no more than 35, unbelievably helpful — and, a rarity, she also has talent for organization. Late at night by the light of a petroleum lamp I hang pictures and curtains and Antonio makes supports for the curtain rods. Satisfied, we climb up the hill towards home. The inauguration is tomorrow.

13 August 1979 — The ambulatorio's inauguration day.

At ten o'clock the first cars come carrying the invited guests. Meeting point: the escolinha, for those who wouldn't find the favela or the ambulatorio. I ran up quickly to the loft and changed. I greeted some people not even knowing who they were, until it turned out they were a delegation from the prefecture of Campo Lindo with the newly elected regional administrator, Alcides. I showed them the escolinha and accompanied them to the favela. We were overtaken by two cars: Dr. Sauer, President of Volkswagen do Brazil, and his entourage. He was very accessible to the favela people. I was happy for the favelados, who were receiving such "prominent" guests: all kinds of directors, Waldorf School teachers, doctors, school parents, our volunteer group. etc.

The Martin Luther King choir sang to open the ceremonies. Then Dr. Michael gave a short speech and I handed a plaque to the helpers from the favela with photographs and a dedication (which their children later read to them as most of them can't read). Then came the play, directed by Cido and thought up by the children: "The Abused Slave". At twelve o'clock the crowd gradually left. A thousand handshakes, here a word, there a word, congratulations, explanations, thanks for the medicine, etc.

Confusion and then suddenly peace. But no. Who is that sliding down into the favela in a long dress placing each foot carefully after the other? Dona O., a mother from the Waldorf School. I explain everything again. Yes, we have three doctors, each of whom who are available one afternoon a week, without charge. Three times a week a nurse comes in the morning, afternoons a male nurse. Medicine? Mostly samples. We're also trying to get Weleda medicines. Finally we went to the escolinha where Cido was performing a dance with the children for the fathers — it was Father's Day. Dona O. was hungry.

"Isn't there anything to eat here?"

"Yes, the children baked cakes for their fathers."

"Isn't there something more substantial?"

"No."

I brought her a piece of cake, not very politely. None of us had had lunch yet and would have been thankful for anything edible, sweet or sour ... Not only the favela children have a lot to learn!

Mid-August 1979

The last day in Brazil before my German "tour". Early in the morning I went to Barbara's for a working breakfast. Terrible! Either you have breakfast or you work, but both together ...? Barbara gave me a pile of addresses (BMZ, GTZ, IBZ), all organizations which might help us.

From there I rushed over to see Dona Edda, who will take care of buying provisions for the kindergarten and escolinha. Then back home in a packed bus. Packing, if one can call that packing: I threw everything in and thought I would repack properly in London. Then to Blaich, who had just returned from Germany. We went to the escolinha to get some building tips from him and so he could see the new buildings: kindergarten, carpentry shop and ambulatorio.

"Well, my girl, a year ago you had nothing and now you have a whole factory!" When you're involved in the daily tasks you don't notice how quickly everything has grown. But he, after a two-month absence, sees the difference between then and now.

Back home. I gave Antonio and Francisco last minute "admonishments". Then I washed my hair, with anti-lice additive just in case, to avoid the possibility of importing lice into civilized Germany. Outside it was pouring. All the rainclouds in Brazil seem to have massed at the moment of my departure. I had to go out anyway in order to say goodbye to the favela and to the children. I arrived soaking wet, dried my clothes and hair at an open fire. Everyone was touchingly attentive. We stood around sadly and finally had to say goodbye. The children changed their clothes, for we had planned an excursion to the airport. Then the minibus that was to take us there didn't arrive on time. I was suddenly pressed for time and just made it to the airport. But in what a state: Soaking wet and splattered with mud.

I got off the plane in London. From the favela direct to Heathrow airport. Nervous, with a stomach-ache from impatience and uncertainty whether F. would be there. How he would be. If we should greet each other seriously or embrace?

Of course everything was quite different. Suddenly I saw a waving hand, a head behind the waiting crowd. I rolled my luggage cart there: "You look the same." "You, too." It had been eighteen years. Years full of life, but somehow vanished. We laughed, were happy. We were out of breath from carrying luggage, laughing, embracing, upstairs, downstairs, looking for the car. We felt like eighteen-year-olds who were in love for the first time.

22 August 1979

A letter from Renate, the kindergarten teacher: "Today was turbulent in the kindergarten. After the usual opening with the children in a circle and drawing, some boys from the favela were to sandpaper the chairs and others to prepare carrots and lettuce for the snack. You can imagine how it looked. When they were hard at work, Dona Regina (the sewing teacher) suddenly ran in and said that Josenildo had struck Lucimera on the head over near the sandbox. That happens fairly often so I didn't take it very seriously, especially as I was occupied with the little ones. When I went over to look however, Lucimera was bleeding quite a lot and I had a fright. But it turned out to be not so bad. It seems the metal slide fell on her head and left a small cut. Luckily Dona Regina was there. She cut the hair away and bandaged the wound nicely. She also washed Lucimera's dress so that the mother wouldn't be too shocked. When I returned to my cooking soup you can imagine was it was like. The large wash-bowl full of water (to wash the lettuce) was full of parsley snips, lettuce leaves and pieces of carrot. Gilmar stirred the brew enthusiastically and I had all I could do to fish out what was still usable. Nevertheless, the salad turned out well and the children ate it with relish. On the last day the morning snack is the most important event in the kindergarten. Yesterday we had cheese salad sandwiches and the day before muesli with lots of fruit, nuts, etc."

The Children's Aid Society of Duisberg now donates $20 per child per month. That's why we can now afford to give the children a good morning snack and relieve somewhat their vitamin deficiency. Nuts = brain-food.

Germany, September 1979

For two weeks I have been in Switzerland with my mother and Lotti and her two children, Michael, four years old, and Tamara, two. We hiked in the mountains, mostly with the children. Tamara especially was full of energy that let her spring fearlessly over stones, walls and brooks. When she saw a wall or a fence she'd cry wall go! wall go! and climbed up with a great show of strength. She was red with exertion and excitement, but she was on top and she called out triumphantly: up, up, and stood on her toes and stretched her hands to the sky in order to look even taller and bigger. When she overcame an obstacle her eyes lighted up with joy.

Why do I tell this? Because the contrast between a childlike Tamara, who grows up in normal circumstances, and a childlike Ademir from the favela is painfully apparent. What a difference between these lively, adventure-loving eyes and the calm, dull look of many favela children. At two years of age,

Tamara climbs over fences and tree-stumps while Ademir at the same age sat apathetically in a corner of his shack or crawled on the only bed. Tamara talks constantly and you can see how she combines her words in an ungrammatically pregnant way. Ademir began to speak at three-and-a-half in kindergarten. Tamara is as big now as Ademir is at three-and-a-half.

"Why is that?" a doctor in Germany asked me. "I don't know, but I think that it's partially due to poor nutrition during early childhood and also to the lack of stimulation it receives from its parents and environment to which the child can react."

I thought of Ingrid, a Bavarian housewife, feeding her little Vroni carrot porridge which the child devoured with relish. And all in a clean, orderly environment.

"What else do you give him to eat?" I asked Ingrid. "Milk, porridge, vegetables, porridge again and evenings milk again." That's what's lacking. Vitamins, mineral salts, a varied diet.

"What do the children in Brazil get to eat?"

"Milk, but what a battle to obtain it. Often it's Nestle powdered milk, which is very diluted. Or mother's milk, weakened by many feedings. No additional nutrition, practically nothing vitamin-rich, and later nothing proper to bite on."

We take care that Claudemir, our favela foster child, receives nutritious food. We were often disappointed that he seemed to be a few months behind in development during his first year. But now, after two years of earthly existence, he's far from being as exuberant as Tamara or most German children, but he laughs, plays and relates to his environment — and is often fresh. You can see that he has an inner life. Of course nutrition isn't everything. And his environment? What does a such a mite see when it first opens its eyes and looks at something? His mother, except when it's born into a family that the father has abandoned and the mother must work.

His brothers and sisters. Thank God that the brothers and sisters fervently love each other and lovingly care for each other. This warm loving web that is spun from one to the other is the salvation of many children. Such a family is all right despite poverty; in such an atmosphere the children can grow. Mostly they are intellectually weak, but can become honest, straightforward human beings. But this isn't the case when chaos, revolt and thievery take the upper hand.

What else does such a child see? A dark, sooty wall, hanging wash, an open fire, boxes and suitcases in which miserable possessions are packed, perhaps a torn couch, a toy car without wheels, a torn-up floor — everything gray, brown, black. Hardly any color or beautiful forms. How should a sense of beauty develop? How shall such a child be stimulated?

October 1979 — Hamburg

At five o'clock I went to the post office and mailed twenty letters to the children, volunteers, teachers in Brazil, as well as "Bread for the World", "Terre des Hommes", "Regional Office for Development Aid", etc. Five o'clock, autumn, almost winter, this semi-darkness, these sounds muffled by damp fog, the people returning from work, emerging from the U-bahn, going home with their briefcases, wrapped in coats and hats. Memories of this daily routine when I worked in a publishing house and had to drop the correspondence in the mailbox after office hours. How lucky I am to have found a different path!

Almost all the letters were over-weight. Patiently the clerk weighed one after the other. I watched him doing it, which must have pleased him, for he smiled at me. I thought again how happy I am not to have to do such workday in and day out. And a kind of thankfulness that he does this work for me. Of course he gets paid for it, but that's beside the point.

And so I went home, brushed the autumn leaves off and thought again: We're privileged, not so much by being able to be free from dedication to material gain, but because of the chance we have to lead a different life, one which is more fulfilling. Privileged as well because of the ability to have doubts about our way of life, to suffer, to be troubled.

It's something that H. listened to in revolt when I reproached him: this quarreling with our destiny, which we in fact control. Everything — not only money, education, but also this ability to doubt and to formulate the doubts and to build bridges over the abyss of confusion and meaninglessness.

If I lived in Germany I think I would settle in the Ruhr area and do something there for the workers' children. What has been done to these children that their spiritual hunger is stilled by sensational journalism? Germany: children committing suicide, 600 deaths per year from heroin, psychological help for children per telephone, unemployment of the young, alcoholism etc.

On the other hand there are young people who think, who participate, discuss problems, much more aware than Brazilian youth. Young people who don't only think in terms of revolution, but also see solutions in small actions. New forms of community living. It's encouraging when you see how the young people in the Anthroposophical youth seminar in Stuttgart try to practice community living, not only by reading Rudolf Steiner, but also by cleaning up in the kitchen. And I get a warm feeling when I see, for example in the Zeist (Holland) Waldorf School, but also in all the schools where I have spoken about Brazil, how the pupils are so enthusiastic about work in the favelas and have suggestions about how they can contribute.

A phone call from Switzerland: US $15,000 in donations have been received. No, I couldn't believe it!

End of November 1979

A side-trip to Bogotá on the way back from Europe to Brazil.

Stop-over in Caracas — first impression approaching the airport. One can easily forget certain details about Brazil or South America in general: the typical eroded hills that are dotted from top to bottom by shacks, sparse at the top, crowded towards the bottom; everywhere the naked red earth surrounded by brush and weeds, buildings set down any which way, the unkempt land between the airport runways.

Bogotá. First night in South America

You know even in the dark, with closed eyes, that you're no longer in Germany: the barking dogs going from one garbage pile to the other looking for food. Things don't work any more: electricity out, the water in the shower doesn't get hot — the first signs that I'm approaching São Paulo.

The four Dominican sisters work in the barrio (neighborhood) Meissen with over 100,000 inhabitants. A desolate conglomeration of brick huts. It's not like São Paulo, where the favelas are built on unpaid-for city land. Here the poorest shacks are mixed in with other somewhat better ones belonging to lower middle-class people, but all on individually owned land. No tree, no bush, nothing green. Unpaved streets, huge potholes, garbage and filth everywhere.

The sisters' work is admirable. A kindergarten with 150 children and eight kindergarten teachers who come from the Barrio Miessen. A clinic with several branches; people from the barrio are taught to be nurses and take over the inoculation campaign, for example. There are also courses in cooking, knitting, sewing; help with schoolwork, catechism, etc. What they do comes from the situation and needs. How it is done is the hard part: taking the people who are in need seriously, the human image which is the basis of the work. It is a question of whether they are only "treated" or whether they are really considered as equals. You teach them but at the same time you realize that you are also learning and advancing.

I could sense this attitude in the sisters. They take on a lot of responsibility, for example in the clinic and in the kindergarten. They trust the abilities of the others, even though they do not have the educational background usually expected for such work. It sounds easy, but it implies an inner struggle with one own ideals. I can imagine how the kindergarten sister must pull her hair when the locally trained teachers stand around during the breaks instead of remaining active. You have to keep a strong grip on yourself in order not to explode. You have to understand why they are that way and cannot yet give all that you expect them to give.

To see how others are working on the "front" was consoling. Everything isn't perfect and most people are concerned with their own advantage and don't understand what the real objectives of social work are. But one goes on working and is glad of the small steps forward.

In Germany there was a lot of talk about the voluntary efforts of the poor, solidarity and so on. Here it is also terribly difficult to create enthusiasm for such principles. It's all done in small steps and not, as they suppose in Germany: here are the poor and along comes a social worker, talks with them to awaken their awareness and their awareness springs to life like a spark. No, that's not the way it is. What an illusion to think that the poor are quicker in this respect that we are!

I see the development of awareness so: you accomplish something together and then some words are exchanged about the task achieved which puts it in a context. For example, our ambulatory clinic: working together on Sundays, a short speech at the inauguration, "certification", appreciation through the presence of many guests also from outside the favela. Then forward. For example, who does the cleaning? A few get together to take on the cleaning chores. Christmas. We could make a manger scene after all. Some women and children build the manger, it's fun. It's our ambulatorio, we decorate it. From outside it doesn't seem a great success, but what goes on inside those people is important.

Or: theater, a small newspaper with biographies, poems, stories which describe the real situation. Or: explain to the ill what their illness is, why they have it, which organs are involved where the pain is.

For me this is developing awareness. But it's invisible.

Cuando otros lloran sangre, qué derecho tengo yo para llorar lágrimas? — When others cry blood, what right have I to cry tears. (José, Marti, Cuban writer).

November 26, 1979

Back in São Paulo! What a joy to embrace the children, the teachers and Cido and Zeca at the airport!

January 1, 1980 In the train from Londrina to São Paulo.

The Eighties. What will we make of them? My first day of the decade looked like this. As has become traditional, I celebrated a delayed Christmas with Dona Isaura's children and other Londrina children. We made short excursions to the Igapó dam, to a playground, to a sitio, etc. The children's' "cultural Program" is concentrated in my twice-yearly visits.

Finally, however, I had to think about São Paulo, on the expansion and improvements of the escolinha, the grass that must be planted, the teachers we have to find, etc. But oh, what a shock — the buses to São Paulo were full! Therefore I had to confront the train. With the word train one thinks of something comfortable, quick and punctual. The associations brought to mind by the word train, however, are the opposite. It was supposed to leave at nine p.m. At 11 o'clock it finally condescended to enter the station with its blinding lights puffing and blowing off steam. Masses of people streamed out of it. I was relieved, for this must mean that there would be some seats free. But there was nothing, which meant a twenty-hour journey standing up.

From minute to minute I surrender more to my destiny. There is simply nothing I can do to change my present destiny. I have only to wait and hope. I feel in myself the same resignation that is to be seen on most of the faces around me, especially the mothers with children in their arms, on their laps or in baby-slings.

Next to me sat a surly looking man with a child that sat on the second seat and slept, leaving a small space free, which I, as well as the other nearby standees, greedily watched. "Move the child over a bit so I can also sit," a man said hopefully. "No! I stood for hours with the child in my arms and have now finally managed to get a seat," he answered rudely. Nevertheless, I thought that his heart might soften and he would offer me the remaining space.

Finally it happened: "Sit down." No one could have said anything nicer to me after three hours of standing. What happiness! A place to sit in a shaking train and a dark-blue shade over your head to block the light. Sometimes it's all so simple ...

I doze and look at the people. For example a wild looking man, half Indio, half Black, with tangled hair and a matted beard, his daughter playing on his lap: blond and blue-eyed. You can only see this in Brazil. There are also many young people who work in São Paulo and visit their families during the holidays. Also those with their possessions and children who are moving to São Paulo in search of a better life.

Now as I write this we are near Sorocaba, two hours from São Paulo. When you travel through this area — hard earth, scrub, termite hills, some eucalyptus trees — it's hard to imagine that it was all jungle not too long ago. Dona Ana, who was born in Russia, told me about her life; she spent the first years in Brazil in this area.

Her father owned a small farm in Russia and heard that Brazil was wonderful. He rented his farm — "In case it doesn't work out in Brazil I can always return." He probably had no idea of the enormous distance involved. Then he boarded an immigrant ship and sailed for weeks across the sea. Once arrived here, he found nothing of the wonder he had been told to expect. The family had to work hard as laborers on a coffee plantation. At that time the government sold pieces of jungle to foreigners. Many Russians bought pieces of land and cleared the jungle. In the beginning they slept under the trees, whole families, and cooked in a hole dug in the earth. Mosquitoes, snakes, wild beasts, unknown illnesses for which they had no remedies. It was all drudgery.

"My uncle went into the jungle every day to clear land and his wife brought him food. One day she found him crushed by a huge tree that had fallen the wrong way." Piece by piece the land was cleared, ploughed, planted, mainly coffee. "I grew up, worked as a maid and married. In 1935 the call went out: Paraná, Paraná! There the earth is fertile, there you will become rich. Many sold their land and moved to Paraná. Those who had brought a lot of money with them, for example Germans who had immigrated around that time, bought large tracts of land with fertile red earth. Others worked as plantation laborers or in brick-works, which is just about the most miserable work you can do."

> Later Dona Ana wound up in the favela, which Frei Nereu and we development workers then transformed into the Vila da Fraternidade.

And now? 1980? Now the call is to Mato Grosso, Goias, Rondonia, always farther west. This has its advantages as the areas are opened up. But the earth they leave behind is usually worked out. I remember a story that Mouzart from Londrina told me. A family — man, wife and children — moved from their roca in Minas Gerais. The woman had never lived anywhere but in her adobe hut. As they boarded the train she asked respectfully if she should remove her shoes. They rode slowly along until one of the children had to go to the toilet. She didn't know that the train had one, so she held the child over the platform of a station they stopped at. The train left and she stood there with her child and nothing else, not knowing at what station they were to change trains, nor even the name of the station nearest her home. Finally a railroad employee put them in a train to Bahia. They traveled a day or two, then went back, for it was the wrong direction. After much asking around, she finally found her way back to her hometown in Minas Gerais. The rest of the family was in São Paulo. The woman could not be persuaded to ever set foot alone again in a train, so her husband had to go and get her. Thus unprepared, hundreds, thousands, tens of thousands arrive in the big city.

January 29, 1980

Today is registration day. Mothers come with their children to register for the various activities: kindergarten, pre-school, sewing course, carpentry. And so many of them came!

After two hours of unremitting questions (How many children? family income? father's work? illnesses, etc.) there's no more room. But mothers keep coming wanting to register their children. No, the school is already full. Putting them off till next year. If only we had more kindergartens and didn't have to always give the same disappointing answer. When you see these mothers, how they arrive with such hope and go away disappointed, you can feel the pressure of necessity and are ready to give up the idea of an (almost) perfect kindergarten for more and less perfect ones.

But where are the people who can take on this job? Where is the money? And the appropriate land?

Help will come. Confidence. Of course it will never be such an ideal kindergarten as we have now with Renate. But anything is better than what the children have now: no stimulation to play, lack of nutrition, filth and so on. The Bogotá kindergarten gives us encouragement: many small kindergarten groups. Girls and mothers with pedagogical talent and love for the children take over the groups. Renate circulates from group to group and does the difficult parts, for example the rhythmic part, painting, play groups, etc., and the local kindergarten teachers do the simple handwork. It's not ideal, but it multiplies Renate's abilities and more children are exposed to a humanized education.

February 1980

Today Renate had her parents' meeting. As usual it has been raining or, as today, heavy rainclouds cover the sky and it threatens to rain any minute. Only one father came to the meeting. I ran down to the favela where some mothers came to meet me. I went from hut to hut, called out: today there's a *reunião*, it's important! Yes, but it's about to rain. That doesn't matter, it's dry there. Finally most of them decided to come after all. I passed Luciene's hut and the devastation hit me like a blow. Most of the hut had fallen down into the ditch. The heavy rains in the past weeks carried earth away and gradually weakened the foundation, which gave way and the outhouse and kitchen slid down. The father had worked all last year on this hut, worked overtime in the factory in order to buy roof-tiling, cement, wood, etc. On Sundays you would always see him there working together with the children. And now it was all for nothing. And my garden, the woman said. All gone. The children were carrying mud away in a wheelbarrow. I could have cried when I saw the ruins. But not the children. Everything will be back the way it was in a few weeks, Ivonie said.

It's understandable that many don't even begin to improve their huts or try to fight against their destiny of poverty. If it all ends in a pile of mud anyway and all the work is for nothing, why do anything at all? You need a lot of strength and courage to start again afresh.

April 1980

Recently someone asked me: "Why do you keep this diary?" I was taken aback, because I have been writing for so long about how I live. "To vindicate yourself?" he asked. No. "To attest to your work?" No. — Why? Yes, Why?

Much of it I wrote as letters, to my mother, so that she could participate in my life with the favela children. Then I often wrote about the children themselves. Often they were difficult children, who had been severely buffeted by life. In daily activity we often rub against each other the wrong way. So I wrote in order to maintain a distance so I would not be seeing them only superficially; to have an insight into what really lives under that crust of revolt, the rebellion of the spirit which tries to realize itself.

And I wrote about the destiny of individual families. I sat in their huts and suddenly a mother would start to tell me about her life on the land: too little food, no doctor, no school, giving birth without assistance, the move to São Paulo, etc. I had the feeling that all these destinies which are lived out in Brazil in the thousands and probably in the whole world in a similar way, that such destinies shouldn't be left to expire unheard, that they should somehow be preserved, because it is the destiny of thousands who can't make themselves heard in the tumult of world events. Only when someone breaks out violently in robbery or murder do they make the headlines.

Human beings who are driven from the land to the cities. Children. Wherever you go — on the streets, at the market, in parks, in museums, in schools — the hordes of children are everywhere. (What a contrast to Germany with its many vigorous, active elderly people.) What kind of souls are these who incarnate in such weak bodies and in such squalid conditions? What meaning is behind the fact that they must preserve their human dignity through all this misery, or lose it?

I wrote what I saw, also to clarify to myself the reason for our work and the spirit from which such activity springs. Later, when we inaugurated the escolinha, and more and more volunteers came to help us, I found that these diary sketches helped them understand the children and adults in the favela. Therefore the sketches made the rounds among the co-workers. Someone asked me if I had thought about publishing them. No, not really. But perhaps it would make sense, perhaps it would encourage some to make their own problems less important and open themselves to others. But then it is also necessary to see how you must wrestle with yourself, how one has doubts and overcomes these doubts. It's not enough to see only the visible side of the work, but also one's own development. It costs something to admit this.

During the past few months some young people, experienced in development work, approached us offering to help. A girl came and taught some children to weave. It was a great success. We had always intended to do this, but never had the time nor the courage to start. Then she came and started the ball rolling. At the moment weave-itis has broken out, from kindergarten to the older boys — everybody weaves. Shortly before she traveled to Germany we had a longer conversation.

"Why do you do social work, and since when?" she asked. "When I realized that all these people, all these children and youths want self-realization, exactly as we want it. Previously I saw only the poverty and its side-effects: filth, sickness, hovels, etc. At a certain moment I understood that they are also human beings who, like me, are looking for a path in life, who want to fulfill their destiny — and not merely survive, not merely stay alive. Mostly this seeking for the meaning of life is suffocated by the need to earn money, already in childhood. When I really felt this in my inner being, not only theoretically but through and through, I began to put my own life in the background in order to concern myself with these people, not only outwardly, but inwardly as well."

"I'm happy that I could work here, and I now know better what I will do later on." I thought: perhaps we should tell many people, especially young people, what we can do in life.

Another said: "I admire your patience." That embarrassed me, for I may have patience in the long run, but how often have I lost my patience where the little things are concerned.

And yet another: "What about your own feelings, sex, your wish to have your own children?"

Gradually it dawned on me, and I should also write it, that I have exactly the same needs, the same despairs, the same wish to find myself as all the others. That the temptation always exists to live for myself, that I also love, live, suffer, with the only difference that I realize I have no right to place these doubts and feelings of hopelessness in the center of my life as long as there are children who live in slums, as long as there are children who work in mines and practically never see the light of day.

May 1980

I am reading Rudolf Steiner's *Knowledge of the Higher Worlds*. So high-sounding, but it was written for daily life. I realize how important it is now, when I am no longer surrounded only by children, and when the escolinha is becoming a larger organism in which adults work and must understand each other. Adults from various countries with differing social and educational backgrounds, black, brown, white. They are all here to do something in the favela. The motives which bring them also differ: compassion for the children, an escape from their own problems, the need to do something beyond the merely personal. All justifiable motives. And all these people must be brought under one umbrella so that they can put their personal affairs in the background.

By occult training one imagines something very mysterious. But it is really quite normal, something through which you can deal better with daily life. "I must develop in myself the ability to let the impressions of the outside world affect me in a manner which only I determine." For example, to remove the wounding barb from angry words; to transform impatience into useful observation during waiting times, etc.

"Especially important for the occult student is the way in which he listens to another person." Silencing his own being, absorbing what the other has to say, without sympathetic or antipathetic comments. Dominating his own feelings, willing, even, to rethink his thoughts in the interest of objectivity. To let the other speak out, listening carefully, understanding why he is as he is, fighting one's own prejudices in respect to so-called national characteristics or educational levels. That means to take someone inwardly seriously, who only went to primary school, who perhaps only learned to read as an adult and is black to boot.

Surely it's hard to discover the human core under all those layers. That's why I was so glad when a volunteer recently told me: "I don't even notice any more if someone is black or white. You can see through the outer appearances."

Is it an exaggeration if we don't only try to find work for a young person, but also try to see that it's a humane activity? Shouldn't we limit ourselves to ensuring that the basic conditions for survival are met, without worrying about whether or not they correspond to human needs? The eternal question: Should we help a few children as much as possible, or help many children a little? Quality or quantity. In any case, I'm not in favor of quick courses of 40 to 50 hours in which the young are taught sewing, fabric coloring, knitting, carpentry, etc. This accomplishes practical proficiency, but the children aren't really educated. After a few months it may all be forgotten. I always must think of St. Exupéry's words: "*Seul l'esprit qui souffle sur la glaise peut créer l'Homme.*" (Only the spirit which breathes over the clay can create man.)

Maybe you can get used to filth and poverty in the course of life, because you have no choice and you can't get excited about it every day anew. When we go into the favela as neophytes, it's what immediately attracts our attention and awakens our compassion or our disgust: the rivulets of indefinable water, the outhouses, the rats that scurry by and whose bite-marks you sometimes see on small children's' ears; or the smell of the earth evenings, when all smells become stronger and when the good smell of damp earth no longer rises, but one of filth and excrement. One wants to change all that because it seems impossible to live that way. But the more you occupy yourself with the people and the favela in general, the more it seems that something else is more important: the impossibility of developing into a real human being under such conditions, or at least the terrible difficulty of developing what has been implanted in us as potentiality and ability. When I see a child, who with shining eyes for the first time reverently digs up a beautiful stone, I ask myself: What happened to this brilliance and reverence in the men who only drink, beat their wives and play pool? Where did this coarseness come from? I know that it's not only a favela problem and isn't necessarily related only to rich and poor, rather with education and values. But I believe that it's especially difficult under the favela conditions to preserve the human essence under the crusts of hardening and truncation.

What depresses me most is that these people are also born with rich possibilities and that this wealth of life crumbles away year by year. They are so limited, so one-sided, that hardly anything remains of what Juracy, Arnaldo, Mario and others might have become.

In Germany you see many pictures of slum areas, you read articles with statistics about the difference between rich and poor countries. But the pictures and statistics touch us only superficially until we inwardly realize that they are human beings like us. That they don't only want to survive, but they need to realize themselves just as we do. That they are singular individuals, beings who want to live out their personal destinies. Once you really feel this, that these people are seeking a way, just as we are, in their work, in love, in life in general, then the fact that they are impeded by the extremely difficult circumstances in which they grow up doesn't leave you in peace. Now I see more clearly that the material circumstances must change, for they are the basis of human dignity, but they are only the prerequisite for what is essential: the path to becoming truly human. Somehow we must try to work on two levels: to improve the material conditions and, at the same time, to think how to awaken the spiritual element in the people. I believe it is wrong to think that we should first occupy ourselves with improving the material circumstances, and only afterwards worry about the spiritual, the human element. I think about the well dressed, well situated, sated people in Europe. But fulfillment as human beings isn't achieved there either. I never before had such a feeling of compassion as during my last trip to Europe for those well-dressed people who have everything a favelado could desire — but they read only the trashiest newspaper. And what is accomplished? The basis has been achieved, but how is it used?

Raimundo

I don't know much about Raimundo. He's about 35, lives in the favela, is unmarried, has two wives, one in the favela and the other somewhere else. He has no children though, because he has a serious case of syphilis. He spent several years in jail because he killed someone. He is *valente*, as his father says. Proud, obstinate, brave — there is no German word to correctly express *valente*.

His grandfather was a real Indio who hunted in the jungle and ate the animals raw. His look is sinister, dark, he doesn't smile, speaks in one-syllable words, pulls his cap far down over his forehead, likes to be well dressed, usually in black, takes no notice of others. When he's not in the mood, he simply isn't in the mood. He's his own master, but a master who isn't free. He gives the impression of a caged predator who has been denied the freedom of the steppes. Gloomy, taciturn, as though there was a wall around him.

But he sings. When he speaks he has a breaking voice, but when he sings it becomes full. It isn't the tone of his voice that makes such an impression however, but the expression he puts into his songs. Perhaps it's sentimental, but it seems as if his soul is breaking out of him, out of his body and his failure of a life.

I would like to understand what goes on in such a human soul. Recently I saw him in his hut, alone. We spoke about prison and his life on the land; he told me about it. I wasn't at all afraid, it didn't occur to me that I was sitting with a murderer. It was all normal, nothing evil.

What happens in a human life, inside a man, that he can kill another? Somehow such people are out of place in the city. In the jungle, on the land, they can live out their wildness; they can hunt or go to war. In the right place they could be brave, valente. What can he do with his savagery in the city, on the assembly line, or as a day-laborer?

A short while ago Raimundo planted the grass at the escolinha. I told him: Be careful, these flowers mustn't be harmed. He said: *o lirio de São João,* the St. John lily. I was astonished because it was the first time a Brazilian had named a Brazilian plant to me. I told him so. He looked up at me and smiled, a ray of sunshine through thunderclouds. A small break in the wall. The wall is ugly, stained with robberies and other crimes; but behind it something is hidden that flashes and shines as it does in other people — his soul, his destiny. It reminds me of the fairy tale Snow White and Red Rose — gold flashes through the shaggy bear's coat. The bear is redeemed. Who will free this man?

Serginho

Serginho is five years old. Since he was three he has played in the curve of a paved road and only his guardian angel can have prevented his being run over. He's blond, though neither his father nor his mother are blond. He mostly goes about naked or in pieces of clothing that are much too big for him and that he drags behind him. His father is dead and his mother and older sister work in a factory. A nine-year-old girl looks after the little ones. Two brothers of fourteen and thirteen years of age are in reform school.

Sergio senses when it's time to prepare himself for kindergarten. He washes superficially at the common water faucet, hangs on some clothes and moves off in the direction of the kindergarten. Usually he's one of the first to arrive. On the way he steals a large flower and gives it to Renate.

Recently he has been terribly weak with sores all over and a huge boil on his forehead. I decided to bring him to our ambulatorio. It was Easter and all the children had received an Easter basket. He gave me one hand and with the other held tightly onto his Easter basket. We walked slowly — slowly — down the street to the favela. It was quite pleasant to walk so calmly. Then I thought: What good will it do if we give him medication from the ambulatorio if no one is there to see that he takes it regularly. A kind of sanitarium is needed for such rundown children who have no one at home to care for them, a place where they can recuperate for a week or so and gain new strength.

The idea has been born. Now we must see how it can be realized.

Sergio and Divino
Poema Para Rezar

Senhor, por que me mandaste amar todos os homens, meus irmãos?
Senhor, estava tão tranquilo em minha casa, tinha organizado,
Já'me achava instalada
Meu lar mobiliado, e lá'dentro
sentia-me tão bem
Sózinho, estava de acordo comingo mesmo:
Mas na minha fortaleza descobriste, Senhor, uma brecha.
Obrigaste me a entreabrir a porta.
Lá fora os homens me espreitavam.

Não sabia que estavam tão perto.
Entraram os primeiros.
Acolhi-os.
Até, aí era razonável.
Mas os que vinham depois,
Senhor, os outros homens, eu não tinha visto,
ocultos por trás dos primeiros!

Nada mais posso fazer;
quanto mais chegam,
mais a porta se abre ...
Poem to pray to:

Lord, why do you command me to love all people,
all my brothers?
Lord, I lived so peacefully in my home,
had everything organized,
comfortably arranged and furnished,
and I felt so good:
Alone I was in agreement with myself.
But you found a crack in my defenses
and I had to open the door a crack:

Outside the people were looking at me.

I hadn't realized they were so near.
The first ones entered.
I sheltered them.
There was no problem at first,
but those that came after,
Lord, I hadn't seen them
hidden behind the first ones.

I can do nothing to prevent it,
The more that come, the more
the door opens.

The Favela Monte Azul swarms with children who are left on their own because their mothers must work. Dona Ifigenia, for example, has eight children and her husband is dead. She leaves home for work at five o'clock in the morning. Her day begins battling with the bus — people hang like bunches of grapes at the doors. As a woman she barely has the strength to hang on, but somehow she does it. At six o'clock work begins: cleaning. She works eight hours a day plus overtime, so she comes home around ten at night. She only sees her children sleeping, except on Sundays. She works in order to keep these children alive. But she has become so deadened by life, suffering and the problems that are beyond her capacity to deal with, that she has lost her relation to her children. Deep down she surely loves them, but outwardly she has been deadened. Perhaps this is the only way she can survive. For how should she otherwise bear the fact that her oldest boys left home long ago, are often arrested by the police and sent to reform schools from which they are always escaping? Recently as she was leaving work she saw her own son sleeping on the sidewalk on newspapers covered with filth. She leaves her smaller children, aged one to ten, by themselves. Cida, ten years old, cooks and does the wash, which is too much for her. Five-year-old Serginho and four-year-old Divino play on a curve in the street. It's a real miracle that they aren't run over.

One of the children is always sick and, as the mother isn't there, nothing is done until they must be brought urgently to the hospital, from where they seldom leave completely cured. And everything is borne stoically. Recently Cida was burned on her back and it took a week before the mother discovered the purulent wound. Until then the child bore it quietly. But what does to bear mean? She is deadened to pain, but also to other things that the environment brings her. Also to learning and to beauty.

May 1981

Life has changed completely now that Sergio and Divino live here. I have never had such small children, five and six years old, living here. I sometimes think I'm developing backwards. Whereas normally one brings up children from small to big, it's just the opposite with me: first adolescents lived here, then school-age children, now kindergarten children. We'll see if I get to babies next.

The first thing I hear upon waking early mornings is Divino's voice: *qui, qui, qui*. Somebody wants something from him and he is furious. He's always furious when you want him to do something. Then the battle continues: *sou primeiro!* I'm first. Or, I saw it first, or I was here first, or I knew Ute first, or I woke up first etc. Then it goes on: *é meu*. Everything is mine, mine, mine! I, I, I! The struggle for survival is already impregnated in their bodies and in their souls. How can one attain to normal togetherness, to sharing, to we? They consume huge amounts of food in breakneck speed. As much as possible as quickly as possible. It's safe from others once in the stomach. When there's absolutely no more room, the remains are hidden in some corner, hoarded. When I was cleaning the house recently I found a crust of bread in the chimney and a banana behind the bed.

Toys don't exist to play with, but to possess. Both of them, Divino as well as Sergio, grab so many things and because of full hands and arms have no hand left to play with the rocking horse or toy house. Divino is especially bad in this respect.

I don't have a moment's peace. You can hear the racket in the next room, things falling down, Divino screams. Or João storms indignantly into the room: "Where's my pen?" After searching and asking it turns out that Divino threw it on top of the closet. Or Bea comes and says politely, but irritated: "Please tell him to stop now" (throwing stones at her door). Yet there are moving moments like when Sergio and Divino hold my hands to go to the escolinha. Or when Divino sits on my lap of his own accord and instead of being stone hard, nestles softly against me. Peace, peace is what they need, a relaxed atmosphere in which they don't have to be always on the defensive and fighting, in which something besides cruelty, noise and rawness can flow into them.

It would be good if they could hear music. Before the bedtime story I always play something for them on the pentatonic flute. But I have the feeling that a lyre would be better, purer. Perhaps mornings, when they are softer and not so defensive. But where do I find time for such things?

Their voices: Sergio has a shrill voice that pierces my ear to the extent that it hurts. Divino's voice is hard to describe, grating, deeper than Sergio's, like a radio voice. His speech is choppy and he pronounces the soft consonants hard. What is he trying to express in the sound of that voice?

Both like to paint. Sergio paints very nicely, always in light colors and with confident strength in the strokes. Divino is still in the scribbling stage and his colors are mostly dark. (After a month Sergio's voice became clear and soft, almost tender.)

Sergio's somewhat malicious smile, looking at me from the side, Divino's deathly earnest gaze ... What is hidden behind them? He knows exactly how to anger someone. He throws stones when he's forbidden to do something, spits, curses using the foulest words, urinates on Sybille's shoe in fury at not being allowed to open her bag. Divino is more obdurate, doesn't answer when you want something from him. In this respect Sergio is more accessible. He understands that certain rules must be respected.

The house and garden were overflowing with banana peels. "Divino, pick up the banana skins and throw them in the garbage can."

No reaction.

"Divino, pick up the banana skins!"

No reaction.

One must be firm now and insist, despite there being a thousand detours before he does it. He often thinks I've forgotten. but I mustn't forget, not even a half-hour later. Very wearisome for the educator. Divino comes and asks if he can have an orange. Yes, but first pick up the banana skins. Be firm, or else he'll never learn to obey. Sometimes Sergio has pity on him and says:

"Eu faço para ele". "I'll do it for him."

He almost always obeys and even does the things Divino should do. He's not nearly as obdurate as Divino. Yet I have the feeling that the mishandling and spiritual deprivation have penetrated so deeply in him that mere "fondness" cannot be the only cure for him. He has lost far less of his hardness than Divino. He reminds me of the mummies of Ramses when he sleeps. I was shocked the first night. During the day he has that knowing smile and that look to see how I will react.

They notice everything, the good and the bad. Already after the first days here they had better table manners and knew that they were to brush their teeth and say their prayers before sleeping. They absorb everything like a sponge. But of course not only now. Also in the favela and on the street. When they were four or five years old they already knew how to survive by cursing, fighting and stealing.

On the very first day I found a fifty cruzeiro note in Sergio's pocket that he had stolen from me. From fear of hunger they hid their stock in every corner of the house, in the chimney, under the bed, in the closet: pieces of banana, bread-crusts, oranges. Everything must be snatched away — and never given away.

(Now, a year later, as I read this Divino is preparing a present for Bettina: a piece of cake, a drawing and a sugar cube. It would have been impossible for him to give something of his away before, especially something edible. Nevertheless, he hasn't yet been cured of stuffing himself with food. If I'm not watching him he stuffs so much food into his mouth that his cheeks blow up like a hamster's.)

They didn't know how to play. Divino was especially egoistic in this respect. In kindergarten he would come in clutching a bunch of wheel-less toy cars, very stiff, afraid someone would take them from him. At home there was continuous strife when both wanted to play with the same toy. But today they are playing nicely. They built a little house under the kitchen table with cloths and pillows. "vem tia, na minha casa!" "Come in my house." I crawled under the table, Divino covered me and we slept peacefully in the little house. But the peace didn't last long. The game changed. Running from the bookcase to the garden, from the garden to the washbasin, from the washbasin to my desk, then onto João's bed and so on. Everything is turned upside down, experimented with, hidden, used as toys. Damage: a shattered vase, a broken doll cradle. But in the beginning you can't hang up "don't touch" signs everywhere.

Yesterday I hid two leftover Easter eggs in the grass and told them they could hunt for them. They found two huge wooden spoons in the kitchen and ran into the garden with them where they hacked at the grass like wild men as if they wanted to hack out the weeds and turn over all the earth. They didn't give up. Divino looked like a dwarf hunting for gold. What strength and stamina this child has. They hacked around until they found one egg, then the other. Today they were at it again: *Procurar ovos de Páscoa!*

Hunt for Easter eggs!

Ten days later, May 17th

After ten days it's hard to imagine how Sergio and Divino used to come to kindergarten: pants hanging down, filthy dirty from head to toe, their sweaters (when they had them) much too big and hanging off their shoulders. Divino's strange sideways walk down the steps to Renate and the kindergarten, his deathly serious face which neither words nor smiles could soften. Now and then Neuza or Lucia took pity on them and washed them in the washbasin. When I entered Divino was always squatting in a corner or playing alone on the chairs; he seldom participated.

Today as I was conducting a "tour" for some people who are interested in our work, I was very pleased with the kindergarten: Sergio and Divino were there and glad when I came in. But I was surely happier than they. Divino stood with the others in the round, the São João Round, and participated in a completely natural way, moved his lips with the verse and songs, and went around with the circle. I was terribly proud. I asked Renate and she said he was much better.

When they come home from Kindergarten I can hear their skipping and chattering from far away. They storm into the kitchen, stop, look at me, and I take them into my arms and then the chattering goes on. Divino laughs a lot now and you can almost forget how serious he always was. Only occasionally he looks at me so seriously, like recently at bedtime when he ripped off his chest-pack and I, losing my temper, said, "So keep your cough!" He immediately closed up, the happy smile was gone, his large round brown eyes looked at me so sadly that I felt sorry. He seemed to be saying: these grown-ups, this terrible adult world, full of impatience and lovelessness.

Severity gets you nowhere. Singing, embracing, playing and whatever else you can think of must be used instead of orders. To requests and orders he only replies: *não, não*. The whole world seems to be a single "no" to him. In reality he's right, for what is the world worth without the love which he has never experienced? You can see though how he's beginning to thaw and relax, and his hard crust is becoming permeable. You can notice it when he wakes up. During the first days they both stayed in bed awake; when Divino heard me get up he staggered into the kitchen. I bent over to embrace him and he fell into my arms with that deathly earnest look on his face. He stayed in my arms until I had to free myself in order to make breakfast. That's all changed. Early mornings you hear the happy chattering, playing in bed, talking to Joãoão. In some ways Sergio is easier, in others more difficult. Although he's only one year older, he's much more advanced in awareness than Divino. He doesn't only feel, like Divino, that he's better off here. It was his idea to move here permanently.

After twelve days Sergio suddenly disappeared. His older brother dragged him home and the next morning they were underway to collect and sell scrap iron. Probably Valdir needed him to push the cart and also to sneak into gardens to steal old iron. At midday I went to their mother and told her that she could visit Sergio any time she wanted, but that his brother couldn't simply come and take him away. Then Sergio and I went to the kindergarten and he said he wanted to stay with me. The same thing happened with Divino today when we took a walk on the *Praça da Republica* and he was obviously tired. I asked him:

"Shall we go home?"

"Não."

"Do you want to stay here?"

"Não."

"Do you want to go home?"

"Não"

Then I realized that he might have understood home to his mother. So I asked him: "Do you want to go to my house?"

"Yes!"

As is so often the case with favela children, I have the feeling that they and not their parents take their destinies into their hands and make the decisions. How strange that Sergio and Divino decided by themselves to come home with me in that certain tone that is characteristic of them:

"*Vou na casa da tia.*" "I'm going to Ute's house." And Divino's repetition: "*Vou na casa da tia.*" Day in and day out they repeated it until it became a reality. They decided themselves: We want to live with Ute. But stranger still is that they only said this at the moment I had decided that I was willing to take them in. How had they known that? What protective power leads these children to the places they need to be?

Although I thought I had no free time, I do spend hours with them, pick them up, play with them, tell them fairy tales, cook with them, etc. Every task which is not absolutely necessary is left undone or waits for some kindly soul to do it. A child from the favela who washes the dishes, or Maristela, who sometimes does the wash and of course Bea, who is a big help to me and is ideal with children.

Divino

Divino will be five years old on July 3rd. He's very short for his age, but strong. When he stands up straight his belly sticks out a bit, he has a mild forward curvature of the spine and he's somewhat bow-legged. His feet are very short but muscular and the soles have a heavy callous covering from walking barefoot so much. His insteps are still filled out with fat as is the case with smaller children and his toes are extremely short. His backside sticks out somewhat, is very hard and somehow tense. His belly is rounded like a baby's but not at all soft. His arms are short and strong, hands also short but wide and muscular. The fingers are very short. His head is round and nicely formed and sits on a short, thin neck. His face is round. He has a fine, roundish chin and a small mouth. His nose is nicely formed, neither too large nor too small. He has large, always wide-open brown eyes, barely visible eyebrows and an almost square forehead. He has blonde curly hair.

He walks with short, heavy steps as though his body were pressing him to the ground with every step. He hardly ever jumps up but likes to jump down from a height. He likes to turn somersaults and tries to do cartwheels, but without any lightness. He climbs well. Divino almost always plays alone. He tries to accumulate as many toys as possible, retreats by himself into the farthest corner and builds his empire there. If someone tries to take something away from him he breaks out in a baby-like howl. His playhouses are so small that only he fits into them. When he feels secure he is totally absorbed and converses with himself. Colored cloths are his favorite playthings, they are the first things he runs to. Recently he started to play with the puppet theater, sometimes even with other children. But his speech is unclear as though it was being squeezed from his chest without breathing. When he hurts himself he screams until he can no longer breathe. He becomes almost blue. Even when he's absorbed in playing he hardly ever smiles. In reality he can only laugh maliciously, when he makes fun of someone or hurts them. He seldom participates in the round in kindergarten. Sometimes he suddenly joins in though, and when he forgets himself makes nice, almost devotional movements. If he's annoyed by something though, either he begins to deliberately disturb the activity or crawls under a table and no longer participates.

Although he has such a hard outer surface, inside he's soft and wants to be close. You have to trick him into it though, for he doesn't let himself be hugged or taken onto my lap so easily. Once it's accomplished his hard body relaxes and he can even be cuddly. Divino likes to draw. He prefers dark colors, but doesn't press hard. He doesn't yet draw graphically. He likes to work with wax and clay and does it very well.

I was just looking through my books but couldn't find the place about bed-wetting. Dr. Simonis writes only that control of the elimination processes has to do with the soul's penetration of the body. At three years of age this penetration should be so far advanced that the child is dry day and night. There are children, however, who must be put on the pot every night until school age, when they learn to get up to go to the toilet by themselves. I think it would help Divino overcome the baby stage by letting him sleep without diapers and putting him on the pot at night.

When my mother was here and we often went sightseeing around the city and surroundings, Divino and Sergio usually accompanied us. Sergio saw everything: birds, beautiful blooming trees, a horse-drawn cart, the buses, traffic lights, everything. And he yelled everything out, in that shrill voice he sometimes still has, directly into my mother's ear.

"Fala mais baixinho, tia !"

"Don't shout!"

"*Olha, uma estrela*", "Look, a star," he screamed again.

"*Olha, dois ónibus ultrapasando! Olha, avião!*" "Look, two buses going by! "Look, an airplane."

"Olha! Olha!" Look! Look!

For Divino only one thing of importance exists: *janelas*, windows. Every few minutes he would cry: "*O, uma janela*!" Of course we passed thousands of windows. I asked myself why he only notices windows, of all things. They're nothing special. But perhaps they are special, not the windows themselves but the opening on the world that a window represents. He finds the window in his spirit and opens it to the world. I couldn't explain it any other way. He continually draws curls and says they're windows. And he is becoming less obdurate and more open. The wall he built around himself as protection from the world that had brought him nothing of beauty, no love, no warmth, is gradually crumbling. He feels better, has become more childish, even babyish. I have the feeling that he wants to make up for what he never experienced: what it's like to be a baby.

MOTHERS DAY, 1981

As has already become traditional, we invited the mothers of the favela to go on an excursion. The Ens family allowed us to use their sitio (country house). My group of children had rehearsed a play to present to the mothers. During this month "Freeing of Slaves Day" also occurs. Therefore the play is about two brothers, one black, the other white, both very handsome, who become separated and the white one sells the black one. Then the history of the slave trade, compulsory labor on the plantations and, finally, liberation.

Sergio was the herald who announced to the white brother: "*Meu amo esta chegando, ele quer conversar com seu irmão preto.*" "My master is coming, he wants to talk to his black brother." He put his hobbyhorse between his legs and came galloping up. Divino came behind him and said everything right, although he had hardly rehearsed.

How close they are to each other. Divino imitates everything Sergio does. It is a little frightening, for how will he escape Sergio's leadership and become his own person? On the other hand, they probably would never have survived if they hadn't had each other for support. Sergio as leader, full of ideas who thought out where and how they should find food, who instinctively knew when it was market day and ran there to pick up the leavings from the ground and probably stole some things from the tables. Divino as follower, who kept his brother company, so to speak, so he wouldn't be alone.

What can you do for children who must grow up without beauty, adequate nutrition or peace for their development?

> "The brain is still developing its plastic form until the seventh year; what has not developed of these fine formations by then is lost forever. Because the brain is the instrument through which the spirit manifests itself, it is of extreme importance that this instrument be developed and prepared as perfectly as possible during the first seven years. For with an insufficiently developed brain not even the greatest genius can begin to think, just as the greatest pianist cannot play well on a badly tuned piano. Just as rickets manifests itself in a malformation of the bone structure, it also appears as a malformation in the glandular system and in the mucous membrane; that is, children affected by rickets often have swollen glands, adenoids, etc. The third symptom which one notices in these children is that they are mentally backward, they are inattentive in school, can be outright stupid. All this is the result of this deficient development of the physical brain, especially the so-called cortex, which in these years must be developed in its most delicate intricacy." (Rudolf Steiner)

How naive is the opinion that intellectual weakness in favela children is hereditary. I think that people are seldom born stupid. They become stupid because of the environment in which they grow up. Stupidity is rather stunted intelligence. If someone is intelligent under these circumstances, it is despite them. His self is so strong that he has fought his way through all this adversity, all these physical and spiritual deficiencies. I have this impression where Sergio is concerned. A strong personality who prevails and subconsciously seeks the best way for himself, the best way for his "inner self" to be born. It was not for nothing that he took the initiative to enroll himself in the kindergarten or to live with me.

August 1981

Divino at night: He often screams and sometimes he calls, *"Mae! Mae!"* (Mother, Mother). I took him into my bed and calmed him. Was it a nightmare or was he longing for his home and his mother? I don't know. One never knows if it's right to take children away from their mother. It looks as though it was a correct decision, they are developing so well. But you can't really know until ten, twenty, thirty years from now. Perhaps it's right for now and in ten years it will become apparent that it was wrong. Or something can seem wrong now and in twenty years you see that it was correct after all. You can feel how limited a person is. How can you know if a decision which affects a human being's whole future is correct if you can't see into the future?

I have the feeling that Sergio and Divino belong to my life, to me; just as a child "seeks" his parents before his birth, these children sought me after their birth. Or perhaps this is an illusion I have because I love them so. It could also be a kind of arrogance because I think that I can give them more than others could.

Supplement 1982

At first the children never wanted to visit their mother, especially Divino fought against it. "*Não vou!*" "I'm not going."

"Por Que?" "Why not?"

"Não quero!" "I don't want to."

Sergio was more neutral. I had to practically force Divino to visit his mother now and then on Sundays. Although they often returned with plastic pistols and full of horror stories — real or from television — I find it important that they don't lose the relation to their parents and to the place and milieu in which they passed the first years of their lives. They should still respect and like their mother and they shouldn't consider themselves better than the other favela children just because they no longer have to live in the favela. At first neither Sergio nor Divino liked their mother. She was "nobody" for them. Once I played a finger game with Divino: each finger was someone from their family — Chide, Valdir, Andrew, Veranda, that is, all the brothers and sisters, then Ifigenia, the mother. He didn't say *Minha mãe* (my mother), but Ifigenia.

Gradually I noticed that they attained a normal relationship with their mother. They began to like going home: "*Hoje vamos na casa da nossa mae!*" "Today we're going to our mother's house." They now say Mae and also thinkãof her more often, as for example when Divino recently said that there is no toilet paper at home: *Na casa da nossa mãe não tem papel higienico, posso levar?"* (At home there is no toilet paper. Can I bring her some?")

I consider that positive. You can't simply deny their previous life but build on it and see how things can be improved for them. I can't say: You can't visit your mother anymore. You belong here now in order to start anew. In any case that could only be done superficially: new clothes, better manners, a bed for each child, etc. That's all important, but it's more important that they face and manage their own destiny. The memories of their first five or six years are a part of that destiny. Also that they were born in a favela. It's no good to try to erase all that. Perhaps it's important. Why is a child born in a favela and then has the chance to leave it? Only for himself?

September 1981

It was a beautiful day at the Ens' country house. The children, along with some volunteers, were invited. Swimming, sun, not thinking about problems — only peace with the children. They played very nicely and were, as Mrs. Ens said, unrecognizable. Such praise pleases me of course.

That afternoon, at home, I was preparing myself for a meeting of the Finance Commission (which supports anthroposophical institutions), where I was to describe the situation in the favela. Sergio was playing in the garden, Divino in the hall. He was playing "light", that is, he tied a string (representing an electric cable) to a ladder at one end and the doorknob at the other. The remains of an old flashlight dangled in the middle. About a month ago he had seen electricity being installed in the favela and had now invented his game. I was pleased at how creatively he now played.

Suddenly Sergio came storming in, yelled "*meu*" (it's mine), meaning the flashlight, and wanted to ruin the game.

"Sergio, let Divino play, he'll give you the flashlight back later." I tried to control him with a stern look, because I had no time for conversation. I had to fly to the bus in order to arrive in time at the Finance Commission.

"No, no, when you leave I'll break everything down, I'll break it all," he growled.

If I leave now it will take Dorle and João three hours to put the children to bed. After some useless talk, I put Sergio on my lap and rocked him, trying to calm him with the steady motion. He continued to scream. Amidst all this bustle and screaming, Divino came in, undisturbed by the racket. *"Tia, vem ver a luz do São Miguel Arcanjo!"* (Aunt, come and see St. Michael Archangel's light.) It was a candle that he had mounted on his electric cable.

Sergio screamed louder. *"Eu vou na rua, na avenida, para a casa da minha mae!"* (I'm going on the street, on the avenue, to my mother's house.)

"OK, let's go." He shouldn't have the feeling that I'm forcing him to stay. With some effort I put his shoes and a sweater on. I took his hand and we went down the hill to the bus station. I stopped there to wait for the bus. Sergio went on up the other side of the hill to the favela.

What should I do? Let him go? Oh God, this doubt whether what I'm doing is right, even when I see them thrive. What, for example, did Divino do before with his creativity at playing when he never played, only sat around and grumbled? Who answered Sergio's questions about God, angels, etc.? Where could they sit on someone's lap, like today on the bus as both sat on my lap and bombarded me with questions? And yet, is it right?

Sergio gradually disappeared up the steep hill. Damn the Finance Commission, I thought, I'll just be late. I went after Sergio. I caught up with him and took his hand in mine and together we continued up the hill. Then came the decision: either left down to the favela, he alone to his hut, or right and back to my house. I turned right and felt no resistance on my hand.

And then came redemption. Until that moment neither of us had said anything, and now suddenly we both saw a glorious sunset in the most beautiful colors and cloud formations.

Olha o céu, I said. Look at the sky.

Are the angels there?

Yes.

Do they like us?

Yes, very much.

And my guardian angel?

He is also there looking after you.

Look, it looks like the Archangel Michael's sword.

Yes, golden.

Is the sword made from Sunlight?

Yes.

Doesn't Saint Michael get burned by the sun?

No, he likes the sun, he lives there.

Yes, but he's also on the earth, isn't he?

Yes, he helps us to fight against the dragon. Against everything evil, when we lie or steal or fight.

And does he also help the other angels?

Yes, the smaller angels.

My guardian angel?

Yes, also your guardian angel.

The darkness seemed to have fallen away from him, forgotten. He was only light now. Calmly we went home. Uli drove me to the Finance Commission in the VW van. Late at night, at home, I wrote it all down, as an act of contrition toward Sergio for almost having given him up.

St. Michael's Day, September 29, 1981

Sergio rises with the sun, runs into the garden and calls to me, much impressed by something: *"Tia, olhe, o São Miguel está chegando na nuvem!"* (Look, St. Michael is coming from the clouds.)

I run out and he says: *"Olhe, a luz do sol!"* (Look at the sunlight!) The sunlight breaks through the dark clouds — like a dark curtain that opens and frees the light.

In the evening, after prayers, Sergio asks: *"O São Miguel Arcanjo da força para min, se eu peço a ele?"* (Does St Michael the Archangel give me strength if I ask him?)

"Dá, sim." (Yes, he does.)

"Ele da força para os anjos menores também?" (Does he also give the smaller angels strength?)

"Yes."

Then he fell asleep.

A Waldorf School teacher once said to me: The problems tend to be resolved around Michaelmas. Afterwards everything is easier. This year I thought of these words and hoped that Michaelmas would come soon. Everything seemed to move so slowly. Sergio and Divino were becoming difficult again, Cido seemed to have lost his enthusiasm, Zeca had his eternal personal problems to contend with, Dora and Bea had difficulties with their *noivos* (boyfriends) and I had the feeling: Oh God, when will someone fall from heaven to do all the things I can't do, but which are expected of me — a partner, a teacher, a person who knows how to deal with directors of multinational companies, aggressive "representatives", government officials. etc., as well as being a speaker for our cause and a pedagogical consultant. Where is the person who really knows how to do these things and doesn't simply do them as I do, because they must be done, although I don't know how. Then, unknown and humble, I could take over a class or group again and together with the children learn more about human nature in order to understand better what kind of education must be developed for the favela children.

On one hand all those admiring letters, admiring visitors, the popularity and fame; on the other hand a feeling of helplessness, a burden of failure and of having exceeded my own capabilities. Then come my doubts about Sergio and Divino. Should they go to the Adventist school, or to an SOS village, to F. in Germany, or should they stay with me. That would mean, though, that I would be bound to these two children for at least the next ten years, which could have a negative effect on my other work. Then F.K. came from Germany and wanted to adopt them. We were eating lunch and she said it suddenly. It was like a blow. I couldn't help thinking at that moment what was a pure stupidity: now that they are more or less mannerly and nice with their hard shells having been broken and their spiritually starved souls shining through, all as the result of a thoughtful and methodical educational process — now everyone thinks they're nice and wants to continue the process. Before they came to live with me, we looked for over a year for a place and found no one willing to take them. In any case, the problem now is: would it be right to send these children, who are old enough to remember their own family and country, to Europe?

Apparently it hasn't occurred to anyone that I haven't only "brought them up" but have also grown to love them and that it would hurt to be parted from them. But then I also recognize that I can't give them all of what they need, for example a father, a room of their own, the knowledge that I am there only for them day and night, etc.

St. Michael's day came. My group had prepared a play *"A Queda de Lucifer"* (The Fall of Lucifer) and we went to the Waldorf School to perform it for the third grade. Damião was *Deus Pai* (God the Father) Elias the Archangel

Michael, Paulo Lucifer and Sergio and Divino were two irresistible angels. Jura, Vania, Adailton and Chaga were the troop of angels. Paulo played his part uncannily well, fearfully, as he rose up from hell and called out to the class: *Um trono só para mim, quero um trono só para mim.* (I want a throne for me alone.) He shouted Lucifer's revolt against God with startling inner strength. That boy, who has practically nothing except a wooden hut with its earth floor and his grandmother, called out with an inner conviction that was fearful: "A throne for me!" And in an environment where all the other children look quite different than those from Monte Azul — white, many with eyeglasses, as one child noted, none with the sores of poverty. What will become of this savage strength if it turns to fury against the world's injustice?

After the performance the children played in the schoolyard, where they were accosted by an older boy who said that was no place for beggars and they should play somewhere else. At such moments it is clear to me how important it would be to cultivate relations with the Waldorf School, with the upper classes in general. They are full of prejudices; nothing will ever be improved in the social order until the people on both sides have learned to think, feel and act free of prejudice. This is also a question of education. The problem of favelas and of poverty in general must be resolved not only in the favelas, but also in the privileged classes, not only in the third world, but also in the so-called first world. Why do we have volunteers from Europe? Partly for this reason.

As we made our way back to the bus I was happy again. I felt free and unburdened, no longer so oppressed. I haven't thought it out rationally, but being constantly occupied with São Miguel Arcanjo and the weighing of good and evil for the past two weeks together with my group allowed this feeling of liberation to arise in me, of renewed confidence that despite my defects and lack of experience, help will come for Monte Azul that will give us inner strength. (Now as I type this for publication, I realize that it was just as well I didn't know then that the uncertainty would last two years. At that moment I felt myself to be on a hill, a month later back down in a valley, and it went up and down like that until 1983/84.)

November 1981

I feel that it's too much for me. It's terrible when they all stare at me and expect a solution to some problem and I don't have a clue; especially since because of my book* people think I'm some kind of hero. But I'm not and I disappoint them and destroy their idea that a style of life exists which is exemplary or meaningful. For example, someone wrote that they wanted to see what the person who does such things looks like. How awful. I hoped to God the letter-writer would never come here! But one day there she was standing at my door. I'd just come from class, dragging Divino, Sergio and Cesar behind me. There were other children visiting: Reinaldo, Mauricio, Antonio, Feliciano. I had to wash the dishes first and she, Gisela, waited expectantly. Divino and Sergio were building a circus with meter-long cords and colored cloth. "Look, Ute!" They constantly wanted to show what they had invented. I went and admired their circus tent. Meanwhile Gisela wanted to know how I came to be doing this kind of work. I said a few sentences and the telephone rang. After that I said a few clarifying words about our work. In reality I wasn't at all in the mood to talk, but then I thought that she might be disappointed and I was dampening her enthusiasm or taking away her belief that it's possible to do something without always thinking about yourself and material gain. In between I had to smooth over an argument between Sergio and Divino. With one ear I was outside where the other children were playing and I was thinking about what had to be done this afternoon. Someone clapped at the front door. The Indio had come and wanted to sell his hut.

I knew that Gisela would like to talk to me more, but how could I with all that activity going on around me? Is she disappointed to learn how the person who she saw as an example in the book is in real life? I don't know. I can't change anything and I feel incapable of explaining to an outsider how it is to be pushed and pulled by a thousand people, all of whom want something from you. Perhaps she had the impression that this Ute is somewhat nervous and taciturn. There was also nothing to eat and the floor hadn't been swept.

The same feeling that I cannot fulfill expectations is present everywhere, in meetings or with the children who live with me. I would like to dedicate more time to them, also consider what can be done to help with each one's problems, be closer to them, but there is too little time. And the correspondence: often letters come with interesting questions about the meaning of development work or the meaning of life itself. I answer them all, but there is too little time to go deeply into the problems. It's always the same — doing half the job and a guilty conscience about it not being done right because it's only half done. On the other hand, I don't know what I can drop. In any case I don't want to be only an administrator. The children, the people, should always be in the center and in direct contact, in doing.

Signs of progress

June 1981: Divino is learning to button his clothes. With perseverance and cries of "Look, Ute," he buttons his pajamas.

July 1981: I hear Divino and Sergio sing for the first time. Divino hops around while singing. It seems as though he breathes more freely, that the pressure on him has lessened.

July 1981: Sergio and Divino squat on the carpet in the living-room and paint. Sergio says this about Divino: "He used to be lazy in kindergarten. He didn't want to paint at all. Like he only wanted to eat. Now he plays, the laziness is over." The observation was correct. It is true that Divino didn't participate in things in kindergarten — except eating. Now, since he has lived with me and feels good, he plays intensively and is always occupied. The conversation continued: "Does the guardian angel help to find children who are lost?" "Yes, he helped find Divino."

At the beginning of the year Divino was kidnapped. He disappeared for three days, we looked all over for him, reported him missing to the police. Finally Conceição found him in desolate circumstances with some woman. Divino never spoke about those days. His mother bawled him out when he was brought home. He didn't speak for days. I visited him the next day in his hut and took him on my lap. He sat there like a block of wood, unmoving and staring straight ahead. I could have cried. What can you do with such a child? Sergio was jumping on the bed. The mother said we should find a home for them both. Yes, but where? For months we'd been trying all the homes. At that moment I was prepared to take them home with me, although I knew that it wouldn't be ideal for them or for me. I didn't say anything though, because I wanted to talk it over with the other escolinha workers. It was brought up at the next meeting and practically everyone was against it, saying it would be too much work. I knew they were right. So we inquired at another home, but inwardly I had already decided to take them in. One day Sergio decided that he wanted to live with me and the problem was solved.

Sergio remembers the moment Divino was found: "His clothes were ripped to shreds." I venture a question: "Did you have anything to eat in that woman's house?" Divino says nothing, only shakes his head.

August 1981: For the first time Sergio said grace. Divino, who always just sat there looking dumb, without folding his hands, said it two days later. Now, a year later, he reminds me to say grace if I forget: *"E rezar, tia?"*

18 Aug. 1981: Divino lit a candle this morning and placed a piece of bread at its base. *Para Deus. Vou rezar para Deus e o pão.* (I will pray for God and for the bread), he says. At midday he plucked some beans from the garden and placed them, together with stones and flowers, on the windowsill.

D: *Vou rezar para Deus.* (I will pray for God.)

S: *Vou rezar para meu anjo de guarda.* (I'll pray for my guardian angel.)

Later they looked for beetles and grasshoppers in the garden. "What does God say when a grasshopper sits on his shoulder"?

Sometimes such concrete questions are too much for me!

October 1981: As usual, the mailman brings a pile of mail from Germany. Sergio says: "The mailman is good".

And Divino: "The mailman is a man of love".

The environment is no longer the enemy. Their feeling for other people has changed.

June 1982: We were eating supper: Cesar, Sergio, Divino and I. There was salad, eggs and wheat grains. Cesar asked:

C: How do eggs grow?

U: They grow in a hen.

C: But how do they grow inside?

U: God made hens so that eggs can grow inside them.

C: Oh yes, just as God made women so babies can grow in them.

D: Is there a baby in my stomach?

C: No, only in women.

U: But the man must help or it can't be born.

S: And how does the child come out of the stomach?

D: You have to cut the stomach open.

U: No, it opens and the mother does a kind of gymnastics and the baby too, and then the head comes out. Then the child looks around and is happy and wants to come out completely.

S: Is it always happy?

U: No, not always.

S: Do they have to operate to take it out?

U: Yes, sometimes, but mostly it's happy and comes out alone.

S: Maybe it sees a little duck and is happy and comes out and then squeezes back into the mother.

C: No, that doesn't work.

U: But it wants to go into a warm crib so it can be as warm as in its mother's stomach.

D: Why don't you have a child?

U: Because I'm not married.

D: Why don't you get married?

U: Would you like me to get married?

D: Yes!

U: To whom?

All: T.

D: And then you'll have a child and we'll have to buy toys for it.

S: We already have toys, we'll give them to him.

C: And it will sleep in our room so we can play with it. There's plenty of room. (by Brazilian standards.)

S: No, in your room. It's quieter there.

C: If it's twins, one can sleep in your room and one in ours.

S: That would be a lot of work though.

Someone changed the subject, but we soon returned to a similar theme.

S: When I die I'll go to heaven, stay there a while, then come back, *não, tia?* isn't that right?

U: Yes.

C: My little brother is already in heaven, an angel, I have an angel for a brother.

D: Me too. Two.

U: Who?

D: My father and my grandfather, two angels.

S: Will I be born in Minas?

U: No, I don't think so, perhaps in Germany.

S: Wow!

C: And did I ever live before?

U: Yes.

C: Was I white?

U: Yes, probably.

D: Me too?

U: Maybe you were black.

Sergio laughs stupidly.

U: Why? Black is beautiful, there's nothing to laugh about.

C: looks at his hands and says: Yes, I'm brown and my fingernails are so white they shine (as an exception). But why don't I remember that I was born before.

U: One doesn't remember that.

S: I do! (Naturally he can't admit that there's something he doesn't know.)

Did you also live before?

U: Yes, we all lived before, somewhere else, and now we're all here together.

They brushed their teeth and we went through the usual evening ritual. Then Divino said: "Let's light the candle in the living room tonight and sing for Mary and Joseph".

U: Fine.

The three of them prepared everything in front of the fireplace: a little Bethlehem with candles, flowers and a little house made of clay and silver paper.

S: Mary comes from this side and sees the flowers first. And the star is over the little house.

D: But she sees my flowers too.

Divino had laid some stones in water and now he comes reverentially and says: "Look how they shine, tia. They shine now more than before".

I told them a story and then we sang Christmas carols. They had been singing these songs all afternoon and playing at Christmas. They decorated a branch for Christmas. I said, "But it's St. John's now," so they played outside.

Sergio lay in the wheelbarrow as the Christ-child, wrapped in batik veils, with flowers, leaves and grass all around him. Cesar and Divino were the angels, trailing long veils in the wind. They flew to the Christ-child and sang Christmas carols, Divino gently, but Cesar at the top of his lungs, almost exploding with joy (at a cost to musical quality). Divino cried: "The wind, the wind, it's stronger than the veils!"

I don't know how often I had to get up, called by them, in order to admire their Bethlehem crib. It was really funny to see Sergio, not especially clean, lying in the wheelbarrow with angels flying around him. But for the children it was serious.

As they were playing, I was reading a book about Punks. Lonely, alienated; the future: a black hole without content, uncertainty, fear. Probably those children lacked what Sergio, Divino and Cesar have: the certainty that something spiritual exists.

1983

Dear Dorle,

I have been waiting many days for the letter you said on the phone you would write. I hope you haven't thrown it in the waste-paper basket. You couldn't guess where I am: at the sitio Ens, absolutely alone on vacation for ten days — finally. The children are at Campos de Jordão in Zimpel's vacation colony. I'm sitting here on the veranda, the palm trees, roses and azaleas before me and above me the bluest sky imaginable — so near the megapolis São Paulo that it seems a miracle. I'm surrounded by 50 kilos of Steiner books, diary notes, writing paper, watercolors and in the kitchen there is something to eat.

Apropos children: I had to take Sergio out of the Waldorf School and put him in another school. It made my heart bleed, but better any school than none at all. He hardly went though, first because it rained uninterruptedly for three weeks and the whole favela was swimming in mud. Later because he probably realized that it's no easy life there and that you can't even turn around during class, let alone make trouble. He went to live at home in the favela. I visited him now and then, but it was awful to see him there sitting before the TV with his tin plate of rice and beans on his lap. He knew exactly what I thought of that, but I wanted to leave him free and not give the impression that I wanted to bring him back, because he would only become more stubborn; he didn't even want to go to Renate's for an afternoon. God knows what he wanted, I simply couldn't understand what was happening to him. I could imagine that he wanted the unlimited freedom of the favela, the complete absence of demands on him, the bumming around in the market and on the streets (he was seen begging) and in the bars. Perhaps he just didn't want to go anymore to the fine Waldorf School where he immediately realized that they are all well-to-do there and belong to another class. But all these reasons, assuming that they existed, are superficial. I have the impression that Sergio is either an angel or a devil. In theater, when he plays the king or an archangel, he glows, and often also in daily life he glows; not, as is often said, with joy, but more profoundly glowing, and it is almost evident that a spiritual being is incarnated in him. Don't think I'm crazy, but I have this impression often. And then there are moments when it seems he is possessed by the devil, when he flies suddenly into such a fit of wrath for no reason at all and screams and kicks.

Once during such a fit I slapped him and he seemed to come to his senses, came exhausted to me and fell asleep on my lap. These battles for his soul rage in his small body and he doesn't know how to overcome them. That's why the St. Michael stories and all the other stories that show how human weakness are overcome through the spirit are so good for him.

During the first months of 1983 Sergio, and Divino by imitation, showed a strong tendency to return to the favela. He wanted to go home to his mother on Sundays, sometimes Saturdays as well, which was a complete change. My mood regarding him was one of disappointment, because I had never thought that he would have difficulty in the Waldorf School. I thought he would learn to read and write easily and adapt relatively easily. Although I never stopped loving him, my disappointment conveyed itself to him. He started saying, when he didn't like something: *Então vou na casa da minha mae.* Then I'll go to my mother's house. Probably he also knew that that wounded me. However, these were only temporary explosions and things went back to normal.

Often he came home late at night filthy dirty and the next morning I had to put him under the shower and scrub him before sending him to the Waldorf School. Every time it happened I told him it wouldn't do, and I spoke to his mother. There was always a great hue and cry, but it didn't help.

Finally, when he came home so late again, I told him it couldn't go on and he turned around and left. It happened in such calm that Chistoph, with whom I had been talking, probably didn't even notice anything. Divino began to scream heartbreakingly for Sergio, so I let him run after him.

So they were gone. *Acabou,* finished. They were here exactly two years, then they vanished without ceremony. I saw them running around in the favela covered with mud. Divino continued going to the escolinha wearing ripped clothing, or clothes too big for him, as he did before he lived with me. When he saw me he looked at me sadly but didn't say a word.

After three weeks, when I had already brought their toys and clothes to the escolinha and was wondering what I would do with this suddenly over-large house, Divino came back with his plastic bag of clothes. It was surely the first independent, Sergio-free decision of his life. I was relieved that at least one of them wouldn't have to live in that total chaos and I admired Divino's act of independence. Then life went on normally, as though nothing had happened. Divino played alone, built his *casinha,* little house, without difficulty and didn't want to go home to his mother Sundays. At night he went to bed and I told him a story, but he woke during the night and crept into my bed. He was very tender during this period.

We visited Sergio now and then in the favela. Wild horses couldn't drag him back to the Waldorf School. Taking him out and placing him in the other school was pure torture and I felt truly sorry that he was ruining his future for unknown, unintelligible reasons, and that he seemed to have no desire for the things he had before. I don't mean the material things, for in that respect the difference between the favela and me isn't that great. They have things in the favela that I don't have — television, candy and scraps of meat, for example. But what about the other things like storytelling, excursions, creative games, the answers to a thousand questions about the world and the heavens. My guilty conscience that I couldn't give the children enough of what they needed because of lack of time became unbearable.

I thought about him every night, not in the sense of "I hope you come back", but I imagined him as he was, from head to foot, what his feet are like, his hands, his head, his eyes, his expression, his gestures — and the atmosphere in which he now lives: the favela. his hut, the bed — the only one in the hut — on which he sits and watches TV.

When we had our São João celebration, Sergio came. His large eyes stared out of the unkempt, wild hair and the filthy body. When G. said he looked so depraved, my heart broke again. Julia, who stayed with me after the festivities, brought him with her. During the night I heard someone cough and thought, that sounds like Sergio. When I woke up in the morning it was really him. "*Agora vou ficar de nove.*" Now I'll stay here again. With that everything was settled for him. I only said, *"Mas aqui voce tem que ir pra escola."* But here you must go to school. In the beginning he was terribly "uncivilized" and very rude to Divino and the other children. As much as I was happy that he had found his way back, the first days were terrible. I had to practically start from scratch.

Once he had such a fight with Cesar that there were pools of blood in the children's room, the bathroom and the kitchen from bleeding noses.

Sergio went, reluctantly, to school, and things went back to normal. But I still felt that I had failed and that no one liked the children except me. They all nagged and complained (with justification, of course). I would have liked to take them to the mato (jungle) and rear them alone, without them having contact with other adults. Of course that was stupid, an escape. But that was my mood — close the door, only the children and me, then I would succeed with them. But, illogically, I didn't really trust myself to educate them or any other children and felt it would be better to find a good children's home for them. That's how the endless thinking began about whether they should stay here or not, go to the Demetria farm, or to Belo Horizonte, or somewhere else. There was also the shame that they had run away and I thought about what the others must think, that I mishandle the children or don't pay any attention to them, give them something to eat and throw them in bed and that's it. The "others" became ever more important to me, what they thought about the children, what they said and gossiped about them.

One day the explosion came. B. had been invited for supper, the children were playing with their hens outside and came by every now and then to tell about their experiences.

We're going to eat now, I saidã

Just once more.

All right.

A half-hour went by and they hadn't come. I became nervous because I knew what would happen — they would come too late, I must admonish them, they say: *Então vou na casa da minha mãe.* Then I'll go to my mother. B. would hear it all, especially the last part and I was ashamed already in advance. Then I went looking for them, didn't find them. Finally I looked for them with the car and found them. I approached them and they came calmly with their hens in a *carrinho de feira* (shopping cart). When Sergio actually said: *Então vou na casa da minha mãe,* I slapped him one.

B. left, the children went to bed without a sound. I had never felt so ashamed as at that moment. In front of B., in front of the children, in front of myself. I didn't want to have anything more to do with children, or with social work, because I simply didn't consider myself capable of it. Why am I writing this in such detail? I think I had touched bottom. The last two years had been mentally disastrous. I was definitely fed up. If there had been some reasonable way to disappear from Monte Azul, I would have done it.

The next day we began our long-planned trip to Novo Friburgo and Juiz de Fora, with Wagner, Divino, Sergio, Cesar, Vilmar and Maristela, in order to find a home there for the children. It was the merriest trip I ever took with the children. They went from one enthusiasm to the next — the bus ride to Rio, the early morning sea, the Pão de Açucar (Sugarloaf) and the cable car, the airport on the sea, the long bridge to Niteroi, the mountains, Novo Friburgo and Luis, who received the children so nicely, Dr. Wesley's apartment in Juiz de Fora. It was all experience, even the throwing up on the curvy mountain road was triumphantly celebrated. We couldn't stop laughing. I saw how fit, how fit for life these children are, probably more so than other, better brought up children. Everyone who saw us smiled, was happy and helped us. That trip cured us. I learned not to be affected by the opinions of others, who can only judge things from outside. I could accept the children again as they are and as they inwardly want to be and not as others want them to be. I had the same relationship to them as when they first came to me.

Sergio has been gentle since then and continuously wants to do something nice for me, a *surpresa* (surprise). I feel again the unity between the two of them and with me.

When I think back on this year, I know that I have learnt something essential (which is why I am writing this in detail): that the thoughts one has about children have just as much influence on them as what one does outwardly with them, what one says to them, plays with them, what one gives them to eat, etc. Even if you don't express your mood and thoughts, they have their effect. It is especially noticeable in Sergio's case. When I was sad about him, or, rather, disappointed, he became distant from me and with what tied him to me, the Waldorf School, for example, and returned to the favela surroundings. Of course other things also played a part, such as what the teachers, children and parents in the Waldorf School thought about him. Then there was the lure of the unrestricted freedom in the favela, without pressure or duties. But the essential things were the thoughts surrounding him.

During the time he was in the favela, about two months, I never outwardly tried to bring him back, but I thought about him every night in a liberating way. Probably he returned because I was inwardly with him. After the explosion and the trip, the outside pressure is gone and I am completely with the children again, and it is noticeable in everything. He never again said in anger that he would go back to his mother; he goes to the favela on Sundays, but returns early and is really very nice now.

March 25, 1983

Today, Sunday, the children returned from their mother's. The first thing they said was: *Mataram uma bicha.* A bicha was killed. (bicha = homosexual, bicho = animal).

I thought I hadn't heard right, that perhaps a dog or a cat had been killed. No, it was a "bicha" who went around dressed in women's clothes. Chilling, it was like in the Old Testament.

Such a person doesn't fit in, debilitates men's self-importance, so get rid of him. I don't know exactly what happened, but it's obvious how far we are from a Christian ethic that doesn't throw the first stone, but understands and forgives, accepts the other without discriminating on all levels. The favelados are discriminated against, pushed to the periphery of society, but they do the same to others, the homosexuals, for example, or the "fallen" women. At our last meeting of fifty people who do social work we considered the direction in which we want to work. What are the first steps in the direction of a new society? Gradually, during the course of the discussion, we came to the conclusion that we must start with ourselves and not get involved in attempts to overthrow the old order. Today's event provided a good example. What good would it do to make rulers of the poor when they haven't learned to rid themselves of feelings of separation, discrimination and revenge.

I felt sorry for the children. They must watch terrible things. The dead man was naked, probably they tore off his clothes. And what they had to listen to. All three were afraid and slept together in one bed. After the story I said we could say an Our Father for the dead man. As I closed the door I saw Divino take the picture of Mary and Jesus and hang it over the bed. That's for the dead man, Cesar said.

They are continuously going back and forth between horror and the sublime.

September 1984

Sergio disappeared again. Overnight, so to speak. He went home to his mother on Sunday, the last day of vacation. I had to almost force him to do it, because he hadn't been there during the whole vacation period. He didn't come back on Monday, probably because it was the first day of school.

Since then I have only seen him only once, on the avenue pushing a huge cart full of scrap iron. Meanwhile he has also given that up, which was at least a useful activity. After the effort of collecting and pushing, they get some money from the scrap dealer. Now I hear from everyone that they've seen him in the most God-forsaken state begging at traffic lights or in restaurants. His mother and Divino tell me that he leaves early in the morning and comes home after midnight, traveling alone in the bus. Divino told me today that some other street children stole some candy for him and the police shot at them as they ran away.

"I bet they were mad, right"?

"Yeah, people are always mad when someone steals".

"Ali's father has a revolver to kill thieves".

"I prefer to pray than to have a revolver".

That's the kind of conversation that goes on at breakfast. Right after that Divino bowed over the beans he had planted and said: *O sol e a força da terra que ajudam nascer, ne tia?* The sun gives the earth strength to help them grow, right?

You could see in his face how his soul was enlivened by those thoughts of sun and earth forces which allow the plants to grow. But he and Sergio and the other children who grow up in the favela are also exposed to terrible brutality. "Katja", the homosexual who was dismembered before their eyes; the police who torture; automobile accidents; the "Alemão", who they poured a can of gasoline over and burned to death as the thief Vicente's act of revenge; the daily radio and TV reports about murders in the night with all the sordid details. It all pours into their souls and destroys, destroys. The outward destruction of nature, the erosion of the Amazon, the air, the climate, the city — it all goes farther: the destruction of the family by the illusions of television, the working mothers, etc. It bores down into the soul.

Is it all then of no use?

What can be done against it? The small light of Monte Azul or, in the case of Divino and the children in the escolinha: the constructive strength of growing, the experience of courage and the overcoming of fear in the Archangel Michael stories. The experience of growing, self-development and transformation in many fairy tales and the certainty of something spiritual hidden behind animal nature; as in tales like Snow White and Rose Red. But that all seems to be so little compared to the overwhelming destructive fury of the inhuman.

Sergio seems to me to be a battleground between these two forces. I have never seen a child who so strongly embodies the "holy" and the "chaotic". Almost in the same moment that he places a banana and a drawing on the windowsill for St. Nicholas or the Archangel Michael and has no doubt that they will take these gifts, he can be possessed by a passionate fit of anger and begin to beat Divino mercilessly. Sometimes he completely loses control for a half-hour and kicks and swings at everything within reach like a raving madman and you can only subdue him with great effort. On a larger scale, he seems to be seized every year and then he must disappear into the favela or, like now, onto the streets. He curses, fights, begs, runs around with stinking pants and a black crust of filth on his skin, with feverish eyes, barefoot — it's all the same to him. Not even his sponsor's visit from Germany, who brought him a watch, affected him, no excursion, nothing. He appears to want to destroy himself with all his strength.

And I must watch and can do nothing, expect inwardly not let him fall.

October 1984

Sergio just returned from his two-month escapade, together with Claudemir. He acted as though nothing had happened, just looked at me with his big brown eyes. Lauro pleaded for him, saying he is ashamed to say so, but he wants to live here again. I didn't send him away, I said. Then came an avalanche of good advice from Lauro and João as to how he should behave in the future. João said he should talk to his mother about it. He went to the favela to get her, but now, three hours later, she still hasn't appeared.

They played, showered and had dinner. Then the news was exchanged. João and Divino told about the theater play, the excursion to the Chácara and the kittens that were born. Sergio told us about an automobile accident in which a car went up in flames and another accident in which a man was killed when he swerved to avoid hitting a child: "He lost his life to save the child." We played at hiding, I told the story of the Golden Youth and they went to sleep.

To the embarrassing question if Sergio would go to school in the morning, he answered that he had no school material.

It really puzzles me. What does he find in that life, begging, freezing, filthy? Adventure, danger, lack of control? But then how can he listen to a story with such intensity and also believe in its contents? There doesn't seem to be any contradiction as far as he's concerned, they're just parts of his life. On one hand the hard reality of the city and its streets, the favela, muggings, accidents, dying people; and on the other hand a story like the Golden Youth, who during a part of his life wears a bearskin, only to put it aside later. If it could only be the same with him, that finally the "golden" part would win out. I have no doubt now that he will have to go through everything that the city and the civilization of the end of the twentieth century have to offer. He will try everything: drugs, stealing, etc. But when he has come through it, then perhaps it will have been worth the effort and he may be able to really do something in his life for the favela, which is something I have always sensed.

One day Jos and Candido came to the escolinha and asked if we had room for this boy — he pointed to a blonde boy about twelve years of age. His name was André, he had no home and Jos had taken him in for a few days, but he had nothing for his own family and it was very difficult. It's true that his is one of the poorest families in the favela. He has eight children and can't work because he has leprosy. He occupies himself cutting wood and such things, but because of his deadened nerves he is always cutting himself. His wife works but is often unemployed and comes to the escolinha kitchen to wash vegetables in order to take a basket of food home. What a place for this homeless boy to be taken in. It is strange how the greatest misery seeks out the greatest misery. I didn't know what to do. I gave them some food and said I would think about it. That night I went to Argentina for a congress and forgot about the boy. Ten days later he stood before my door, dragged in by Divino and Sergio.

"Here's someone who could live with us," Sergio said enthusiastically (I less so).

"Where did you come from?" I asked André.

He told his story: He had no father and his mother died. He had a twin brother and he lived in Diadema at the other end of the city. Now he lived wherever he could, being careful that they don't put him in the state orphanage.

The children showered, we ate dinner, I told them a story and they went to sleep. He liked that of course. I didn't know what to do with him, telephoned all the children's homes, but nobody wanted him. Divino was very jealous and the wrangling was continuous. André didn't know how to play and only bothered Divino's playing. But could I simply put him out on the street in this gigantic city? One day I came home and André was already in the kitchen cooking.

How did you get in?

He beat around the bush and after a long interrogation I found out that he had broken the lock with a chisel and hammer. That was very clever, but you could see that he had already learned something, unfortunately.

I couldn't get anything done because of the endless fighting. One day he didn't come home. He disappeared without a trace. As I didn't know his last name I couldn't inquire with the police or the youth magistrate whether he had landed there.

A month later Sergio said: there's a boy outside crying. It was already dark.

Bring him in.

Can he stay with us?

Sergio is always happy to have children live with us.

The boy was about seven years old and sobbed constantly. He said that he had waited all day for his mother. She went looking for work because she had lost her previous job and there was nothing to eat at home and there was a baby there which he always minded. Now he was looking for his mother because she hadn't returned. He lived quite far away, had ridden the bus, then here.

I gave him something to eat and something to take with him and said: "Go right home, or you mother will be looking for you. If you don't find your house, you can come back here".

He didn't return. I hope he found his mother.

What becomes of such children when they no longer have homes? They beg, stand at traffic lights selling crackers, flowers or chewing gum, get together with other boys and wash cars outside fine restaurants, shine shoes in the city center (though the sneakers fad has seriously affected the profitability of this occupation). Then they begin to steal. When they are a little older they come into contact with drug dealers who use them. Somehow they get a revolver and hold people up, even kill.

Dio, a woman from the favela, wrote a poem about such a child:

Poesia do menino pobre

Aquele menino pobre
que nasceu só pro sofrer
pelas ruas da cidade
mendigando quer comer.

Quando volvata para casa
algum dinheiro trazia
entregava sua mae,
a velhinha serria.

Mas um dia mendigando
pela ruta ele encontou
vinha vindo bilheteiro
o bihete ele avistou.

Foi tão grande insistencia
que o bilhete ele comprou
no caminho de sua casa
um caminhão o matou.

Quando a mae soube do fato
como louca ela gritava-
como é vou fazer
meu filihno que me tratava!

Um bilhete de loteria
no seu bolso foi achado,
quando forom conferir
tinha sido premiado.

Aquele meninho pobre
que tirou a grande sorte
amparou sua maezinha
na vida e também na morte.

Poem for a Poor Boy

That poor boy
born only to suffer,
on the city's streets
went begging for food.

When he returned home
he brought some money,
gave it to his mother,
and the old girl smiled.

One day when begging
on the city's streets
a lottery vender came
and offered him a ticket.

So much did he insist
that the boy bought a chance.
On the way to his home
a truck ran him over.

When his mother found out
she almost went mad —
What am I to do,
My son gave me so much.

A lottery ticket was found
in the poor boy's pocket,
When the drawing came
its number was a winner.

That poor boy who won
the final grand prize
helped his old mother
in life and also in death.

November 1984

It's fun to be with Divino, he is blooming and I have the feeling that the ground has been well prepared in kindergarten and pre-school; he has become inwardly mature and everything he has in him is coming out. He is much calmer than before, suddenly paints objectively — a giant step forward. He is continually asking and thinking and the kingdom of numbers has opened itself to him. He is funny, full of humor and enthusiasm. His favorite word is éba (wow!)

Sergio has it harder. He is serious even when he laughs; his mouth seems to have difficulty forming a smile as though it were mixed with shame. He never lives in peace with his environment and with himself. A main problem is school. He knows that he should have learned to write long ago, but can't admit that he has bungled it. He wants to be always playing but also realizes that he is "unoccupied", not sufficiently challenged.

Should we start our own first grade for these children? Wagner, Antonio Neres, Alexandre Fidalgo, Vav, Reinaldo, Elsa, Jovelina, Edson, Lucia, Eliane, Isabel, Marcia? If we could make an agreement with the Secretary of Education that the first grade would be taught in the favela? A kind of experimental class.

Christmas Play in the Waldorf School, São Paulo, December 1984

Vinicio, Gorete, Divino, Sergio, Carlinho, Lauro, Valtair Vanderley, Iz,, Cristina, Andreia, Donato, Paulo, Edvaldo, Pedro — we all left from my house to the bus around 7 o'clock in the evening, relatively well scrubbed in order not to stand out too much before the parents and children in the Waldorf School. As we were waiting at the bus-stop it began to rain and our "dressing up" was washed out. A few of the children were splashed by passing cars, their neatly combed hair became unruly again and their shoes muddy. But it didn't make any difference. We were all excited about seeing the Oberufer Christmas play. Some remembered the previous year and wondered if the devil would appear again in the Paradise play and if anyone would have the nerve to grab him by the tail.

The bus finally came and we squeezed in, most of the children crawling under the crossbar without paying. 15 minutes bus ride, then a 15-minute walk. I had to carry Andreia because she walks too slowly. Our entrance into the theater caused a stir, but a well-intentioned one. We sat closely packed in the first row and waited.

This play is especially appropriate for the children. The shepherds, like the favela people, are happy, easily irritated, scuffle and romp, feel strong. And the children — what destinies! Gorete, who suffered many months with severe burns; Lauro with infantile paralysis; Carlinho, shuffled back and forth between father, mother and grandparents; Iz, who often earns his money by stealing; Sergio and Divino, and then Vinicio. He is the loneliest eight-year-old I have ever seen. He is often seen on the street completely alone, uncertain, for where should he go? That in itself means something, for in Brazil one is seldom alone.

Vinicio sat next to me, now and then put his arm gently around me. Then he lay his head on my shoulder and watched the Paradise play from that position. His frizzy hair, his fine, sensitive features, his slight body, and his gaze, which is more than sad: resigned, of something broken within him. Last year he still reacted strongly against being thrown back and forth between his mother and grandmother. He bellowed, stamped his feet, screamed once for a half-hour uninterruptedly. But now he is apathetic. In an indifferent voice he relates horrors: he smoked marijuana, slept on the street alone, the police arrested him ... And then, as with hope, he puts his arm around me again. If only we could find a home for him. (Shortly thereafter he spent his vacation at the chácara and will be able to stay there with R.)

Meanwhile the devil appeared, Sergio and Donato grabbed his tail, a bit too hard, so that he snorted back at them, whereby the smaller children landed on my lap from fear. After that I had to stop them from taking the apple which Adam threw away in disgust (to eat!). At the birth they were all absorbed and very enthusiastic with the shepherd scene, especially when they threw cookies to the audience ... On the way home each one told how many he had grabbed.

March 1985

The worst thing that can befall an educator of so-called difficult children is when people one values say: this is a hopeless case. Then the hard-earned flame of hope is extinguished and the conviction takes its place that the challenge such a child presents to the educator will not be overcome and that it will all have no meaning for the child's life or for one's own. Faith in the child and in one's self fall apart with such a statement. To overcome it requires a long inner battle of reconstruction. When Sergio escaped from the home at Nova Friburgo, was alone for two days without a penny and traveled in buses as a stowaway and finally appeared here, I heard such statements. Two months later, when he began begging on the streets in order to make some money for his mother and himself, I thought again: it's all for nothing. And even now as I am writing this, I was interrupted by an irate woman who came to complain that Lauro, Sergio and Edson threw stones at her porch.

But hopeless? That they have an uncontrollable, exaggerated will to freedom! That Sergio doesn't integrate into the community, that he picks on other children, that he ruins group work, is all true. But where it will all lead in five, ten years, to the end of his life, that nobody knows. It would be presumptuous now, after ten years of life, to judge the outcome. If he could, as an adult, control the chaotic strength in him, then something could be made of his life. His life, which was born of the favela, his way to me as his own decision when he was only six, but never completely renouncing the favela. It has become clear to me that all this seems hopeless only when one has not recognized his real self, the second I.

> "Picture-like, essence-like, as though it seeks to reveal itself as an individual being, a second self arises from the soul's chaos, and takes its place as a matter of course over the being that one previously considered to be one's self. It takes the role of that self's inspiration. The person flows as this latter self together with the inspiring, superior one ... Only this inspiration is not one of thoughts or interior speech; it works through deeds, processes, happenings. The other self is the one that leads the soul to the particulars of its life's destiny and calls forth its capacities, inclinations and talents". (R. Steiner, *The Gates of the Spiritual World*)

The fact that Sergio was so decisive in saying: I will live with Ute — shows that it was such a step, inspired by his other self. It was, if I may say so without arrogance, a step against the complete hardening of his being through the favela. More accurately, it was his second independent step, the first being his entrance in the kindergarten at four years of age. It is always easier to recognize such other self acts in retrospect, and to differentiate between the acts of his "eternal being" and those of his lower self. But in the present it is despairingly difficult. Why, for example, did he run away from the Nova Friburgo home after only two weeks? Was it an act of his higher self: "I don't want to grow up in a bourgeois home with maids and fine food, but near the favela where people suffer and are degraded, where my place is? Or was it simply laziness and lack of desire to integrate. Here opinions differ. Whoever sees only the lower self, or only one self on the whole, will see him as a hopeless case. But in recognizing a higher self, you can see this as a stage in his development. Whether he develops positively or negatively in life will only be known later.

When Sergio gives my desk a furious shove and all the drawers fall out, I am inclined to agree with the "hopeless case" theory. But when I see him give away all his Easter eggs to the children in the Chácara in order to make them happy, I sense what is in him. Yesterday I told the Easter story and he said: "If

I had lived then I would have taken the nails out of Jesus' hands and hidden them from the soldiers."

The conversation went on:

S. And Judas, do you feel sorry for Judas?

U. Yes, he wasn't bad, only weak.

S. Me too, I feel sorry for him.

D. Has Judas returned to the earth?

U. Yes, probably.

D. And does he still betray Jesus?

U. No, I don't think so. He even regretted it then. He wouldn't want to do it again.

The children can be merciful and aggressive at the same time. When you look at Sergio's drawings, you can see the struggle going on in his soul. He never draws concrete, earthly things, almost always inward pictures: the world from the perspective of heaven, with strong strokes and full of color; above arches the sky, either adorned with huge stars or with St. Michael doing battle with the dragon. Sometimes St. Michael has two swords, one in each hand, as though one sword is not enough to fight against all the evil. The struggle between good and evil is omnipresent.

Poem

Your children are not your children.

They are the sons and daughters of life's desire for itself.

They come through you, but they are not from you.

And although they live with you, they don't belong to you.

You can give them your love, but not your thoughts, for they have their own thoughts.

You can shelter their bodies, but not their souls,

for their souls live in the house of tomorrow, which you cannot visit, not even in dreams.

You can try to be like them,

but don't try to make them be like you.

For life does not go backwards and is not detained in the past.

We crowded around a large bowl in which two fish were swimming among stones and flowers, which the children obtained for them as accommodations. One fish died.

The other is suffering, right?

I thought so. Divino thought that the surviving fish was sad about the death of the other. A few hours passed. We had built a fire in order to roast some meat on bamboo sticks. A splinter fell into the fishbowl and the little fish seemed to be wounded, didn't move, seemed dead.

Divino: *Não adianta mesmo.* It doesn't make any difference.

Ute: What?

Divino: *Ele vai sofrer do mesmo jeito.* He would have suffered anyway.

Ute: But he wants to live anyway. When your grandfather died you were sad, but you want to live anyway.

His comment shocked me. It wasn't at all childish. When you die, at least you no longer have to suffer, was the intuition that seemed to underlie it. But this from the mouth of an eight-year-old. Live is suffering in any case. Suffering, illness, death, pain are deeply ingrained in these children's lives. In his eight years Divino has seen more death that I have in 47.

And when it isn't suffering in its purest form, it's the battle for survival. Another conversation:

-*Minha mãe vai arrumar serviço para min.* My mother will look for a job for me.

-*Onde?* Where?

-*Vou trablhar no supermercardo. Vou poras compras no carinho.* I will work in the supermarket. I will put the goods in the shopping carts.

This is of course pure illusion, for those jobs are reserved for boys twelve and over and are very coveted. But what he does do and his mother approves, is beg at traffic lights, as well as in restaurants. If it were really necessary one could understand it. But it isn't necessary and she is ruining her children's future through short-sightedness.

Sergio and Divino's story could be understood as one without a happy ending. But it is a true story, one which is being lived on in every instant as one reads it. It will come to an end when they both somehow reach the moment of death. Only then will it be possible to say if their living with me had meaning and that so many people worried about them. In the depths of my heart I am convinced that there is always a meaning to things even though there are no apparent visible results. A human life is not an exercise in book-keeping: something is invested here, so there must be a result there. In reality one can only plant. No one can know when the harvest will take place. But that is no reason to be discouraged from planting and harvesting. I write this because I had to go through this process of discouragement time and again and sometimes agreed with those who said: You take such pains and over-exert yourself, but it's no use: *O pau que nasce torto, fica torto*. The tree that is born twisted, stays twisted. This saying is a seducer, and despite all its inherent logic, should not be succumbed to.

I write these true life histories in order to help those who have the courage not to withhold their confidence, not even from street children, thieves and prison inmates.

HOPE FOR A HUMAN LIFE

Once upon a time there was a child who lived in heaven, where it rested a very long time and slept. The greatest brilliance came from the area around God's throne. But the light shone so brightly that it was blinding, so the child of heaven never went near God's throne.

One day the child awoke, looked down and saw something terrible: pitch-black clouds, iridescent violet waves, fire battling against water, lightning flashes that destroyed houses, burning forests, and in the midst of this chaos the child saw people trying to save others.

The boy was so frightened by all this that he called his Guardian Angel and asked:

- What does the chaos down there mean? Where is this abomination happening?

- On Earth, was the Guardian Angel's answer.

- And what does it mean? the child wanted to know.

- The people who live on the Earth have become alienated from each other. What you see are the consequences of the discord and the egoism of the people who live there. They are impatient and want to have everything immediately; each thinks only of himself. You see what has come of it: the forests have burned, the land has dried out, the seas have become polluted, the animals are dying out, the birds can no longer fly, the fish disappear and many people live in wretched huts in dire poverty while others live in glacial stone palaces.

- That's terrible, cried the child. But what is going to happen? They will all die in such poverty, there won't be anything to eat, no clean water or air, no fertile land and no people who love each other!

- Yes, said the Guardian Angel, it looks like the end is near. I don't know either what is going to happen. I will ask the Archangel Michael.

The guardian angel went to where the light shone brighter, where he met the Archangel Michael and said:

- The heavenly child asked me how it will be possible to continue to live on the Earth.

The Archangel answered:

- Tell the heavenly child he should betake himself to the Earth and fight against the chaos. If he does that I will stand by him. I cannot defeat evil alone; human beings must help.

The Archangel returned to the child and said:

- This is what the Archangel told me: If you want to save the Earth you must betake yourself there. The Archangel Michael will help you to fight against the evil you encounter. He needs your help to defeat evil.

- In that darkness and chaos! cried the child fearfully.

- Be courageous, said the angel, do not think about it too long, just dive into the all the misery and the Archangel Michael will stand by you. Have courage!

The midnight light filled the heavenly child and it drew courage. Then it began its journey.

*

In the middle of the favela, in a poor hut, a child was born. It was called Sergio. His mother was very happy when she saw the child. It seemed to her as though light encircled his head. But when Sergio opened his eyes he saw something ugly. He didn't know what it was. His body began to ache and he had stomach pains.

Where is the light, where is the warmth that enveloped me in heaven? All was ugly and loud, the air was heavy, mosquitos buzzed around him and rats scurried across the floor. Sergio began bitterly to cry. What will become of me?

Then his mother came and took him in her arms and he felt protected. And thus he grew.

One day he became aware of something terrible: his mother disappeared for hours at a time. He waited and waited; gradually he began to lose hope that she would ever return. Then he realized that she had to work all day in order to buy milk and food for the children. No one had time for him. Slowly he became angry, bitterly angry that his mother had to work all day in order to eat some rice and beans at night. Sometimes he remembered the wonderful times in heaven. But he had completely forgotten the Archangel Michael.

One day a boy from the neighboring hut said to him: Do you know what I saw today? We celebrated Saint Michael's Day. Saint Michael was there and he carried the scales of good and evil. Each child took a piece of crystal and laid it on the scale of the good. And do you know what happened? The scale of the good became heavy, much heavier than the evil side. We children of the kindergarten did it, together with the Archangel Michael.

Sergio remained still as he listened to the boy. A memory awoke in his mind and he sensed immediately: I want to learn in that school too. The next day he spoke with the teacher and since then went to the school every day. Many things from his heavenly past that he had forgotten were woken anew. Sergio became happier and more settled every day. The light began to shine again around his head.

He saw much evil outside the school, however.

There were days when he was all light and love. On other days he was like a wild bull. What angered him so? He didn't know himself. We knew though. What he saw and heard was not like his past. He saw people die, he saw how people killed or mistreated other people, he heard people curse or speak nonsense, how they got drunk in bars. Then a thief crept through a hole in the wall of his house in order to steal food and kicked his sister. On the streets he saw accidents and burning cars and on television he saw violence.

Was this what the child had hoped for from the world? Often the heavenly light went out and his face was dark.

At the next Saint Michael's Day celebration he told the teacher: I would like to play the prince and fight against the dragon.

Why, Sergio?

Because I want to defeat evil. When I am grown up I will fight against evil.

As he said this a ray of light shone on his face. And like a flash he remembered: Yes, it is so: I am on the Earth to fight against everything I see that is ugly and false.

After he said that Sergio made a beautiful drawing of the Archangel Michael slaying the dragon with his sword.

The years went by. When Sergio was nine years old life in the favela became noticeably worse. The women were hungry, the children also. Many died from diseases such as measles, pneumonia and dysentery. The time came again for the Saint Michael's Day celebration. The teachers prepared for it. This, however, was a very special celebration. For the first time in the whole world the celebration took place in a favela, among the poor huts. But in the hall made for the celebration it was all marvelously beautiful. Flowers in spiral form decorated the wooden floor, candles lighted the hall and high above beamed the Archangel. Many, many children of all ages, along with their parents, admired the flowers and the candles. The teachers sang and the children, in pairs holding hands, passed through the spiral of flowers, picked a crystal, came out of the spiral and laid the crystal on the scale of good. — How beautiful it is, I thought.

Suddenly a shot was heard outside. It was a criminal who lived in the favela. Then it was quiet again, the music played and the children continued to lay their crystals on the scale. And the Archangel put the amethyst on the scale of the good, so it would win.

The celebration was over. Everyone left. But Sergio returned to the hall, looked up to the Archangel's place and asked, wondering:

Where is he?

He has gone.

Where? To the favela?

Yes, to the favela. First he went to the favela, then he rose into heaven.

During the celebration we ask the Archangel Michael for strength and light. We need this island of peace and light in order to withstand the world of misery.

Sergio grew older, he entered the world, he fell deep into the abyss, he got lost in the forest. Without losing his courage he climbed to the highest mountain-top. Where did the courage come from? Sometimes it seemed as if he wanted to challenge the world because he didn't love it; for him who had come from heaven, it was too evil, too ugly. But sometimes one had the impression that the Archangel Michael himself comforted him: Test your strength, your ability, have spirit! At other times it seemed that he would sink in the vortex of life and never escape from this hell. But when he did find his way out of the abyss the pure light shined once more.

Many years later, when Sergio was grown up, he returned to the favela, where he first saw the light of day. He started to build beautiful houses for the people of the favela, he showed them how the houses should be furnished and embellished; and he taught them to love. He cared especially for the forgotten ones: the aged, the cripples, but also the delinquents and the drug addicts, the criminals and the pickpockets.

One day Sergio died and went back to heaven. The Guardian angel asked him:

What have you brought from the Earth?

I have a present for the Archangel Michael, was the answer.

What is it?

A little bowl full of pieces of crystals for the scale of the good.

How did you obtain it?

I always tried to understand people, to love and not to mistreat them. I never condemned anyone, Sergio added.

Sergio handed the bowl to the Archangel.

Did you never injure anyone or act falsely.

Yes, Sergio admitted, forgive me. I learned through my own mistakes to understand people better, to love and not to condemn.

The Archangel Michael blessed him and laid the pieces of crystal on the side of the good.

***

The theme of violence by young people is being discussed everywhere, because brutality and cruelty in schools, on the streets, in "reform" schools and youth prisons is on the increase. On the bus to work violence is subject number one: everyone has a story to tell, how he or she was assaulted, how drugs are sold openly in schools, how young people in prison revolt and cut off another prisoner's head, how someone goes to the bank to pick up his salary and is mugged on leaving, how another has his running shoes ripped off — all of course accompanied by threats with guns, usually by drug addicts.

I returned from the television studio by taxi — on arrival the favela people asked: "Where are you coming from, so well dressed?" — "From television, the favela must be well represented, with high-heeled shoes and a dress if necessary."

That afternoon I gave a course for the teachers of the curative education school in Monte Azul. And in the evening we had our *reunião,* our regular meeting of about 40 longtime co-workers. We wanted to talk about Monte Azul's future, what we imagine the 21st century will be like and how to organize our work. We can't simply continue as we have been doing, but must have a sense for what new steps the future demands.

This vision of the future had an abrupt end when I arrived home after the meeting. Someone banged on my door. I opened the window and saw a masked figure who held a revolver to the neck of Stefan — a Swiss volunteer — and yelled for me open the door immediately. I had no choice, the bandits stormed into the house; one was drunk and fearful, and yelled continuously:

"Where's the safe? Where's the money?" He waved a revolver around while the other one stuck his gun in Stefan's back. "Don't scream so much, I'll give you all I have," I said, and we ran upstairs. 200 dollars were found. "That's too little, it's nothing! Where's the safe?" — "You can search all you want as far as I'm concerned, but there is no more, only papers and books." We were locked in the bathroom and after a while an ex-volunteer with her child were also pushed in as hostages. So we sat there for hours through the night, though a few pillows, blankets and jackets were thrown in to us. We tried to think of something. Gradually we realized that there were only two bandits who rummaged around the house and now and then came into the bathroom and screamed at me, where my damned money was. Then there was the one guarding us, who said that the most dangerous members of their gang were waiting outside on the street. They kept running outside for instructions because they couldn't find anything and were more and more afraid because they wouldn't be able to carry out their "mission", for which they could pay with their lives. We could hear them yelling outside the bathroom door: "*vamos matar, vamos matar!*" (We'll kill them!)

Thank God we kept calm. The child with its shock of blonde hair shone like the sun. We negotiated with the bandits and made suggestions: checks, or we could call someone to bring money. But they insisted doggedly on the non-existent safe. Well, I thought, whatever happens will happen, and I reminded myself of my morning verse: "..that today be an image of your destiny's ordering will." I did not want to lose my presence of mind, because you can get used even to such unnatural situations and miss the right moment when a solution could come.

I had a lot of time to think. In great haste I had taken a few books, paper, pencil and a thermos with me. I went back over my almost 33 years in Brazil. At 27/28 I went as a social worker to a favela in the interior; when I was 33 I began working as a class and language teacher in the São Paulo Waldorf School, which lasted for nine years. At 37 (second moon node) I began the favela work together with pupils of the São Paulo Waldorf School; at 56 (third moon node) I became a member of the executive committee of the Anthroposophical Society in Brazil; since then I have been adviser to and have helped found various small social initiatives.

"Dear Ute, when you left last week, the air seemed to congeal. It was strange. And even I, who never cry, couldn't hold back the stream of tears during the meeting. Yet that *reunião* had something "light" to it, because in some of us suddenly a force seemed to work, that will simply only go forward. [...] Because of this whole story many people have taken a giant step forward. Although the opposing forces will also be there — but that will only give the scales new movement, and Monte Azul seems to have become mature." Or, in another letter: "I think after 30 years of work, also considering the end of the millennium, that this is a trial. This separation has a meaning, and surely you will return different than when you left. And also in Monte Azul the people will be more alert in their work."

A step towards humanity in general:

- I had previously expressed the intention of working more outside Brazil: For example the idea of organizing a Multicultural Congress of all anthroposophical social initiatives. It would bring together the initiators, wherever in the world they are on the social front.
- To really forgive the thieves and to empathize with the tragedy of their lives — and to pray for them.
- To know that it is only possible to transform the earth's destiny when you don't *only* consider the earthly.

The story told here is taken from life and — as they say in Brazil: *"Só Deus sabe como vai terminar"* (Only God knows how it will end ...). It is only an example of the innumerable untold stories in the world.

Editor's note: Ute Craemer has since returned to Brazil (June 2000) after spending several months abroad lecturing. She has taken up her work again there, but will also continue to travel the world in order to spread the Monte Azul educational and social message.

WHAT IT MEANS TO BE BORN IN A FAVELA

When a human being enters upon earthly life he delivers himself up completely, with all his senses and feelings. For the child the world is good, therefore it imitates everything in its surroundings. Later, at around six or seven years of age, the child acquires a certain independence, but even then it perceives the world through the deeds, feelings and thoughts of its educators. They are the bridge which unites the child to the world and through them it perceives what is good or evil, beautiful or ugly, true or false. It is only during adolescence that the human being begins to look at the world critically, searching for an ideal, a meaning to life.

The question arises: And in a favela? How are these laws of development affected under such adverse conditions? The laws of development are universal, but the environment affects the individual in different ways, favoring or impeding his development.

A child like Divino, born in a favela, is deeply marked by his environment and conditions of life. When a child is born in a favela the mother, sisters and brothers, the whole family is happy and a climate of love reigns around the newly-born. It is received just as any child is, regardless of social class. After a few days, however (and this is one of the most painful phenomena we meet in the favela), that same child has already been marked by the scars of poverty: dysentery, skin lesions, fever or potentially fatal illnesses such as dehydration or pneumonia. Nutrition is deficient, especially if the mother is not able to nurse the child, sense impressions are deplorable: noisy, ugly huts, always humid and very hot in summer, "decorated" with pages torn from magazines.

When the child is still very small it doesn't differentiate his surroundings from himself. He assimilates all these impressions, and these form the "instrument" through which he will act, feel and think in life. It is important to emphasize that all the child's organs, especially the brain, are formed during this phase and that this formation is deficient in the case of favela children due to the conditions mentioned. This is one of the main causes of poor performance in school and not, as is often said, stupidity or laziness.

At the age of seven, totally unprepared, the child goes to school with the joyful expectation of finding something important for his life. For the majority however, school life becomes a burden. Aside from not having anyone at home to help him, the teaching does not relate to his external life, not to mention his internal life. The child is forced to pass through an arid desert of facts without meaning for him and lacking a loved person who he can respect and who can give him the chance to discover the world's beauty, as well as educate him by means of art, crafts and religion.

Soon the child leaves school and begins to work. He is transformed into a miniature adult, submerged in the ferocious battle for survival. His natural development is interrupted, his childhood sacrificed. In becoming a precocious adult, he skips over an important phase of development.

Overburdened by their lives, adolescents frequently feel that the moment of freedom has arrived. The more burdensome life is, the more quickly they fall into the first passion. Universal love is reduced to sexual desire, children come almost immediately, very early and "by accident".

An adolescent who lives in a favela rarely finds the opportunity to find ideals or a profession which corresponds to his personality. Therefore he idolizes anyone "different" or "modern" whom he meets or sees on television. Aside from the singers on television, the idols of the favelas are the drug dealers and the gangsters. Usually the first work by which some money can be earned is immediately accepted. In truth, it is the labor market which determines the occupation and not the individual's aptitudes and wishes.

It seems to be a no-win situation. In fact, the obstacles to a healthy, creative and integrated life are immense. We could easily make the mistake of thinking that it is a vicious circle and that it isn't worthwhile trying to do something about it:

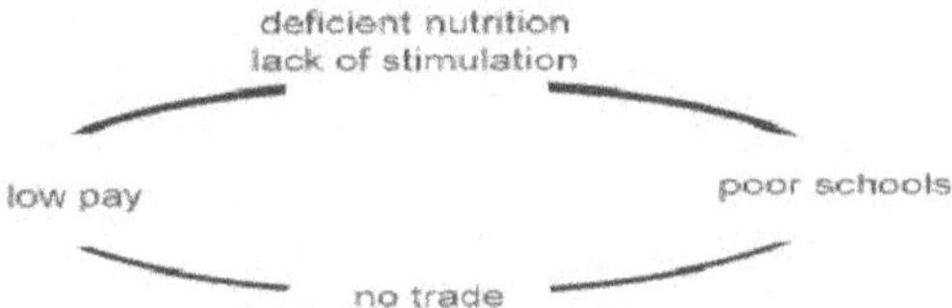

However, this vicious circle can be broken by two forces: The individual's Self (incarnated in a favela) and love for the other.

It is truly painful to experience the deep wounds which the hard life in a favela leaves on human beings. On the other hand, it is gratifying to see how many are able to retain their dignity under the worst conditions, keeping their spiritual flame burning. Many are able to learn a trade and leave the favela.

The second force is neighborly love, or, to avoid an over-used expression, a deep interest in the developing human being; also the firm conviction that there is potential for growth in every individual.

Every seed requires fertile soil, air, water and sun in order to unfold. The human being needs love and trust in order to awaken. Just as a seed can rarely break through a layer of cement and grow without water and sunlight, it is also very rare that a human being is able to lift himself up alone. Every human being needs help to grow and develop — especially those who are born in an infertile soil, with their air and water polluted and a "spiritual sun" which shines with difficulty through the obstacles imposed by life in the favela.

The social work we are doing in the favelas is an attempt to help each human being to live.

UPDATE

About 37 years have passed since I first got in touch with the children of the Monte Azul slum. They used to come with plastic bags and knock on my door, saying, *Voc tem alguma coisa para dar?* (Do you have something to give us?) I asked myself for a long time what I could do for those poor children. I had not yet met any of them, but I had seen them begging on the streets. At that time, I was teaching at the São Paulo Waldorf School, where my middle- and upper-class students had their own social and psychological problems. I wondered if I could help them by giving them the opportunity to do something for others.

The greatest challenge was how to transform physical and mental suffering into something positive and empowering, i.e. how to transform a burden into something which eventually might help a person grow. My main focus has been the human being between light and darkness, or, between spirit and matter.

While studying Anthroposophy and Waldorf Pedagogy over the years, I have found that Rudolf Steiner's writings express exactly how I feel about almost everything.

"... We wish to do material things in the light of the spirit, and we wish to find the light of the spirit, so that it produces warmth for our practical activities."

Building Bridges

Building bridges between different worlds has always been a basic motive of our work at Monte Azul. That is the way it all began: bridges between different social classes — the students of the São Paulo Waldorf School and the children of the favela Monte Azul. Later we started building bridges between different peoples and cultures: young volunteers from Europe, Japan and

North America came in order to explore their ideas about life and to contribute to the work with groups of children, the health center, the bakery, etc. Then came the bridges between anthroposophical initiatives and people who had never heard of Waldorf education, anthroposophical medicine, or Anthroposophy itself. Many of these people found this new approach extremely helpful. We taught Waldorf pedagogy in many places, even way up in the north of Brazil, published two books and accepted a number of practitioners who were interested in Waldorf education for the favelas. Participating in congresses on anthroposophical pedagogy or medicine has also been a beneficial learning experience.

Building bridges in itself has also been successful, especially between favela residents and people from other places. Of course problems sometimes arise when people from very different backgrounds, ways of life and experiences come together, but this can also be extremely rewarding and lead to a better understanding and appreciation for different cultures.

Development

Development is another important topic that has been guiding us since we started work here. In every person, as well as in every group of people, the possibility for development exists: you can try to bring to light what could be hidden; you can make sure that each and every organism, be it a person or a group of people, contains a spiritual core. You may presume it exists and it might develop as long as it is carefully fostered, encouraged and cultivated. It may have to be trimmed, but it will surely appear again somehow, somewhere, in a different shape. This is the principal motif of our work.

Here are some points linked to the development of the Monte Azul social organism:

1) The "people concerned", i.e. those who live in the favelas, participate more and more in study groups, discussions, debate and biography work, all of which encompass their "growing up" process, so that they begin to co-operate and contribute to important decisions.

2) The relationship to people who live on the margins of society, such as criminals, can be dangerous.

3) Dealing with conflicts among collaborators, or with those who are unable to accomplish an assignment.

Workshops

Learning is closely linked to health. We have observed that although a person might be eager to learn, he or she frequently is not strong enough to concentrate because of chronicle health problems, such as parasites, anemia, dysentery, bronchitis or pneumonia. The will to learn exists, but the body is weak. Some mothers told us that they wished to have a doctor at the favela and a room where he could attend to their needs. Many people helped to make this dream come true. With some old wooden containers, they hammered together a small clinic. We found a doctor who practiced anthroposophical medicine and who was willing to help even under such precarious conditions, without water or light and even without medications. He was available once a week.

This tiny, primitive "doctor's office", which a visitor called a "doghouse", in time became a two-story building with tests for parasites, treatment of wounds, gynecology, psychological care, chiropractics, ultrasound examinations and dentistry.

A midwife is available for childbirth, family planning and counseling mothers. Prophylactic campaigns are helping to prevent AIDS, cholera, caries, etc.

Neither the responsible doctors nor the midwife or therapist are from the favela, but the nurses come from there. They were able to work at the health center while taking their training course.

Thanks to the good quality of anthroposophical medicine and the individual care of each patient, the health center has received people from far and near. It appears as an island of humanity in a sea of suffering due to bureaucracy and poor treatment in public hospitals.

Cultural Center

At the "escolinha" (after-school) the children participate in all kinds of play. For most holidays they put on a performance, such as Christmas plays, legends, Brazilian historical plays (emphasizing the contribution of Africans and Brazilian Indians to their country's history). This activity led to the planning and realization of the Cultural Center, where our co-workers and other favela residents write and rehearse plays, most of which refer to the social situation (problems of migration of country people to the big cities, street-children, women's rights, the colonization of Brazil, etc.) There is also an adult choir active at parties and funerals, a children's choir and a small orchestra.

Personal Relationships

The poet Christian Morgenstern said that one should not reject whatever is evil but provide love instead of hatred. We have often tried to do just that when dealing with people considered to be criminals. Certainly most people who live in favelas are normal human beings who have a job or are looking for work, but their low income does not permit them to pay the rent for even a very small house or apartment. Nevertheless, a favela is an ideal place for criminal elements to hide. People who sell or buy drugs meet and hide there; thieves offer stolen goods for sale, unhindered by the police. This causes a lot of trouble and is a constant problem for the favela families. We meet people who rob and steal, both youngsters and adults. It is very difficult to find equilibrium between strength and protective measures on the one hand and understanding the kind of life these people live on the other – for example when young drug addicts rob and plunder our nurseries. Emotions like rage, helplessness, revenge or punishment versus the feeling that even this human being was once a child born to realize something; he too, according to Morgenstern, was "woven of light".

We have tried to include people in our meditations or, upon release from prison to provide work for them through a drug-withdrawal institution, but a feeling of weakness and impotence remains while facing the heavy burden of destiny. You feel it when you accompany such a person to his grave, killed by another guy just as disturbed and unable to succeed. Sometimes one feels that there is no other solution but to "start life all over again". In spite of the often tragic ending of such a life, we believe that perhaps the seed of what we planted into this person when we tried to awaken his good qualities might have been of some benefit to guide him.

Our Co-workers

The idea of "development to the greatest possible extent" has become increasingly significant in that co-workers are becoming more involved in the process of planning and decision-making. In an anthroposophical enterprise this would be obvious. However, it is worth mentioning here, since about two-thirds of our staff come from the favela. This leads in many cases to certain limitations, due to little or no schooling, great stress because of bad living conditions, and a lack of opportunities to withdraw and concentrate on something special. Many difficulties arise, such as serious family problems, children, relatives who come from the north of Brazil looking for help, a husband who does not appreciate his wife becoming independent, or who is even involved in dishonest dealings and becomes dangerous. And are such members of the staff, in spite of all such restrictions, able to co-operate in the process of favela development? The answer is yes, if in each case personal development can progress and the person can accept more and more responsibility, step by step, up to the limits of his or her capabilities depending on circumstances. A person might be able to join a committee to organize a festival or celebration. The weekly meeting must be planned, the stipends distributed and the health funds administered. All of these are opportunities for a person to become engaged beyond his or her specific activities.

Moreover, we have what we call "reunião de area," the weekly discussions, for example, at the health center, the nursery, the "escolinha", the cultural center and the therapy group. Here we consider problems related to a specific field of activities, as long as they are not related to fundamental changes or to financial consequences. During these meetings, everyone can share his or her own opinion and share responsibilities with all the others. It is important that there be a parallel "study group" meeting, which considers and studies pedagogy, social questions, Anthroposophy, etc.

We also have "reunião de metas," a weekly meeting to consider and plan the most important aims and purposes. It is a gathering of a group of people of long-time standing and responsibility for planning and controlling all activities. It has been very difficult to find favelados (favela dwellers) who feel they can be responsible, observe and help plan the activities in two favelas and the workers' settlement at Horizonte Azul. Only about 30 people, half of them favelados, have been able to join the group in the past three years. The purpose and meaning of the work (social threefold organization), damage caused by television, the elementary beings, etc.) is most important for a real and conscious understanding of our work.

Summing up: We currently have the following activities at the Favelas Monte Azul, Peinha, and Horizonte Azul:

1. For children

   Nurseries, daycare, kindergartens, pre-school, after-school programs, libraries, Waldorf primary school

2. For Adolescents

   Professional training and production of different workshops: carpentry, weaving, bakery, paper recycling, doll making and electrical work.

3. For Adults

   Training for kindergarten and nursery teachers. Theater group.

Also:

> Medical and dental care; midwifery; production of biodynamic vegetables at Horizonte Azul; garbage recycling; co-operation with other social worker organizations in Brazil and abroad; congresses; a housing co-operative; books, lectures, etc.

Work with approximately 1200 Children

In the infants ward, the 8 full-time nurseries, and the 6 kindergartens, the children feel safe and secure. Their day has a certain rhythm: round dances, fairy-tales, free games and plays, and regular meals, all of which provide a feeling of security and self-confidence. The children help with cleaning, cooking, and dishwashing, and they learn to keep themselves clean (brush their teeth, wash their hands). We celebrate the four great yearly holidays: Easter, St. John's, Michaelmas and Christmas; they are important events for the children.

The *Associação Comunitária Monte Azul* prepares the 6 to 7 year-old children for public school with form-drawing, painting, and ABC stories. Once they start school, we complement their studies at the "escolinha" (after-school care), where they also learn handicrafts, singing and dancing, stage plays and organize festivities. When needed, we help them with their homework. On certain dates the children interact with special Brazilian topics, such as Afro-Brazilians, Brazilian Indians, ecology and their own problems and favela background.

Education and Training

Associação Comunitária Monte Azul offers training courses for youngsters and adults, which help provide opportunities for them to find work in order to overcome the problems of favela life and avoid drifting into marginality.

In the two carpentry workshop courses (one in the morning and one in the afternoon), thirty 12 to 17 year-olds learn all possible skills from making a simple wooden spoon to movable toys, and all kinds of furniture. They also have special courses in drawing and in cost calculation. SENAI, the official Chamber of Industries, endorses the curriculum and, on graduation, bestows official diplomas. At the moment, quite a few former students, now journeymen, work in the 200 square-meter workshop and earn their livelihood.

In the weaving shop, 25 boys and girls — some of whom are handicapped- learn how to weave, dye wool etc. The sale of their products brings them a small income.

In the bakery, students produce ryebread, among other things, which is sold in schools and some shops. As a result, they can sell wheat bread at a lower cost to the favela people. The children in our nurseries learn to appreciate ryebread and introduce it at home.

We have a course for educators on Saturday mornings which includes the rhythmic planning of daily activities, correct nutrition, round dances, saying grace before and after meals, song preparation, and the seasonal festivities.

Improving Living Conditions

Medical care:

In 1985 a two-story building replaced the primitive little wooden shack. Anthroposophic doctors and dentists have daily office hours at the Health Center. A midwife, working full time, provides instructions on family planning and contraceptive devices, childbirth and the care of infants. The nurses, two of whom come from the favela, give injections, dress wounds, provide information about problems of hygiene vermin (lice, ascarid) etc.

Cleanliness:

Many *favelados* help improve conditions, remove garbage, clean the gutters, build steps to substitute for slippery, sloping, muddy paths and provide drinking water for the huts. They have started sorting garbage (paper, glass, plastics, metals) to sell it — the first project of this type in this huge city.

Rudolf Steiner's Anthroposophy is fundamental for all of this work.

APPENDIX

Ute's report to her many friends and supporters thirty years later.

I'm now back in Brazil and Monte Azul, full of many encounters, conversations and interviews which span whole generations. This trip was poignant, I felt as if a great arc was straddling 30 years, years full of life, work, joy, disappointments and transformation. Hundreds and hundreds of people of different cultures, also transformation of living places.

The first lecture about Monte Azul took place in the nineteen-eighties as a result of the book *Favela Kinder*. I traveled alone across Germany, Holland and Switzerland with my suitcase and a case full of slides, the trip having been organized by the Monte Azul friend Frank Thomas Smith – at that time still using the telephone.

For me this trip was part of my birthday celebration: 75th year of life, 44 of them in social work – not only in Monte Azul by the way, also for "Kinder und Jugendheim" [Children and Youth Home] with more than 50 children and youths over 20 years old, the work with the Alliance for Childhood, in the study group Pindorama, consulting for many social work organizations, etc. The celebration took place in the Centro Cultural Monte Azul: life stories adorned with Hayek's poem, recited by our cook Edson, Brazilian songs which pertain to my life, like a *desparada ("eu vim pra consertar"* – I have come to improve*)*, photo displays and much more.

The European trip continued in Brussels with a meeting about the situation of the Alliance for Childhood as an international movement for the protection of children *Aliança pela infancia.*

From there I went to Dornach, where I was received by a group of Japanese volunteers.

And let's not forget the Daxi Theater presentation about the life of Darcy Ribeiro by Marcelo and Vital.

In the Goetheanum important meetings took place with the Social Science Section, the Youth and Pedagogical Sections and various culturally creative people. Subject: the possibility of a World Social Initiative Forum.

Then the seven lectures in the GLS [anthroposophical bank] branches (Freiburg, Munich, Stuttgart, Hamburg and Berlin), sometimes with the Folia de Reis [Three Kings Festival] or with the St. Francis song. The focus of these lectures was to make the Monte Azul Foundation Fund known.

Also lectures in Waldorf Schools, the Christian Community, interviews, conversations. And always meeting with friends of Brazil and volunteers, even some of the first ones from 1980!

Wonderful was the re-encounter with the students of the Music School Montabaur and the Neuwied Waldorf School, who had visited us in June and together with our students of the Escola de Música and the Indio Culture Center Arapoty and the pupils of the Escola Rudolf Steiner organized the Music/Eurythmy festival.

In Hamburg I had a very interesting conversation with a group of teachers who have taken upon themselves the task of founding a Waldorf School in a difficult part of the city, and with state financing, because parents there, partly with immigrant backgrounds, cannot pay school fees.

Many questions arose during the lectures:
What does "resilience school" mean?
Where does the strength and trust come from?
How are these initiatives financed?
How does one deal with violence?
What about political participation?
And drugs?
Often after a lecture people came to me with intentions for similar projects or were having difficulties and needed courage ...

There was never enough time to answer all the questions and to speak with all those people.

I would like to end this report with the Monte Azul verse, which was born in the year 2000, as I was banned from Brazil, so to speak!

Oração da Monte Azul
Possa a oração para os seres humanos ligados
à Associação Comunitária Monte Azul
ser ouvida em espírito.
Possa a força auxiliadora do Cristo
Iluminar nossas metas.
Que sempre mantenhamos os nossos pés bem firmes
no chão da realidade do mundo.
Que em nossa cabeça resplandeça
A luz da nossa estrela guia,
Para que possamos escutar a
íntima voz do nosso coração
Que nos abre às intuições necessárias
Para agir com amor e consciência,
E assim transformar as forças destruidoras
Em nós e nos outros em forças criativas sanantes.

The Monte Azul Prayer

May this prayer in spirit be heard by the people
united with the Monte Azul Community Association.
May the guiding strength of Christ enlighten our goals,
that we always have our feet planted firmly
on the ground of the world's reality,
so that in our heads does shine the light of our guiding star,
so that we may hear the intimate voice of our hearts,
that we may be open to living intuition,
to work lovingly and aware, and thus transform
the destructive forces in us and in others
into creative healthy forces.

Ute Craemer

Ute Craemer now (2021) devotes much of her time to the *Alliance for Childhood* as well as being a consultant for similar initiatives. Until the Covid-19 pandemic, she had also been traveling the world consulting and giving lectures. She intends to continue this activity when it becomes possible again. [Editor]

OTHER BOOKS

authored or translated by

Frank Thomas Smith

All titles available at Amazon.com

ANTHROPOSOPHICAL FANTASIES (by Roberto Fox, as told to Frank Thomas Smith): Anthroposophy, also known as Spiritual Science, is not known for fantastic literature, or fiction at all. So how can stories with titles like "Life on Mars," or "The Girl in the Floppy Hat," or "To Hunt a Nazi" qualify as anthroposophical. They do not — until now. Therefore, this book is groundbreaking. You may smile at times, even laugh; other stories may cause a lump in your throat ...
ISBN: 978-1948302104

CORONAVIRUS PANDEMIC II (by Judith von Halle, translated by Frank Thomas Smith): In this book, the main focus is not on the distressing social developments that have arisen as consequence of the coronavirus pandemic – and for good reason: Although there are already (thankfully) many quality descriptions and articles about this complex of problems and questions, at the same time on the other hand a dangerous knowledge-vacuum has arisen. Therefore in this book I will refrain from elaborating on the problems already made widely visible in favor of this knowledge-vacuum, which will be outlined as an addition to what has already been described in Vol. I.
ISBN: 978-1948302357

ESOTERIC LESSONS FOR THE FIRST CLASS Volumes I, II, and III (Rudolf Steiner, translated by Frank Thomas Smith): During the re-founding of the Anthroposophical Society at Christmas 1923, Rudolf Steiner also reconstituted the 'Esoteric School' which had originally functioned in Germany from 1904 until 1914, when the outset of the First World War made it's continuance impossible. Twenty-eight lectures in three Volumes with in-line illustrations and blackboard drawings.
ISBN: 978-1948302289 (vol. 1), 978-1948302302 (vol. 2), 978-1948302333 (vol. 3)

THE HISTORY AND ACTUALITY OF IMPERIALISM (Rudolf Steiner, translated by Frank Thomas Smith): In 1920 Rudolf Steiner had already foreseen that the future imperialism would be economic rather than military or nationalistic. In these three lectures he describes the history of imperialism from ancient times to the present and into the future. The Anglo-American would play an increasingly important role in future developments, so the English visitors who attended must have been especially attentive.
ISBN: 978-1948302203

JOURNEY TO THE STARS (by Frank Thomas Smith): The protagonists of these 12 stories are involved in fascinating adventures, which will delight young readers and leave an indelible impression on their minds and hearts. For children from 9 years old on up.

ISBN: 978-1948302395

THE MAGIC MOUND (by Frank Thomas Smith): Sergio and his younger brother, Divino are poor children who live in a favela (slum) in São Paulo, Brazil. They go on vacation with their revered teacher, dona Ute (pronounced oo-teh), to the country house of one of Ute's friends. Once there, they leave the house together to fetch kindling wood. They cross a stream and discover a strange round mound surrounded by white stones ... for children from 9 years old on up.

ISBN: 978-1948302258

TOWARD A THREEFOLD SOCIETY (Rudolf Steiner, translated by Frank Thomas Smith): This work, written late in the life of Rudolf Steiner, makes use of a threefold analysis of the human individual and of human society. Man as an individual, or in a group, functions basically in three modes: thinking/perceiving, feeling/valuing, and willing/planning/acting. A unit of functioning, whether a part of an individual or part of a society has its proper role. Each role needs a certain respect from other areas if it is to function properly ...

ISBN: 978-1-948302-16-6

www.ingramcontent.com/pod-product-compliance
Lightning Source LLC
Chambersburg PA
CBHW062127020426
42335CB00013B/1127

* 9 7 8 1 9 4 8 3 0 2 4 2 5 *